W9-CKA-833

HC
59.3
.P48
2006

The Coming First World Debt Crisis

DISCARD

DISCARD

The Coming First World Debt Crisis

Ann Pettifor

© Ann Pettifor 2006

All rights reserved. No reproduction, copy or transmission of this
publication may be made without written permission.

No paragraph of this publication may be reproduced, copied or transmitted
save with written permission or in accordance with the provisions of the
Copyright, Designs and Patents Act 1988, or under the terms of any licence
permitting limited copying issued by the Copyright Licensing Agency,
90 Tottenham Court Road, London W1T 4LP.

Any person who does any unauthorised act in relation to this publication
may be liable to criminal prosecution and civil claims for damages.

The author has asserted her right to be identified as the author of this work
in accordance with the Copyright, Designs and Patents Act 1988.

First published 2006 by
PALGRAVE MACMILLAN
Houndmills, Basingstoke, Hampshire RG21 6XS and
175 Fifth Avenue, New York, N.Y. 10010
Companies and representatives throughout the world

PALGRAVE MACMILLAN is the global academic imprint of the
Palgrave Macmillan division of St. Martin's Press, LLC and of
Palgrave Macmillan Ltd.
Macmillan® is a registered trademark in the United States,
United Kingdom and other countries. Palgrave is a registered
trademark in the European Union and other countries.

ISBN-13: 978–0–230–00785–7 hardback
ISBN-10: 0–230–00785–6 hardback
ISBN-13: 978–0–230–00784–0 paperback
ISBN-10: 0–230–00784–8 paperback

This book is printed on paper suitable for recycling and
made from fully managed and sustained forest sources.

A catalogue record for this book is available from the British Library.

Library of Congress Cataloging-in-Publication Data
Pettifor, Ann.
  The coming First World debt crisis / by Ann Pettifor.
    p. cm.
  Contents: The international financial system : at the root of the crisis —
Understanding money — Debt : personal, household, corporate, and
sovereign — The bubble and the coming de(b)tonation — Debt and
ethics : an age-old struggle — What is to be done? — Conclusion.
    ISBN 0–230–00785–6 (cloth) — ISBN 0–230–00784–8 (pbk.)
    1. Economic history—21st century. 2. International finance. 3.
Globalization. 4. Debts, External—Developed countries. 5. Debts, Public—
Developed countries. I. Title.

HC59.3.P48 2006
332'.042—dc22   2006050315

10   9   8   7   6   5   4   3   2   1
16 15 14 13 12 11 10 09 08 07

Printed and bound in Great Britain by
Antony Rowe Ltd, Chippenham and Eastbourne

Contents

Acknowledgements   vi

Introduction   1
1   Globalization: the House that Finance Built   26
2   Costless Money and Costly Credit   56
3   Easy Credit: Costly Debts   84
4   Poor Country Debt Crises: Causes and Parallels   108
5   Moneytheism and Lawless Finance   120
6   Debtonation? When and Why will it Happen?   145
7   Things Don't Have to be This Way   163

Index   182

Acknowledgements

This book is an attempt to guide lay readers through the apparently impenetrable forest of Finance, screened and guarded as it is by formidable bankers, financiers and orthodox economists. But first I had to find my own way. I looked for guidance from some brilliant thinkers and economists; from idealists and pragmatists; from 'bears' and 'bulls'; from theorists, practitioners and commentators. My guides included Aristotle, Luther, Marx, Keynes and their followers. But also a range of monetarists whose concerns about the explosion in credit I share, even though, while we agree on likely effects, we do not share the same conclusions about causes. Christian and Islamic teachers were important guides, as were historians and environmentalists. I doubt that I have done them all full credit; but I owe them debts of gratitude.

My most immediate guide through the tangled forest was Dr Geoff Tily, an expert on Keynes' monetary theory and on the monetary policies he espoused. Dr Tily is an economist and statistician with a heart and soul, and with a proper concern for social justice. I am grateful to him for sharing his research into Keynes' monetary policies; and indebted for the guidance he offered through the thickets of economic theory, statistics and data. While his contribution is credited in the book, he cannot be held responsible for the way in which I have interpreted theories, analysed data or presented statistics.

While Dr Tily's guidance was invaluable, it was the economist and historian Karl Polanyi, through his famous work *The Great Transformation* that initially provided me with the lens through which to examine contemporary finance and economics. I have since been privileged to meet and discuss Polanyi's work with his daughter, the eminent development economist, Prof. Kari Polanyi Levitt, of McGill University, Canada, and of the University of the West Indies. I thank her for her support and inspiration. We have a shared ambition: to establish a Karl Polanyi Institute in Britain that will further erode Hayek's intellectual legacy and rival the Adam Smith Institute in its influence on contemporary economics.

While visiting New York's Anglican Mission to the United Nations in 1999 on behalf of Jubilee 2000, I first heard and met Prof. Herman Daly. Until 1994 Prof. Daly was Senior Economist in the Environment Department of the World Bank, and is now Professor of Public Policy at the University of Maryland. He is an economist and environmentalist; but also a philosopher, physicist, theologian, sociologist and chemist. Hearing him speak with modesty and wit, about his faith, economics and the ecosystem on that hot summer's day in New York, was one of those life-changing moments for me. This book has drawn extensively, and I hope not too clumsily, on his ideas, particularly those espoused in his famous work *Steady-State Economics*.

Another to whom I owe a considerable debt is Michael Hudson, once a bond trader on Wall Street; but now an authority on 'the economic archaeology of debt'. I am humbled by his extensive knowledge of debt systems, and thank him for generously sharing his work with me, and for stimulating discussions on subjects as diverse as debt in Babylonian and Sumerian civilizations and today's international bond markets.

There are many other intellectuals to whom I owe thanks, including Eric Helleiner, Jane d'Arista, Dean Baker and Nouriel Roubini. The latter first introduced me to the wonders of the world wide web back in 1995 with his Stern University (New York) website tracking global economic developments and later, the 1997/98 financial crisis. Roubini's Global Economics Monitor <www.rgemonitor.com> is now as important a start to my day as Claudia's cappuccinos.

While I have gained much from these esteemed economists and thinkers, this book would never have been written without my experience of a powerful movement of campaigners for social justice, millions of whom came together under the umbrella of Jubilee 2000. That campaign taught all of us involved in it, that millions of people could, appropriately briefed, come to grips with supposedly complex international financial policies and concepts – policies and concepts that financial elites would prefer remained elusive and exclusive. Jubilee 2000 campaigners used their understanding of sovereign debt to challenge powerful international institutions, officials and politicians – and change their policies. They gave me the confidence to write this book, and I thank them for that.

Between 2001 and 2004, colleagues at London's new economics foundation (nef), including Ed Mayo, Elna Kotze, Andrew Simms and Stewart Wallis, gave me the chance to recover from the rigours of a global campaign; to deepen my understanding of international finance; and to augment and integrate this with an understanding of the limits to our ecosystem: the need for us all to 'return to scale' <www.neweconomics. org/gen/z_sys_PublicationDetail.aspx?pid=158>. I thank them heartily for that.

Helen Kersley, who has worked in the UK Treasury and the European Central Bank, helped me assemble data and material, and check references. Our lively discussions over coffee in Saporito's obliged me to further hone and refine my arguments, and I thank her for that. I am indebted to Wanja Githendu who supported me throughout the Jubilee 2000 campaign, and also through the writing of this book with her quiet calm and administrative efficiency.

My dear partner, and great friend, Jeremy Smith encouraged me, and gave as always, unstinting practical, intellectual and emotional support as I worked on the book. I thank him with all my heart.

Finally I must thank Amanda Hamilton of Palgrave for her encouragement and support. This book would not have been written if she had not egged me on to do it.

Ann Pettifor
July 2006

Introduction

> Growing domestic and international debt has created the conditions for global economic and financial crises.
>
> Bank for International Settlements (2005)

This book foresees a time, in the not too distant future, when the so-called First World will be mired in the levels of debt that have wreaked such havoc on the economies of so-called Third World economies since the 1980s. This debt crisis, I argue, will hurt millions of ordinary borrowers, and will inflict prolonged dislocation, and economic, social and personal pain on those largely ignorant of the causes of the crisis, and innocent of responsibility for it. This book has been written for those potential victims – 'debtor-spenders' – in the hope of deepening understanding of the causes of the crisis – moral, political and economic – and of stimulating further debate and questioning.

The book is completed at a time (spring 2006) when stock markets in both the US and UK are booming; and Japan appears to be recovering from 15 years of recession and deflation. In the US (the world's 'engine' of economic growth) home-owners and consumers are still flush with cash, increasingly reluctant to save and alarmingly indebted. In the 1970s US household debt-to-income increased at a growth rate of less than 1%. Household debt in the US as a share of disposable income remained below 70% until 1985, with debt-to-income growing at a compound annual growth of less than 1.25%.

Since 2000 the compound growth rate of US household debt is in excess of 5%. In the third quarter of 2005 the growth rate reached an historic high of 13.67%. By 2006, the share of debt to income had risen steeply to 122%! In 2004, the US household sector borrowed more than $1 trillion. This contrasts with the period prior to 2000, during which the household sector borrowed less than half that a year (Papadimitriou et al., 2006).

These US debtor-spenders are stimulating economic growth by boosting consumption and inflating house prices. Personal and household consumption are compounded by high US *government* spending and both are dependent on borrowing, including foreign borrowing. World-wide, China's demand for resources has led to rising prices for key commodities, including oil, and it appears that US consumers are taking the higher oil price in their stride.

By writing this book I want to draw attention to the heroic role US and other First World consumers are playing in propping up both their own economies, but also much of the global economy. In the US, they are doing this with encouragement from the Federal Reserve, and its governor until recently, Alan Greenspan; but also from political leaders, supported by prominent, orthodox economists. The framework for such high levels of borrowing and consumption is set, after all, not by ordinary consumers, but in the first instance by economists, and the policies they espouse; and then by central bankers at the Federal Reserve and politicians in the US government.

By borrowing, shopping, and buying and selling houses consumers, especially in the US, are driving the global economy forward. However, they are also inflating bubbles – in stocks and shares; in property and in other assets. As J.K. Galbraith noted, 'a bubble can easily be punctured. But to incise it with a needle so that it subsides gradually is a task of no small delicacy' (Galbraith, 1954).

Just as in 1928 and 1929, there are many amongst the world's financial elites that are aware of the potential of these bubbles being punctured violently, leading to a crash, and a prolonged crisis. However, they face an intractable problem: if they raise interest rates, say to discourage American consumers from borrowing and spending, they will surely puncture the bubble – and that could be very messy. However, if they do not take action now, things will be much worse when finally the bubble is punctured, as it must be. The dilemma is the same for consumers: if they stop borrowing and spending, the bubble will burst. However, if they carry on borrowing and spending, they store up more trouble for the future. This is a quite terrifying lose-lose game, similar to the one faced by policy-makers before the 1929 crash.

> Some of those in authority wanted the boom to continue. They were making money out of it, and they may have had an intimation of the personal disaster which awaited them when the boom came to an end. But there were also some who saw, however dimly, that a wild speculation was in progress and that something should be done.

For these people, however, every proposal to act raised the same intractable problem. The consequences of successful action seemed almost as terrible as the consequences of inaction, and they could be more horrible for those who took the action. (Galbraith, 1954)

Blame for the victims

When the crisis breaks, US consumers (and much of the world's population) will be punished mercilessly for this excessive borrowing. At the same time I have no doubt that they, the victims, will be *blamed* for the crisis: after all, blaming-the-victim is a favourite game with persecutors.

If democratic societies are to manage and moderate this coming crisis, then it will be necessary to once again constrain and regulate the finance sector, in particular those who create, lend and trade in money. But to do so, it is important for citizens to understand the political and economic roots of their indebtedness; and the reasons behind the recent growth in power and dominance by the finance sector. This book briefly explores those political, ethical and economic roots.

I have been determined not to write a book that aspires to academic status, although it owes much to the scholarly work of many neglected but brilliant economists. Instead, leaning heavily on these scholars and practitioners, I have tried to write a book for ordinary consumers and for those mired in debts.

The book examines the re-engineering of the global economy – away from the 'real' productive sectors of making and growing things – and towards the unproductive finance sector in which money is gambled, compounded and multiplied. It warns of the implications of this re-engineering of the global economy for individuals, households, corporations and governments; for society's well-being; and for the ecosystem's sustainment. The intention is not to alarm and paralyse readers with fear; but to equip those who are, or will be, victims of the debt crisis with some understanding; with a political strategy; and with some common-sense economic solutions.

The rosy picture in 2006

As this book goes to press, to most observers the global economic scene looks pretty rosy. This is enhanced by glowing reports of the gains made by the finance sector of the global economy – banks, and other financial institutions – all enjoying record profits and bonuses. US financial companies have doubled their share of total US corporate profits since the 1950s. The Hong Kong Shanghai Banking Corporation Ltd (HSBC), which began life by providing services during Britain's Opium Wars with China, and which makes 80% of its profits outside the UK – smashed records in March 2006 with its announcement of an 11% rise in profits to $20.96 billion (£11.9 billion) (HSBC, March 2006). HSBC paid record bonuses of $219 million (£126 million) to staff, an increase of 17% on 2004. Total profits for London banks as a whole had, by this date, risen to some $63 billion (£33.3 billion) (*Guardian*, 7 March 2006). Newspapers ran stories about bankers spending £15,000 on a night out at a modish watering hole, paying more than £300 for an exotic cocktail (*Guardian*, 23 November 2005).

HSBC's results were announced at a time (spring 2006) when the British economy was regarded as robust, with the prices of houses and other assets still rising; and many enjoying the good times. Not since the 1950s had the London stock market enjoyed such a long, uninterrupted bull run – three years of capital gains, without corrections, of 10% or more. Things were not just looking good for those lucky enough to hold these assets – they *were* good.

In the January 1928 issue of *World's Work*, Will Payne ... went on to explain the difference between a gambler and an investor. A gambler he pointed out, wins only because someone else loses. Where it is investment, all gain. One investor, he explained buys General Motors at $100, sells it to another at $150, who sells it to a third at $200. Everyone makes money. As Walter Bagehot once observed: 'All people are most credulous when they are most happy.' (Galbraith, 1954)

Despite the euphoria of this 'feel-good' economy HSBC recorded a sizeable increase in write-offs of bad loans, with bad debt charges rising to $7.8 billion (*Guardian*, 7 March 2006). Earlier, in 2005, Barclays, with 9 million credit card customers, reported to the City of London that provisions for bad debts had risen significantly (*Guardian*, 22 February 2006). The number of people in the UK in arrears on their mortgages began to rise for the first time in seven years – and this while interest rates were low and unemployment numbers down. In other words, despite all the apparently good news on the global economy, debts and deficits in rich countries like the UK, continued to climb.

However, this phenomenon went more or less unnoticed by the larger public, thanks to the general economic euphoria. Debates about 'Third World' debts had raged over the previous decade, and, with help from hype by world-wide, grassroots campaigns like Jubilee 2000, which lobbied to alleviate the debts of low-income countries, and 2005's Make Poverty History, these debates continued to grab headlines at G8 Summits. However, the startling growth of 'First World' debts – personal, household, corporate and governmental – had only just begun to receive attention. While awareness of the scale of debts out there was growing, there was, at the time of writing, little public understanding or debate about the role played by the finance sector – central bankers, finance ministries, mortgage lenders, credit card issuers, insurance company managers, foreign exchange dealers, hedge fund operators – in burying millions of citizens, dozens of companies and a number of nations in debt.

At the same time there was not much *public* discussion of the threat these debts pose to global financial stability. But behind the scenes, private and public sector experts and analysts (e.g. Prof. Wynne Godley of Cambridge Endowment for Research in Finance, Tim Geithner of the US Federal Reserve, Stephen Roach at Morgan Stanley, Doug Noland at PrudentBear.com, Paul Krugman at Princeton, Nouriel Roubini and Brad Stetser at Roubini Global Economics) were feverishly debating the timing of what one called the coming 'global economic armageddon'.

They were joined by normally cautious economists at the International Monetary Fund (IMF) and the Bank for International Settlements (BIS) – the bank of the world's central bankers. Raghuram Rajan, the IMF's chief economist, said in April 2006:

> As the US deficit continues to be financed easily, the optimists who think there is nothing to worry about are gaining ground over the pessimists who think an abrupt and costly adjustment is likely. But the optimists have to be right every day while the pessimists need to be right only once. (*Guardian*, 20 April 2006)

Ariel Buira, formerly on the board of the International Monetary Fund and now a director of the Group of 24 countries (including China, India and Brazil) warned in March 2006 that a new global financial crisis caused by a plunge in the dollar is not only possible, but likely, and could be devastating for many developing countries.

All these experts shared grave concerns about the global economy's imbalances – in particular the imbalances caused by deficits and debts, which had proliferated in the decades since 1970. Their warnings were not echoed by presidents, prime ministers, finance ministers or more influential officials, like Anne Krueger, deputy managing director of the IMF. On the contrary, Ms Krueger made a very upbeat speech in April

2006, declaring that 'the world economy has rarely been in better shape than it is today' (Krueger, 2006).

The warnings from the 'bears' (pessimists) were drowned by the optimism of the 'bulls' and made little impact on the millions of consumers and the hundreds of companies in Anglo-American economies who confidently increased their borrowings, assured by politicians and economists that there was no harm in increased lending, in de-regulated credit and in de-regulated capital markets. Debtor-spenders were acting in their own interests and in the interests of the economy, these economists implied. By using this borrowing to finance purchases of shares on the booming stock market, property and consumer goods, they were boosting economic growth in their home economy, and world-wide.

Debtor-spenders were the heroes of the booming global economy.

Easy money and costly credit

The rise in easy, but costly credit after 1980 and its corollary – debt – would be glaringly obvious to anyone economically active in western economies before 1970. In contrast to the earlier period, a massive proliferation of lending through credit cards and other 'innovative' financial services had taken place. The contrast with the tough conditions for obtaining credit in the decades before 1970 could not have been greater.

As I explain in Chapter 1, de-regulation or liberalization in the 1970s of money and credit helped accelerate this process, at the same time as it enriched money-lenders, and indebted those without money. It also led to major imbalances at the global level. Above all it helped ensure that making money from money – whether through lending, speculation, tax avoidance, insurance, mergers and acquisitions (M&As), betting or gambling – had become the dominant activity of a global economy breaking free of its bearings in the real world.

As a result of these radical changes to what is known as the international financial architecture, the world economy is awash with credit 'vast as space' (M. Gustave de Puynode, quoted in Dunning Macleod, 1879) and its counterpart, debt: individual, household, corporate and governmental. This book will explore how the dominant economic policies of the 1980s and 1990s deflated real wages and the prices of consumer goods, largely because economists and bankers worked hard to ensure that governments adopted policies that suppressed such inflation. As a result, by 2006 most economies operated within an environment of disinflation or deflation.

Deflation ... involves a transference of wealth from the rest of the community to the rentier class and to all holders of titles to money; just as inflation involves the opposite. In particular it involves a transference from all borrowers, that is to say from traders, manufacturers, and farmers, to lenders, from the active to the inactive.

But whilst the oppression of the taxpayer for the enrichment of the rentier is the chief lasting result, there is another, more violent, disturbance during the period of transition... Modern business, being carried on largely with borrowed money, must necessarily be brought to a standstill by such a process. The wise man will be he who turns his assets into cash, withdraws from the risks and exertions of activity, and awaits in country retirement the steady appreciation promised him in the value of his cash. (Keynes, 1930, Chapter XXXV 'Problems of International Management' – II. The Gold Standard (Vol. II))

Wages and prices vs assets: rich vs poor

But while most governments now adopt economic policies that help suppress prices and wages, these policies have, at the same time, inflated the prices of assets. Assets include property, stocks and shares, works of art, racehorses, vintage cars and pricey jewellery. 'Intellectual property' or 'brands' are assets too, and increasingly the already-rich earn enormous sums by collecting rent on intellectual property: brands, inventions, music, or new medicines. (And in contrast to, for example, the owners and traders of tomatoes, shoes or hamburgers, the owners of patents or brands increasingly use the state, the law and the World Trade Organization (WTO) to both protect and guarantee extraordinarily high prices for 'rents' on these assets. This does not prevent them attacking the state for its 'nannying' role.)

The average employed citizen lives from a wage or salary; and the average small business-person from the sale of goods and services. Neither group, on the whole, can avoid work. The rich, in contrast, do not on the whole work, and instead live from income earned as rent on their assets.

Credit-fuelled asset price inflation

The availability since the late 1970s of easy and ever-larger sums of credit, lent against assets, has led to the massive inflation of property and other asset prices, and to extraordinary bubbles in these sectors. Those without assets have not found it as easy to turn on the easy credit tap. Instead they are pushed into the clutches of loan sharks offering unsecured loans and tough – very tough – credit conditions.

The availability of easy, if not necessarily cheap credit, compounded by the removal of restraints on the movement of money has generated enormous wealth; but also mountainous quantities of debt; volatility, or turbulence in the international financial system, and with it many financial crises. This has disturbed the Bank for International Settlements.

> ... A combination of deregulation and technological progress has had profound effects on financial systems.
>
> The build-up of debt levels over time, both domestically and internationally, can eventually also lead to economic problems with attendant and often substantial costs. Consider how long it took for Japan and East Asia to recover from their respective financial crises. Recent policy actions by a number of central banks, partly in response to credit-fuelled increases in house prices, indicate a growing recognition of this problem. True, formalising a policy response will be difficult since there is no clear benchmark to indicate when credit growth, debt levels or asset prices are 'too high'. Nevertheless, the stakes are certainly such as to warrant a significant analytical effort in this regard. (Bank for International Settlements, 2005)

As this club of central bankers explained in their 2005 annual report, the household savings rate in many industrial countries has trended sharply downwards; and debt levels have reached record highs. The external imbalances of nations have never been larger in the post-war period: 'The unprecedented size of the US deficit, the speed with which external debts are growing ... and the fact that US borrowing has primarily financed consumption (rather than investment) all suggest an eventual problem', wrote the normally restrained club of central bankers.

These debts include credit and store card debts. (In the US alone, 215 million adults hold more than a trillion credit cards.) There are rising student debts; debts mortgaged against property and other assets; corporate debts mortgaged against future income; the debts of healthcare systems, including government-owned healthcare systems, like Britain's NHS; vast, apparently unpayable debts owed to future pensioners; and sports club debts mortgaged against the gamble of future wins (e.g. Manchester United). Above all there are the enormous private and governmental, domestic and foreign debts of sovereign nations like Iceland, Turkey, New Zealand, Japan, South Korea, Australia and the United States, as well as those of many low-income countries. These debts are mortgaged against the future assets, livelihoods and lives of their people – and against the asset that is the ecosystem as a whole.

The world is truly living on 'borrowed time'.

Debt, de-regulation and the rich

As noted above, there is a strong correlation between the ballooning of these sovereign, corporate and personal debts on the one hand, financial crises on the other, and the de-regulation of finance in the 1970s. There is a particular correlation with the removal of controls over capital flows and credit.

This period contrasts with the three decades following World War II – decades during which finance and credit was regulated, and interest rates – short, medium, long, real, safe and risky – were largely fixed by governments. The decades from 1945 to 1970 have been described as a 'golden era of tranquillity in international capital markets, a fulfilment of the benediction "May you live in dull times"', by the renowned historian, Barry Eichengreen and co-author Peter Lindert (Eichengreen and Lindert, 1991).

Thanks to the liberalization of finance during the 1970s and 1980s (of which more below) the power to a) create unlimited sums of money (at little cost) b) manage flows of money across international borders and c) fix interest rates – was largely transferred by politicians to the private sector, away from the accountable public sector of democratic societies.

As a result of this transfer of massive economic power to the private sector, and of the loosening of controls over credit, money and credit became easily available. This stimulated and drove forward the international trade in goods and finance – celebrated as globalization.

One major consequence of this transformation of the global economy is that the rich have become richer; and the poor, poorer.

I do not believe this to be accidental.

Western nations, corporates and already-rich individuals have become much, much wealthier; but also, as a whole, much more indebted. The burden of debt, however, falls disproportionately on poor nations. In rich nations the burden falls disproportionately on the poor, particularly those who are asset-poor, i.e. without existing houses, racehorses, stocks and shares etc.

The US demonstrates this phenomenon well. The easy availability of credit has led to a rise in the value of assets held by those US households lucky enough to own assets. Their value has risen from $11 trillion in

1980 to $59 trillion in 2004. Over the same period total credit market debt in the US has ballooned from 170% of gross domestic product (GDP) to 313% of GDP (figures derived from Federal Reserve, Flow of Funds Accounts, and Bureau of Economic Analysis, National Income and Product Accounts).

Credit has enriched those who own, or are able to purchase assets like property, but also including money assets, because it enables them to leverage their assets *to obtain more*. This is best exemplified by the experience of those who already own houses. Since 1996 house prices in the US have risen by more than 45%, adjusting for inflation. This bubble has largely been financed by borrowing, as 'easy' but not necessarily cheap money has chased scarce assets like property in Manhattan or San Francisco. As the Center for Economic Policy Research notes, this has generated more than $5 trillion in housing bubble wealth for those who already own houses – the difference between the current market value of housing and the value if house prices had followed past trends and kept pace with inflation (Center for Economic Policy Research, July 2005).

Debt, de-regulation and the asset-poor

However to buy houses or homes in this market, those who do not already own assets have had to borrow well beyond their means. These and other debts have plunged individuals, households and major economies into crisis, often prolonged crisis. In the UK, insolvency and home repossessions are on the increase in 2006 – when the good times still prevail and unemployment is low. In the first quarter of 2006, insolvency soared with individual bankruptcies up 73% compared with the first quarter of 2005 (*Scotland on Sunday*, 7 May 2006).

Enron, WorldCom, GlobalCrossing, Parmalat and General Motors are but some of the prominent corporations that have been capsized by unpayable debts. For some, like Enron, GlobalCrossing, WorldCom and Parmalat, the rise in debt is linked to corruption. The bankruptcies of financial firms like Barings, Drexel Burnham Lambert and the Long-Term Capital Management hedge fund, and the recent trading suspension of the hedge fund Refco, remind us that it is not just individuals and corporations, but also the unregulated, larger and more complex financial institutions that can accumulate debts. The Bank for International Settlements worries that the failure of these institutions could portend a global, systemic crisis. US billionaire investor Warren Buffett has warned that it is the trade in derivatives – complex financial instruments – which is especially dangerous and could push not only companies but entire markets to collapse. He pointed out that governments and central banks could not control or even effectively monitor the risks of these instruments which he famously described as 'financial weapons of mass destruction' (Buffett, 2003).

The sovereign nations that have already endured sustained crises include most African and many Latin American economies whose people and ecosystems continue to suffer the effects of the 1980s and 1990s debt crises. Despite the valiant efforts of a world-wide movement of people clustered around the Jubilee 2000 campaign, rich creditors have made only piecemeal efforts at alleviating the debts of these low-income countries. While there have been small improvements (in historical terms) in the prices of some of their commodity exports, they have had to struggle, simultaneously, with increases in the price of oil. As a result, their foreign debts continue to rise.

But debt crises are not confined to the poorest countries. One such First World debt crisis erupted in Japan in 1990, miring that very rich country in more than 15 years of personal, corporate and government debts, rising unemployment, business bankruptcies and deflation. This economic degradation has led to incalculable and often invisible human anguish and suffering, including rises in alcoholism and family breakdowns. Sixteen years later, Japan had still not fully recovered from the crisis. Other countries that have suffered include the countries of South East Asia, like Indonesia, South Korea and Thailand; but also Russia, all seriously affected by the 1997/98 financial crisis. Another is Argentina, still recovering from its major default on foreign loans in 2001.

The world's biggest debtors

While the US and UK appear to have so far escaped crises, they have nevertheless moved from being the world's biggest creditors, and instead become the world's biggest debtors. The foreign debts of the richest country in the world pose a real and widely recognized threat to the US itself; but also to the global economy. The US external deficit has risen to record levels – 6% of GDP at the time of writing – and this despite a reduction in the real value of the dollar of more than 20% from its peak in 2002. (The US, unlike most poor countries, repays debts in its own currency.) There is no precedent for a country responsible for the world's reserve currency maintaining a current account deficit of such magnitude.

In contrast to the 'golden era of tranquillity' between 1945 and 1970, since 1980 these debts and imbalances have led in turn to political crises within and between nations that have wreaked civil war, pain, unemployment, loss and havoc on the lives of millions of innocent people affected. In 1980 there were 8.4 million refugees world-wide. By 1992 the number had risen to 17.8 million. And by 2005 the total number of people of concern to the United Nations High Commission for Refugees (UNHCR) stood at 19.2 million – people displaced by civil war, disease, famine and ecological disaster (UNHCR, 2005).

Branko Milanovic, one of the World Bank's top economists, demonstrates that the average annualized rate of growth for all *countries*, unweighted by population, was only 0.7% per annum for the period 1980–2002; a full 2 percentage points lower than during the previous 20 years (1960–80) (Milanovic, 2005). He shows that the poorest countries have fallen further behind middle-income and rich countries. This reversal in economic fortunes has led to the loss of livelihoods and of lives; to the loss of opportunities for children and young people, and to the worsening of their life-chances.

However, while these reversals have hurt poor countries, they have not resulted in the kind of generalized economic upheaval that hurts the rich: lenders as much as borrowers. In other words, despite the massive growth of domestic and sovereign debt, despite the immense pain and suffering of the people of poor nations, and of the poor in rich nations, the world has not experienced the 'convulsions of bankruptcy dragging down lenders as well as debtors' witnessed during the debt crisis of the 1920s and 1930s (Hudson, 2005). This may help explain the continued complacency of politicians in rich nations towards the irresponsibility of the finance sector; towards global imbalances and high levels of debt and towards the injustice of current lending and interest-setting practices.

How to 'unwind' the imbalances?

To avoid a financial crisis these debts will have to unwind in the gradual and benign manner preferred by central bankers. For this to happen, asserts the Bank for International Settlements, governments and their citizens may have to 'commit to some unpleasant compromises now' (Bank for International Settlements, 2005).

Such compromises will require government intervention and the adoption of standards, regulations and laws to protect debtors, creditors and the planet, from the consequences of aggressive lending and exploitation. Control over the creation of credit, over flows of capital, and over interest rates will, in my view, have to be transferred away from private individuals, operating through the often irresponsible and unaccountable invisible hand of markets, and restored back to governments, answerable to their people. Such transfers from the private sector back to democratic governments have happened before, as Britain's Hugh Dalton noted: 'during the Napoleonic Wars, during the Great War and again during the Great Slump' of the 1920s and 1930s (Dalton, 1935). The transfer from private to public was confirmed in 1944, with the establishment of the Bretton Woods system, after the immensely destructive period of the Great Depression and World War II.

History may once again be about to repeat itself. Once again, just as in post-1929 US and Europe, there will need to be substantial intervention to protect the industrial and agricultural sectors. To limit unemployment, governments will be obliged to intervene to protect the employees of companies like General Motors whose $453 billion of debt was reduced to junk status in the spring of 2005. Governments will have to intervene to lift the burden from the younger generation of heavily indebted students; to cushion pensioners from the imploding deficits of private sector pension schemes – predicted to rise to $150 billion in the UK alone. Above all, a crisis will require that world leaders finally co-ordinate and co-operate together to prevent a sustained and intractable financial crisis, and possibly a contracted global depression, which will impact most forcefully on the poorest countries.

Recent G8 Summits have been notable for their attention to celebrities, big rock concerts and other forms of media hype, and for their neglect of global imbalances. World leaders have used these PR events to mask their irresponsible failure to work together and intervene to restore stability to the global economy.

The need for ethics

However, co-ordinated intervention by governments, the adoption of standards, regulations and laws are fiercely resisted by the finance sector, and routinely derided by their friends in the economics profession and the media. Unfortunately, their resistance is likely only to be overcome in the event of a crisis, when these same financiers, economists and commentators will do a U-turn, and demand that the 'nanny state' – i.e. innocent taxpayers – provide compensation to shore up their losses.

This book has been written to make the case that western societies have to revive moral standards and set clear *ethical* benchmarks by which to regulate credit and debt, and to rein in the finance sector.

Ethical standards for the regulation of money, interest and credit would normally issue from society's moral sense; from inborn ideas of justice, fairness and harmony; from a sense of that which is right and wrong; and from some understanding of nature's scale and limits. It would be helpful in developing such ethical standards if western society's intellectual, religious and political leaders expressed open antipathy to the ruthless exploitation of the planet's finite physical and human capital. That is, to the exploitation and depletion of nature's limited assets; the pollution of nature's sinks; and the exploitation of those individuals who lack assets, most often poor debtors, by those who hold assets, most often creditors.

It is particularly important that Christian leaders should once again take up the cudgels against usury, and emulate their leader, Christ, in chasing money-lenders from the temples that dominate human communities. Western failure to maintain ethical standards in matters relating to finance is paralleled by Christianity's obsession with arcane matters that belong to the private sphere. This obsession serves as a useful, but dangerous distraction from the public sphere: in particular, finance and economics, money and money-lenders.

The finance sector, I will argue in this book, has, since the time of John Calvin (1509–1564) successfully manipulated, evaded and discredited Christian moral and ethical standards – in particular the concept of usury – that placed limits on the capital gains made by money-lenders and other financial institutions. It should come as no surprise, therefore, that western economies are experiencing historically unprecedented rates of usury. Christianity's neglect of the sin of usury contrasts with Islam's success in discrediting usury. In Islamic societies, interest on lending (*riba*) is still considered odious, and forbidden; and attempts by the finance sector to legitimize the institution of interest have failed.

Renewing and re-invigorating ethical standards that define and condemn usury should then provide the basis for new laws and regulation.

Finance sector activists have not stopped at weakening religious ethics: they have gone further. They have successfully attacked and marginalized those academics and intellectuals who question the dominance of finance; those that call, as Keynes once dared to do, for the 'euthanasia of the rentier' (Keynes, 1936). There is virtually no university department or journal of economics left in the world that challenges 'high finance'. Indeed high finance is not even a subject of economic discourse. Instead, departments of economics and their staff, obliged to become hired guns to finance research, are packed with ideologues inventing arcane theories for obscuring or justifying the activities of their ideological masters. Economic commentators in the financial press possess a blind spot for the finance sector and develop convoluted arguments to explain, for example, the high cost of housing without ever referring to the role of the finance sector and of credit in fuelling housing bubbles.

This growing, secretive power of finance has, not surprisingly, required an increased deference to, and worship of the god of money. But as Midas discovered to his cost, the power to turn all to gold cannot fill our bellies; nor can it grant us love, companionship and community to meet our emotional and spiritual needs; and nor can gold or money provide a healthy, balanced ecosystem to sustain life. For millions of decent, upright people, particularly in rich countries, a widening gap exists between the alienating and exploitative values of the finance sector, and the values we hold dear. These include long-held and civilized values of economic justice, equity, honesty, decency, peace, contentment, dignity, love and respect for those close to us; for our communities and for the earth. *Homo economicus* is, as Herman Daly and John Cobb rightly argue, abstracted from any notion of community, and is now made up of isolated individuals, many millions of them unemployed and ravaged by the indignity of worklessness and poverty (Daly and Cobb, 1989). Those more privileged, live separate, atomized life-styles (often in gated communities) while endlessly seeking redemption in the temples we have built to consumption.

There is a gulf between these atomized privileged individuals – political and financial elites – and their communities. At the same time there is a gulf opening up between our high rates of consumption and environmental sustainability – evidenced by the threat of global warming. Above all, there is a gulf opening up between the productive and unproductive sectors of the global economy; a growing disconnect between the real economy – where food is grown, goods are made and exchanged, value is added through knowledge and skill – and the virtual economy of bank money, gambling, tax evasion, speculation, credit cards and debt.

This disconnect is embodied in the term 'debt' – the concept of living beyond our means; beyond our environmental budgets; of mortgaging the future; of being in hock or enslaved to creditors that are often usurers.

Democracy and the need for a grand alliance

While it is vital to have a robust ethical foundation for laws and regulation, these are not feasible without democratic government. Democratic government is, in turn, not feasible, I argue, if regulation and the allocation of key resources is transferred from elected representatives to invisible, unaccountable and un-electable elites operating through markets.

It is vital, therefore, that democratic, accountable governments, not invisible financiers and speculators, should once again be put in charge of the creation and regulation of, money, interest and credit.

That is, finance sector elites should be ousted from their role as *masters* of the global economy, and instead be returned to their proper role as *servants* to the economy. This can best be done, in my view, through organized political challenges from a grand alliance: an alliance between the productive sectors of the economy, broadly defined as *Industry* – those who research, make, grow and sell goods and services; and *Labour* – anyone who works by hand or brain. In the final chapter I will argue that such an organized political alliance is vital if Finance is to be effectively constrained, regulated and subordinated to the interests of humanity and the ecosystem.

The dual threat of financial and climate melt-downs

If First World debt crises become systemic, as seems likely, the world as a whole is at risk of another Great Depression. This grave threat coincides with another: the threat of climate change, and is in many ways linked.

Humanity's exploitation of the earth – land in its broadest sense – and of labour, is largely driven, I will argue in these pages, by the finance sector's demands for exponential rates of return from the productive (broadly industry and agriculture) sectors of the global economy. These exponential returns – capital gains – differ from the profits made on investment. The dynamics of the latter tend to be volatile, rising and falling in response to increased, or falling costs; increased, or falling sales. The dynamics of capital gains, by contrast, can rise exponentially – to 'celestial spheres' (Hudson et al., 1994). To generate these exponential returns for Finance, both the industrial and the agricultural sectors need, in turn, to increase consumption and with it, their exploitation of Land and Labour.

Finance as parasite

Until recently, the established pattern of agricultural and industrial production meant that profits were used for research and development; for investment in new equipment and for hiring labour. That world is fast disappearing. Instead we live in a world in which profits are largely used to repay debts; or to speculate; or to merge and acquire new assets. As a result, research and investment programmes are cut back; and labour is made redundant. A stark example of such pressure by the finance sector is provided by the oil industry. Oil companies regularly replaced the oil they sold, with new finds. No longer. According to a study in October 2005 by Wood Mackenzie, the oil industry has shed engineers, lowered investment and failed to replace production. Lord Browne, CEO of BP, explains why: 'We are in the business of efficiency', he told the *Wall Street Journal*, 'because we have to maximize the amount of free cash flow available for shareholders (i.e. the finance sector) over the long haul'. Lord Browne had persuaded his board that capital gains could be made through mergers and acquisitions; not through the research and development of new oil fields. His approach was copied by the rest of the oil sector, and cheered on by the finance sector. But this strategy led to a sharp fall in spending on oil exploration, which left the industry unprepared when China's growth dramatically increased demand for oil in 2005.

Today's heavyweight commentators celebrate this power of the finance sector over the productive sector. Lightly-regulated institutions that use borrowed money to gamble and speculate on a grand scale, notably hedge funds, are cheered on because they are simultaneously asset-stripping profitable companies, and making them more 'efficient'. In reality, they are acting parasitically, using their 'hosts' to extract more and more assets for the finance sector. The healthy, real world 'hosts' of small businesses, big global companies or national economies invariably succumb to the predatory instincts of a sector that behaves as an invasive parasite – and often does so using corrupt methods.

To survive, agriculture and industry are increasingly having to turn their backs on research, investment and productive activity, i.e. the business of growing food in a sustainable way: researching, investing, producing, buying and selling useful goods and services. Instead these sectors are turning to the business of making money from money – often to repay accumulating debts.

Many companies and corporations that have been bankrupted by debts have shut down and sacked their workers; others have downsized and laid off workers. The 'if you can't beat them, join them' brigade – from the British Post Office, to supermarkets, department stores (think of store credit cards) – are scaling back on productive activities, and transforming their businesses instead into financial institutions.

This is because making money from money is so much more profitable than say, making money from growing food, providing a postal service, making clothes or building homes.

Capital gains vs profits

There is thus intensifying competition between sectors where profits are made from money, known as *capital gains*, and sectors where *profits* are made from making or growing useful products.

In the past, many people (including Marxists) were concerned both about profits per se, and also about the rate of profit. Today we live in a world in which making a profit from productive activity is no longer something that merits, in my view, criticism from Marxists. Instead it is an increasingly unusual activity, the achievement of often heroic industrialists, manufacturers, retailers and farmers; and their diminishing pools of employed labour. They undertake productive activity using costly, borrowed money; and as a result, build up mountainous debts. It is this debt, not 'structural rigidities' which stands in the way of productive activity.

To make profits, farmers and industrialists have to engage, first, with the land in the broadest sense (i.e. earth's resources). Land is limited, and can be subject to drought, erosion or floods; to shortages and gluts, which can cause costs to rise, as well as fall.

Second, industrialists, farmers and other entrepreneurs have to engage with labour. Labour can help lower or increase the cost of growing or making goods and services. This can lead to increased or decreased competitiveness, and also raise or lower profits.

Bankers, financiers and money-lenders do not face these challenges directly. They do not engage with land and labour in this, the broadest sense, or if they do it is at best in a disconnected way, when, for example, they take control of businesses and extract assets from them. They can make capital gains from creating money, from charging rent (interest) on that money; from buying cheap and selling dear; from tax avoidance, and from speculation and gambling. *All without engaging either with labour or land*. Indeed private banks make immense profits from an activity that is essentially without cost: in other words, by entering numbers into a ledger and creating money. (This helps explain why the headquarters of banks are based in elaborate, formidable-looking buildings that resemble Greek Temples and Roman pantheons – the more to disguise the largely costless activity taking place inside.)

It is this reality – that money can be made from money more profitably than money can be made from engaging with land and labour in productive activity – that often causes entrepreneurs and industrialists to give up productive activity, and diversify into making money from money. Today my local supermarket not only sells tomatoes, trainers and seed packets, it also sells money: bank money, insurance and even credit cards. In other words, my supermarket can, at virtually no cost, sell money for more money.

The additional cost of money

However, while money is able to grow exponentially, the means of repayment of money, rent and interest, lies outside money itself. As I explore later in the book, Aristotle was the first to recognize this. He noted that while the loan of a cow contains within itself the means of repayment (i.e. a calf borne by the cow); and while seeds similarly contain within themselves the means of repayment, metal and other kinds of money are barren, and have no powers of generation (Aristotle, 1962). *Any interest paid in money must originate from some other source or process.* Those sources include the earth's raw materials or commodities; and the processes include human labour. Hence, with the exponential rise of money and/or credit, and the need for compensation or repayment (rent and interest) of those with money, we have exponential increases in other processes of wealth generation: exploitation of the land (in the broadest sense) and labour.

The financial rentier sector is basically a *'free-luncher'* to quote Michael Hudson (Hudson, 2005). While we live with the delusion that the finance sector provides credit and other resource allocation services needed to create tangible wealth, the fact is that a reverse parasitic process takes place.

While many believe that banks create credit by lending out their savings or reserves, the truth is quite different, as this book explains in Chapter 2. It is not lenders, but borrowers that create credit. In other words it is the application for a loan, and the guarantee of that loan against an asset (e.g. a home) that enables a lender/banker to enter a number into a ledger and create money or credit. The asset, or the owner's salary is the tangible wealth and the credit or debt simply becomes a means for draining that wealth from the home-owner to the bank or lender.

The heavy costs of the parasitic sector

Without democratic regulation over, and restraints on the creation of these debts, banks and money-lenders assume a parasitic role on the tangible wealth of the economy, on the well-being of people, and on the ecosystem.

US Iowa State Senator Roger Stewart (D-Preston) describes car title lenders as, 'financial parasites that prey upon individuals and families in financial distress.'

There oughta be a law...

Car title loans – sounds okay – probably something like giving the bank a lien on a new car until it's paid off, right? Wrong! Car title loans are predatory lending schemes that target down-on-their-luck Iowans.

A person needing a loan, usually a few hundred bucks, goes to a car title lender. The borrower hands over their car title and an extra set of keys and immediately gets the loan – which is due in full in 15 days. Predictably, most borrowers are unable to pay the loan off in 15 days. Fees kick in, which, coupled with the 360% annual interest rate, in just a few months drive the balance owed to amounts that quickly double or triple the amount borrowed. Since one missed payment is grounds for repossession, often the car title lender drives away with the borrower's car. Over 1,600 Iowans have lost their cars to car title lenders.

Twenty-seven states have passed laws to make car title loans illegal or to place limits on the rate of interest that can be charged. In 2005, the Iowa Senate, on a unanimous vote, passed a bill setting the maximum interest rate on car title loans at 21%. The bill died in the Iowa House.

This year, Speaker Christopher Rants (R-Sioux City), who controls which bills are debated in the House, has said that restrictions on car title loans are not needed. Coincidentally, Rod Aycox, the owner of car title lender, LoanMax, gave Speaker Rants a $500 contribution in 2005. Another $40,000 was contributed to a political action organization with ties to Speaker Rants.

<www.iowaaflcio.org/vol_06–04.htm>, 10 February 2006

By assuming this bloodsucker role, the finance sector acts, ultimately, against its own interest.

This can perhaps best be demonstrated by examining the role of the finance sector in poor, highly indebted nations. For it is the finance sector that has for several decades dictated what Hudson calls the 'anorexic monetary policies of the IMF...imposing austerity programs to squeeze out a fiscal surplus to pay global creditors' (Hudson et al., 1994). These countries have been (and are) obliged to divert their savings to foreign creditors for ever-increasing debt repayments. These precious, scarce savings could not, and cannot be used therefore to finance domestic investment, boost employment and raise living standards. Instead they are sent abroad to swell the global build-up of finance capital. The privatization or sell-off of vital public assets at often knock-down prices has been just another means by which foreigners can obtain assets cheaply in low-income countries. The effect of these parasitic policies in Africa and Latin America over the decades since the liberalization of finance in the 1980s has led to reversals in economic growth rates, and notable declines in economic activity.

This behaviour by the 'free-lunchers' of the finance sector is not confined to low-income countries. The richest nations are the most deeply indebted of all, if only because they have more assets to pledge, and hence credibility, that is, the belief by creditors that they can be repaid *with interest* for their loan advances. For creditors are not satisfied with draining wealth from an asset; they seek to multiply the value of their take by adding interest, and at times, compounding interest.

In other words, like a parasite the finance sector invades otherwise relatively healthy economic bodies, rich and poor, and manipulates these to generate greater returns (interest and rent) for the finance sector itself. By doing so, it has weakened, and is weakening these host bodies. This includes individuals, from students to home-owners to pensioners. Small and large businesses from the local 'Mom and Pop shops' to Freddie Laker's brave low-cost airline, to Enron. And whole economies: from Argentina to South Korea to the United States.

This parasitic behaviour threatens the economic health of all these economic actors, including, I repeat, ultimately, the health of the finance sector itself.

The shock of 'corrections'

This usury may not be immediately visible to corporations lending money to hedge funds or borrowing huge sums of money in the international capital markets, through bond issues and other financial instruments. Nor is it visible to those in thrall to banks and other dispensers of credit and credit cards, those made delirious by the opportunities that credit provides for endless, relentless consumption.

But the dream-like state of these borrowers and lenders is invariably shattered by what economists call 'corrections' but which we may safely call shocks: unemployment, bankruptcy or a wider financial crisis – over which they may have no control. One need only ask the victims of low-income country debt crises; of the Japanese property bubble which burst after 1990; of the Argentine crisis; or of the Enron, WorldCom or Parmalat debt crises; or indeed those millions in 'booming' western economies who are already facing bankruptcy and the repossession of their homes.

> A father of two killed himself after the Halifax (bank) won a court order to evict his family and repossess their home ... Mr. Beech left a note saying that the Halifax's decision to repossess his home because of mortgage arrears of just £4,714.66 was 'the last straw'. (*Daily Mail*, 15 February 2006)

The finance sector's spin doctors are likely to blame the victims – the debtor-spenders – for high levels of debt. By this means they will not only neutralize and silence victims, but also evade responsibility. This book, in contrast, will try to re-balance the debate. It will examine the roles and responsibilities of lenders and borrowers, citizens, politicians, economists and central bankers for the re-engineered economy and the coming debt crisis.

It is written in the hope that greater understanding of the international financial system will help ordinary members of society challenge and transform the economies we live in; and adopt a more rational response to financial crisis. I believe it vital that we prevent the irrational outbursts of racism and anti-semitism that added war, genocide and devastation to the Anglo-American financial crises of the 1920s and 1930s.

The book's overwhelming case is this: our, local, national and international financial systems do not have to be this way. These financial systems are not a gift from God. They are not a natural phenomenon. They are wholly artificial and man-made. We, the people, can change them. We do not have to passively accept the status quo. We do not have to conduct our lives and economies within a system designed by usurers, those who live parasitically on financially healthy individuals, households, farmers, corporations and national economies – and our ecosystem.

We do not need to live in ways that are uncontrollable, unstable and subject to systemic risk. We do not have to agree to, and encourage an economic system that has burdened millions with debt. That enriches those who already enjoy privileges and advantages. That has therefore made the rich immeasurably richer, and the poor, poorer. Nor do we have to live within a financial system that ignores the limits to our fragile ecosystem.

Above all, we do not have to adopt or live within the moral and ethical codes of a financial system designed by usurers. We can base it on the moral philosophy and intellectual scaffolding provided by brilliant thinkers and economists like Aristotle, Karl Marx, John Stuart Mill, John Maynard Keynes, Karl Polanyi, Ernst Friedrich Schumacher or the great contemporary economists, Jane Jacobs, Kari (Polanyi) Levitt and Herman Daly.

We can base it on values we hold dear – values to do with our respect for the planet, and the rich diversity of all its plants and creatures; our love for families and friends; our responsibility to future generations; our concern for neighbours and communities both near and far; our belief in solidarity and the value of collective action; our commitment to optimal scale, distributive justice and full employment.

Conclusion

Another, more just and sustainable world is indeed possible. First we need to enquire and understand. Then we need to join together to reassert our long-standing values of justice, equity and sustainability. Finally we need to act and to organize – politically – at local, national and international levels. Above all, we need new alliances: between Industry and Labour; between Industry and Labour and faith organizations; between those defending the ecosystem and those working for humanity. We need such alliances to strengthen the spines of our elected politicians, and to challenge the dominance and power of the finance sector.

To return Finance once again to its role as servant to the global economy, and to the ecosystem.

Sources and Suggested Reading

Aristotle, *The Politics*. Re-presented and revised by T.J. Saunders, Penguin Books, 1992. Translation by T.A. Sinclair, first published in 1962.

Bank for International Settlements, 75th Annual Report, 27 June 2005. <www.bis.org/publ/annualreport.htm>.

Buffett, W., Chairman's Letter to Shareholders of Berkshire Hathaway Inc., 21 February 2003. <www.berkshirehathaway.com/letters/2002pdf.pdf>.

Buira, A., quoted in Khor, M., 'Global Trends: Warning of a New Financial Crisis', 20 March 2006. <www.twnside.org.sg/title2/gtrends96.htm>.

Center for Economic Policy Research, 'The Housing Bubble Fact Sheet', July 2005. <www.cepr.net/publications/housing_fact_2005_07.pdf>.

Dalton, Hugh, *Practical Socialism*. G. Routledge, 1935.

Daly, H., *Beyond Growth*. Beacon Press, 1996.

Daly, H., *Steady-State Economics*. W.H. Freeman and Company, 1977.

Daly, H.E. and Cobb, J.B., *For the Common Good: Redirecting the Economy toward Community, the Environment, and a Sustainable Future*. First published by Beacon Press, 1989.

Dunning Macleod, M. *The Theory and Practice of Banking*, Chapter IV: 'The Theory of Credit'. Longmans, London, 1879.

Eichengreen, B., *Globalizing Capital: A History of the International Monetary System*. Princeton University Press, 1996.

Eichengreen, B. and Lindert, P.H., *The International Debt Crisis in Historical Perspective*. MIT Press, 1991.

Galbraith, J.K., *Money: Whence it Came, Where it Went*. Houghton Mifflin Company, 1975.

Galbraith, J.K., *The Great Crash 1929*. First published by Houghton Mifflin Company, 1954.

Guardian, 20 April 2006, 'Leaders risk taking us back to 1930s, says IMF', by Larry Elliott.

Guardian, 7 March 2006, 'HSBC sets European record with £12bn profit', by Fiona Walsh.

Guardian, 22 February 2006, 'Barclaycard sets aside £1bn for bad debts', by Jill Treanor.

Guardian, 23 November 2005, 'It may be beyond passé – but we'll have to do something about the rich', by Jonathan Freedland.

HSBC, *Annual Results Media Release*, 6 March 2006.

Hudson, M. Unpublished essays. 2005.

Hudson, M., *Super Imperialism: The Origin and Fundamentals of U.S. World Dominance*. Pluto Press, 2003.

Hudson, M.; Miller, G.J. and Feder, Kris, from the Prologue to *A Philosophy for a Fair Society* in Georgist Paradigm Series: Editor, Fred Harrison. Published by Shepheard-Walwyn (Publishers) Ltd, in association with Centre for Incentive Taxation Ltd, 1994.

Jacobs, J., *Dark Age Ahead*. First published by Random House, 2004.

Jacobs, J., *The Death and Life of Great American Cities*. First published by Random House, 1961.

Keynes, J.M, *The Collected Writings of John Maynard Keynes*, 30 Volumes. General editors: D.E. Moggridge and E.S. Johnson. Macmillan and Cambridge University Press for the Royal Economics Society, 1971–89.

Keynes, J.M., *The General Theory of Employment, Interest and Money*. First published by Macmillan Cambridge University Press, for the Royal Economic Society, 1936.

Keynes, J.M., *A Treatise on Money*. First published by Macmillan, 1930.

Krueger, Anne, 'A Remarkable Prospect: Opportunities and Challenges for the Modern Global Economy'. IMF, 2 May 2006.

Levitt, K., *Reclaiming Development: Independent Thought and Caribbean Community*. Ian Randle Publishers, 2005.

Levitt, K., *Silent Surrender (New Edition) The Multinational Corporation in Canada*. McGill Queen's University Press, 2002.

Marx, K., *Capital*. First published in 1867.

Marx, K. and Engels, F., *The Communist Manifesto*. First published in English in 1848.

Milanovic, Branko, *Worlds Apart: Measuring International and Global Inequality*. Princeton University Press, 2005.

Mill, J.S., *Principles of Political Economy*. First published in 1848.

Papadimitriou, Dimitri B.; Chilcote, E. and Zezza, G., *Are Housing Prices, Household Debt, and Growth Sustainable?* Strategic Analysis, Levy Economic Institute, Bard College, January 2006.

Polanyi, K., *The Great Transformation: The Political and Economic Origins of Our Time.* First published by Beacon Press, 1944.

Ruskin, J., *Unto This Last.* First published in *Cornhill* Magazine, December 1860.

Schumacher, E.F., *Small is Beautiful.* First published by Blond and Briggs Ltd, 1973.

Scotland on Sunday, 7 May 2006, 'If we're so rich, then why are we all in debt?', by Bill Jameson.

UNHCR, 'Refugees by Numbers', 2005 edition. <www.unhcr.org/cgi-bin/vtx/basics/opendoc.pdf?tbl=BASICS&id=416e3eb24>.

Wood Mackenzie, 'Oil and Gas Exploration, Reserve Replacement Down Worldwide', 3 October 2005. <www.woodmacresearch.com/cgi-bin/corp/portal/corp/corpPressDetail.jsp?BV_SessionID=@@@@1773440703.1148925419@@@@&BV_EngineID=cccdaddhlkhemjmcflgcegjdffjdgih.0&oid=719152>.

1

Globalization: the House that Finance Built

Communities must protect themselves against an imperious international financial trust ... If international finance is to combine, the slavery of labour is inevitable, and the politics of the world will become the will of finance. Finance can command the sluices of every stream that runs to turn the wheels of industry, and can put fetters upon the feet of every Government in existence .... No community can be free until it controls its financial organisation ...

Ramsay MacDonald, Britain's first Labour Prime Minister, 1924, in *Socialism Critical and Constructive*. Quoted in Dalton (1935)

The international financial system – at the root of the crisis

How did we get here? How did Anglo-American economies build up the mountains of debt and the historically high deficits that now threaten to destabilize the global economy? Our international financial system was, until relatively recently, stable, equitable and fair. Lending and borrowing was under control, with high rates of saving in OECD countries. Income inequality was at its lowest. The crisis of the 1920s and 1930s had taught western societies grave lessons about the folly of allowing 'the money-lenders to take over the temple' – the main theme of President Franklin D. Roosevelt's inaugural speech, in 1933 – at the height of the international financial crisis.

a host of unemployed citizens face the grim problem of existence, and an equally great number toil with little return. Only a foolish optimist can deny the dark realities of the moment.

Yet our distress comes from no failure of substance. We are stricken by no plague of locusts ... Nature still offers her bounty and human efforts have multiplied it. Plenty is at our doorstep, but a generous use of it languishes in the very sight of the supply. Primarily this is because the rulers of the exchange of mankind's goods have failed, through their own stubbornness and their own incompetence, have admitted their failure, and abdicated. Practices of the unscrupulous money changers stand indicted in the court of public opinion, rejected by the hearts and minds of men.

... Faced by failure of credit they have proposed only the lending of more money. Stripped of the lure of profit by which to induce our people to follow their false leadership, they have resorted to exhortations, pleading tearfully for restored confidence. They know only the rules of a generation of self-seekers. They have no vision, and when there is no vision the people perish.

The money changers have fled from their high seats in the temple of our civilization. We may now restore that temple to the ancient truths. The measure of the restoration lies in the extent to which we apply social values more noble than mere monetary profit. (Roosevelt, 1933)

Bankers, economists and politicians like Roosevelt had learned painful lessons. They later became the architects of a much more stable, just and regulated post-war system – the Bretton Woods system. It was by no means perfect, but it led to a period of economic and social stability for which there is today genuine nostalgia. Under Bretton Woods elected governments and their people were put in the driving seat. The movement of capital was regulated and, for a brief post-war period, provided the means and mechanisms for governments to set interest rates. Britain's Labour government, led by Clement Attlee, attempted a deliberate cheap money policy. Attlee's Chancellor Hugh Dalton, who succeeded in nationalizing the Bank of England, was, however, challenged by Finance, in the shape of the City of London. In his memoirs he wrote: 'The forces against me, in the City and elsewhere, were very powerful and determined ... I felt I could not count on a good chance of victory. I was not well armed. So I retreated' (Dalton, 1962, p. 239).

The Bretton Woods system also set controls and stabilizers which regulated trade and discouraged countries from building up massive trade deficits – or surpluses for that matter. Nevertheless, citing the WTO, the IMF notes that annual growth rates in world trade reached 12% a year between 1951 and 1975, but never rose above 10% after 1975 (IMF

Anne Krueger, May 2006). These conditions provided the framework for a period of peace, stability, trade expansion and economic growth.

Then, in the early 1970s, this international financial architecture was dramatically, and unilaterally, dismantled (Helleiner, 1994). President Nixon of the US headed up the demolition crew. This might surprise many who believe that the international financial system is 'natural' and has a life of its own; or that it is the construct of big business and the finance sector. It is important for our democracies, and for the empowerment of citizens, to understand that the system has been constructed by political process. It can only be transformed or dismantled by elected politicians, because it involves changes to legislation and regulation put in place by their predecessors.

The presidents, prime ministers, congressmen and -women, who dismantled Bretton Woods, were of course encouraged by the finance sector, by the new breed of neo-liberal economists and by unwise officials. Nevertheless it required elected politicians to make the big changes.

Together these people helped construct a liberalized, ultimately less stable international financial system which has come to be known as globalization. In contrast to the Bretton Woods system, globalization once again strips governments of key powers; prioritizes the interests of the finance sector, in particular creditors, through the free and unregulated flow of capital and trade, and through the implementation of deflationary policies, which lower wages and prices, but increase the cost of debt. This latest system of liberalized finance, globalization, has helped to marginalize the role of elected, democratic states and parliaments; has led to instability and financial crises, lower rates of growth in trade; to protectionism and rising nationalism; and has resulted in much lower real rates of economic growth across the world.

Under the new international financial system, just as under its nineteenth-century predecessor, the gold standard, governments have lost the power to control the flow of capital, to set short- and long-term interest rates; and to control the creation of credit. Just as in the nineteenth century, globalization has led to the de-regulation of trade, and to the build-up of surpluses and deficits. Individuals and corporations have been freed up (by governments, their politicians and officials) to pursue their own interests, regardless of the broader interests of their community or country, or indeed of the global economy.

Globalization has immensely expanded opportunities for both rich and poor countries. However, it has also led to tensions between trading nations, to the demise of multilateralism and to the rise of nationalism and protectionism. (Such nationalism and protectionism is often blamed on local, short-term problems. Francis Fukuyama, for example, suggests that the chaotic outcome of the war in Iraq is feeding US economic nationalism and isolationism (*Guardian*, 21 March 2006). It is much more likely that the economic insecurity encouraged by globalization is feeding US nationalism and isolationism – just as it did before World War I, and in the 1930s.)

Globalization has polarized wealth; it has enriched the rich countries, while the poor have become poorer – both within countries, and also between nations.

It has triggered international debt crises (in e.g. Mexico, Russia, Thailand, South Korea, Brazil, Indonesia and Argentina); and has encouraged the build-up of personal, corporate and governmental debts. It is widely recognized as fragile. Like the levees of New Orleans, the current international financial architecture is unlikely, without some regulation, to withstand coming financial hurricanes – at least according to the bank of central bankers – the Bank for International Settlements in the conclusion of their June 2005 report.

The house that Finance built

The basic concepts underlying the international financial system are comprehensible to anyone who has ever gambled, managed a budget; taken out a mortgage or loan; and handled the exchange of money into foreign currency. Statistics are more challenging. Understanding how statistics are manipulated is a highly developed skill in itself, requiring years of study. Nevertheless it is possible to understand, analyse and follow the workings of the international financial system, by simply grasping the key underlying concepts, and then developing a judgement about the array of statistics that assail us each day.

First, however, it is necessary to briefly survey the recent historical background. In doing so, this chapter will necessarily skate over and simplify many debates taking place within the political and economic spheres. Readers interested in these debates are referred to experts in the reading list at the end of this and other chapters.

The purpose of this chapter is to unravel and analyse one key theme in international financial systems since the nineteenth century – the role of the finance sector in international economic and political crises. This theme is often overlooked, denied or simply ignored by economists, and economic and political historians.

The fantastic machinery of the gold standard

The gold standard put a fantastic machinery of global self-regulation into place.

Block (2001)

The story of how today's international financial system was created goes back some way.

To understand our current system, we need to recall that we are living through just one of a succession of periods defined as globalization – a term that embraces the free, global movement of money, trade and information – but not, on the whole, people. While many of its advocates argue that there is no alternative and that because of new technology globalization cannot be ended abruptly, in fact recent history provides evidence of three abrupt and very unpleasant endings to previous waves of global financial, trade and labour liberalization.

The first wave of globalization began early in the nineteenth century, and was spurred on by the role played by Britain's finance sector in bankrolling railway, commodity and mining projects around the world.

To protect their assets or loans, London bankers needed an international financial system that would guarantee the value of loans made to investors/speculators and/or dictators in far-off places, and that would guarantee the value of the debt repayments too. This was challenging, because investors/speculators/dictators wanted to repay debts in their own local currency (in which they paid wages and purchased supplies). However, the value of these currencies (especially in the emerging markets of that time) could fluctuate in value – depending on domestic political and economic circumstances or external shocks. London bankers could not have their loans or debt repayments fluctuating in value. That would not do. So, to overcome the problem that strangers in far-away places exercised national control over currencies, and therefore over the value of international debts and other assets, they designed what was to become an international monetary framework known as the gold standard – that would effectively bypass national monetary systems and economic policies.

Gold and the British empire

Britain's Bank Charter Act of 1844 decreed that Bank of England notes were to be backed by gold. Under this law, the Bank issued notes, and guaranteed that they could be redeemed by a certain amount of gold.

This, together with a fixed price for gold, laid the foundation for the gold standard. The gold standard, in turn, became the central mechanism for creating and guaranteeing debt – both within Britain, and also internationally.

Over the next century, British foreign policy was to focus on the need to expand London's ability to act as the world's creditor, by expanding gold reserves – the basis of this lending. In effect, this meant that British foreign policy focussed on discovering and extracting gold from colonies, and depositing this gold within the finance sector's vaults in the City of London.

Expanding London's gold reserves enabled the City of London to expand credit internationally, maintaining its pivotal position as the world's banker. This in turn meant extending Britain's old empire into a new, 'virtual' empire of countries like Russia, Argentina, Peru and Uruguay – countries which were not directly occupied, but which became clients of the finance sector.

In 1886 the world's largest known gold reserves were discovered on the Witwatersrand, in the Transvaal, South Africa. London's powerful finance sector, led by Cecil John Rhodes and Lord Alfred Milner, then set about using all the instruments of imperial power, including war, to extract and transfer that gold from South Africa to the vaults of London. In 1887, just one year after the discovery, Rhodes registered and boldly named a new company in London: 'Gold Fields of South Africa Ltd'. In 1899, local resistance from Afrikaner Boers (farmers) led to war, and to the defeat of the British in 1902. But Britain's finance sector went on to win the peace. For by World War I Britain had secured sole purchasing rights to all of South Africa's gold production.

The gold corset

Under the international monetary system of the gold standard established by London's bankers, a nation's credit was linked to the amount of gold stored in the central bank. With time, most countries (even those with few reserves of gold) participated in the system of the gold standard, because a) they needed credit, and/or had individuals or firms that needed credit and b) they needed to repay foreign debts in gold.

To participate in this system, countries had to follow three simple rules of the game. First their central banks had to set the value of the currency in relation to a fixed amount of gold – and had to commit to buying and selling gold at that price.

Second, each country had to base its domestic money supply on the quantity of gold held in the central bank's reserves. In other words, the local money supply rose or fell according to the rise and fall of gold reserves in the central bank. When gold flowed out of the country, for example in repayment of debts, the money supply fell, and with it economic output. When economic output fell, unemployment and depression invariably followed. When gold flowed in, the money supply rose, and with it economic output. There were (theoretically) no mechanisms for checking and balancing inflows and outflows. These depended on the whims or fortunes of traders/investors/speculators importing or exporting goods or money. Governments and central banks were theoretically powerless to intervene. In reality, as explained below, not all governments played by the rules of the game.

This was largely because of the third rule of the game; that each country would give its residents complete freedom to move gold in and out of the country. The principle was that of the invisible hand; if individuals and corporations were given maximum freedom to pursue their own self-interest, everyone would benefit.

We may note in passing, as Herman Daly has reminded us, that while neo-liberal economists from Adam Smith onwards have always urged nations to adhere to economic frameworks which give citizens maximum freedom (freedoms which do not oblige them to take into account the interests of the nation as a whole) no firm or corporation would give its staff the same privileges.

> Every deal that corporation people make has to be vetted up through higher authorities to make sure that it's really in the interest of the larger entity. And so I think the same thing is the case with trade across national boundaries. The reason again goes back to community because if you have the free flow of goods and capital and, increasingly, labour across national boundaries, then you really lose any possibility of policy at the national level. (Daly, 1995)

Under the gold standard, individuals and firms could move gold in and out of the country – without regard to the larger entity.

Creditors insisted on repayment in gold, not in say, Peruvian pesos, Russian roubles or Indian rupees – because these could not be relied upon to maintain their value. Gold would therefore flow out of the country as repayment of debts, and without compensating inflows, this would reduce the amount available for the domestic economy. This would lead to cuts in economic output, which meant factories/farms would cut production or close, unemployment would rise, and wages and prices would fall. The generalized *deflation* would cause great economic and social pain – but international creditors would have protected the value of their assets – they would have got their gold.

To stop the outflow of gold, countries might increase interest rates (to attract new inflows) but this too would hurt the domestic agricultural and industrial sectors. The reverse effects would occur if gold flowed *into* the country – output would rise, followed by employment, prices and then wages. The point was that these economic impacts were not the result of deliberate government policy, but of the uncoordinated actions of thousands of individuals – invariably imbued with the herd instinct.

The periodic and often dramatic adjustments that took place were nineteenth-century versions of IMF-driven structural adjustment policies so unpopular in the late twentieth century. The difference was that in the nineteenth century, adjustments under the gold standard were to be made automatically, with even less regard, effectively, to sovereign governments, industrialists and farmers than was the case in the late twentieth century. It did not take long before political pressures made it difficult for governments to abide by the golden straitjacket. As Fred Block has noted,

> The reality was that the simple rules of the gold standard imposed on people economic costs that were literally unbearable. When a nation's internal price structure diverged from international price levels, the only legitimate means for that country to adjust to the drain of gold reserves was by deflation. This meant allowing its economy to contract until declining wages reduced consumption enough to restore external balance. This implied dramatic declines in wages and farm income, increases in unemployment, and a sharp rise in business and bank failures. It was not just workers and farmers who found the costs of this type of adjustment to be high. The business community itself could not tolerate the resulting uncertainty and instability. Hence, almost as soon as the gold standard mechanism was in place, entire societies began to collude in trying to offset its impact. (Block, 2001)

Both the nineteenth- and twentieth-century versions of these policies, were designed to protect the assets – including loans and debt repayments – of international creditors, and not the interests of nations and their people. Above all, gold and the gold standard system enabled London's bankers to maintain their dominant role in the global economy as the world's creditors.

GARDNER HARVEY LIBRARY
Miami University-Middletown
Middletown, Ohio

The first crisis of globalization – 1873

Soon this period of nineteenth-century globalization came to an abrupt halt, with the first severe international financial crisis, the crisis of 1873, which erupted at the end of the Franco-Prussian war. The shock of this crisis caused, for example, the Gentiles of Vienna who had lost money on the stock exchange, to find scapegoats in Jewish bankers. Anti-semitism was rife, and began to be promoted by the Austrian Christian Social Party, providing a fertile environment for the development of one Adolf Hitler (1890–1945) – an Austrian. Because of the openness of the global economy and the absence of regulation over international capital movements, there is evidence of the 1873 crisis being transmitted globally; from Austria and Germany to Italy, Holland, Belgium and then to the US, and later the UK.

Despite the economic slump experienced in these countries, the lessons were not translated into policy action to control the causes of the crisis in the future. The liberalization of finance, based on the gold standard, continued as a hallmark of the next two periods of globalization before the Great Depression. The first was from the 1880s to 1914; and the second from 1919 to 1929.

The second crisis of globalization – 1914

During the period 1880–1914, financial, trade and labour markets continued to be liberalized, leading to a globally integrated economy. Some economists allege that this period was much more integrated than today's global economy (largely because labour was more mobile at that time than it is today).

Karl Polanyi, the great Hungarian economist, wrote in 1944 that it is a matter of historical record, and also of some irony, that this period of global integration achieved the very opposite of what was apparently intended. Just as today, competition between nations was intensified, fostering division, nationalism and protectionism. Contrary to the aspirations of neo-liberal economists who were keen to sideline or minimize the role of the state, the gold standard before and after 1914 'had the ironic effect of intensifying the importance of the nation as a unified entity' (Block, 2001).

The tensions caused by a rise in protectionism and nationalism ultimately erupted, and the world descended into a prolonged and destructive war. World War I finally brought to an end the system that had been so carefully put in place by London's bankers.

Politicians in 1914 had no choice but to subordinate the interests of the finance sector, to the very survival of nations – through controls over the movement of capital and goods (Hardach, 1977). Legislation was implemented which blocked international transactions. The conversion of bank notes into gold was prohibited by Russia on 27 July, in Germany on 4 August and in France on 5 August, 1914. Germany and Russia banned the export of gold. In London the private export of gold was not banned, but was heavily restricted. Like Britain, the United States abandoned the gold standard in practice while maintaining its outward form.

The bankers press their case: 1918–25

Not long after the end of World War I, bankers and the finance sector once again began to prevail upon sceptical politicians to restore the pre-war system of liberalized finance and trade – using the monetary framework first adopted by Britain back in 1821: the gold standard. John Maynard Keynes was one of the few academic economists to challenge the finance sector and oppose the reinstatement of the gold standard. For this he was vilified and like many who challenge the finance sector 'pretty generally regarded as an extremist' (Kindleberger and Aliber, 2005).

The first countries to re-adopt the gold standard were the United States, Sweden, the Netherlands and a few Latin American countries (Aldcroft, 1977). Memories of the tensions of the pre-war era were fresh, and politicians like Britain's Winston Churchill, backed by Lord Beaverbrook, were deeply sceptical, reluctant to bow to the will of the finance sector and re-adopt the gold standard again. On 29 January 1925, Churchill wrote to Montagu Norman (governor of the Bank of England) and others, expressing his concern for the non-financial sectors of the economy.

> The whole question of a return to the Gold Standard must not be dealt with only upon its financial and currency aspects. The merchant, the manufacturer, the workman and the consumer have interests which, though largely common, do not by any means exactly coincide either with each other or with the financial and currency interests. The maintenance of cheap money is a matter of high consequence. (Quoted in Gilbert, 1991)

However, Churchill, and others, were subject to unrelenting pressure from Montagu Norman, Benjamin Strong, governor of the Federal Bank of New York, and other Federal Reserve officials. Opponents of the gold standard were depicted as inflationists, and marginalized.

Initially many countries adopted a watered-down version. Nevertheless by 1925 all the most important economies of the world were once again tied into a financial system designed by, and for, international creditors. Capital was given the freedom to roam around the world without restraint or regulation. Merchants, manufacturers, workmen and consumers found their interests subordinated to that of the finance sector. And once again countries were obliged to structurally and automatically adjust their economies to the fantastic machinery of the gold standard.

The third crisis of globalization – 1929

The system whereby capital flowed freely, but governments were constrained in their room for manoeuvre, remained in place until it was brought crashing down by the New York stock market crash of 1929 and the Great Depression of the 1930s.

For the third time in 56 years, amidst the vast destruction of financial crises, a prolonged depression and a world war, the system of economic government by international capital markets was discredited and brought to an abrupt end. The cost, in human, social, financial and political terms, was immense, indeed incalculable.

Hugh Dalton, a distinguished economist of the London School of Economics, one of the architects of Britain's welfare state and Labour's Chancellor from 1945, witnessed the debacle of the 1930s and wrote of its causes in 1935:

> The world-wide crash in the price level since 1929, with all its disastrous consequences is a financiers' achievement: the continuous deflation of currency and credit in this country from 1920 onwards was a long series of financiers' decisions, taken without public advertisement or public discussion, or Parliamentary sanction, and imposed upon British industry and agriculture, either unawares or against their will ...
>
> ... our return to the gold standard at the pre-war parity in 1925 was based on the bad advice of Mr. Montagu Norman himself; the British financial crisis of 1931 ... revealed that a number of leading London Acceptance Houses, acting without consultation, either with one another or with the Bank of England ... had borrowed large sums on short term at low rates of interest from France and other foreign countries, and had lent large sums on short term at high rates of interest to Germany. There was no social justification for these operations. They were neither safety first, nor Britain first, nor constructive internationalism. They were mere speculative profit seeking of the crudest and most risky kind.

According to the testimony of Mr. Ramsay MacDonald, it was bankers, British and foreign, who dictated the financial decisions of the British Government, making their credits conditional on the adoption of specific detailed economies, including in particular, a cut in the rates of unemployment benefit.

Add to all this the fact that an unusually large number of financial scandals, both large and small, has come to light in recent years, and it is easy to understand why British opinion has moved far from its old moorings, and lost its old blind trust in the high priests of finance. (Dalton, 1935)

Government by bankers brought to a close – temporarily

In 1944, before the end of World War II, world leaders, and a group of economists, including John Maynard Keynes, gathered at Bretton Woods, and vowed, effectively, never to allow bankers to rule the world again. Instead, they created a new and more stable international financial architecture – the Bretton Woods system. Under this improved, but imperfect system, governments co-ordinated and co-operated to construct an international financial system that:

- imposed controls over the movement of capital – exchange controls;
- restored to governments vital powers to fix interest rates;
- created the key-currency standard whereby, through international co-operation, the dollar helped anchor and co-ordinate the value of world currencies, by linking its value to gold, so each dollar was worth $\frac{1}{35}$ of an ounce of gold, or \$35 an ounce.
- introduced a system of international co-operation and co-ordination to ensure that currencies did not drift too far apart in value;
- which gave governments effective control over exchange rates, which were fixed;
- thereby regaining the initiative for governments, giving them room for manoeuvre, or policy autonomy; and finally
- encouraged governments to ration, or cut back on foreign imports and balance these with exports.

The IMF was created to supervise these arrangements, and to act as a firefighter lending to countries with temporary exchange difficulties, and negotiating any necessary changes to the fixed exchange rates.

John Maynard Keynes, who was now no longer regarded as an extremist and who was Britain's leading negotiator at Bretton Woods, wanted the IMF to have a matching power to draw funds from countries with surpluses – to give it the even-handed capacity to maintain international equilibrium between countries. The US, at the time the only surplus country, vetoed this proposal.

In order to discipline and restrain the international money-lenders that had wreaked such havoc on the global economy in the 1920s and 1930s, and in order to restore policy autonomy to governments, the Bretton Woods architects had recommended capital controls. In June 1931, in the first of the Harris Foundation lectures in the United States, Keynes had explained why this was necessary:

> We are today in the middle of the greatest economic catastrophe – the greatest catastrophe due almost entirely to economic causes – of the modern world ... I see no reason to be in the slightest degree doubtful about the initiating causes of the slump...
>
> The leading characteristic was an extraordinary willingness to borrow money for the purposes of new real investment at very high rates of interest – rates of interest which were extravagantly high on pre-war standards, rates of interest which have never in the history of the world been earned, I should say, over a period of years over the average of enterprise as a whole. This was a phenomenon which was apparent not, indeed, over the whole world but over a very large part of it. (Keynes, 1931)

To correct this state of affairs, Keynes and his fellow Bretton Woods architects argued that democratic states should regain from financial markets the right to control over key levers of the economy, namely the flow of capital, and its corollary, the management of interest rates. In his view: 'the whole management of the domestic economy depends upon being free to have the appropriate rate of interest without reference to the rates prevailing elsewhere in the world. Capital control is a corollary to this' (Keynes, *Collected Writings*, Volume XXV). The aim of domestic monetary policy was to be the cheap money that he saw as necessary to prosperity.

The Bretton Woods Agreement ensured that people should be free to exchange any national currency for any other for purposes of trade or travel. But for the first 14 years after 1945 most governments kept control of their citizens' access to foreign exchange. Some restricted foreign investment and ownership within their territory. Broadly speaking, they did their best to restrict imports to what they could pay for (Milward, 1977).

Under the Bretton Woods system, while the dollar was key, the US government was nevertheless subject to stiff constraints, and was obliged to ration imports in balance with earnings from exports. All governments were obliged to balance their books – their trade and capital accounts – with the rest of the world, and co-operated internationally to ensure that there was no build-up of large deficits or large surpluses.

The Bretton Woods system, though not perfect, and though not implemented in full, remained in place for almost 30 years, until the 1970s. During that period the world, including continents like Africa and Latin America, enjoyed unprecedented economic stability; rising growth in income; and expanded trade. Per capita GDP growth in Latin America, for example, in the years from 1960 to 1980, rose by 80%. By contrast, per capita GDP growth in Latin America since liberalization in 1980 has risen by only 10%. During the Bretton Woods regime, countries did not build up huge deficits or surpluses. At the same time the world enjoyed a period of political stability (helped in part by the Cold War). Barry Eichengreen and Peter Lindert, the distinguished economic historians, have noted that:

> In retrospect, the three decades following World War II seem to have been a golden era of tranquillity in international capital markets, a fulfilment of the benediction 'May you live in dull times' …. Sovereign defaults and liquidity crises were relatively rare. (Eichengreen and Lindert, 1991)

The dismantling of Bretton Woods and the house that Finance built: globalization

Bretton Woods was to be displaced in the 1970s, and replaced by a system still in force today. This system of financial liberalization is different from the old gold standard, in that it is not anchored in gold (or any other commodity for that matter). Instead it is anchored on a system of debt; US debt. Nevertheless it is a system that resembles the earlier periods of globalization in almost every respect. It prioritizes the interests of the finance sector, and in particular the creators of credit. It provides for the unregulated growth of trade – regardless of imbalances between nations; environmental or other impacts, and certainly with little regard for nations, and for those people I will loosely define as 'Industry' and 'Labour' within nations. Using spurious arguments, the finance sector insisted on the de-regulation of capital movements, and on the de-regulation of credit creation. (The arguments are spurious, as I demonstrate in a later chapter, because, since the invention of bank money, investment no longer depends on the transfer of the 'idle savings' of rich countries to poor countries, supposedly bereft of such savings. This argument is wrong because it fails to acknowledge that in a modern economy banks have the ability to *create* credit. In a credit-creating economy a bank is not an organization that holds people's savings and passes them to industry. Credit *creates deposits*, not the other way round (Tily, 2002).)

Globalization has gradually weakened the autonomy of elected governments and their people, and ensured that key areas of policy-making (such as the setting of both short-term and long-term interest rates) are taken by invisible, unaccountable capital markets. Deflationary policies have ensured that prices of goods and wages have fallen as a share of global GDP. Financial assets, on the other hand, have risen as a share of global GDP (Greenhill, 2003). Above all, financial liberalization has fostered global imbalances, deficits and debts, fraud and corruption; and international financial crises.

How was Bretton Woods dismantled? The truth is that it was done stealthily, behind the closed doors of a small group of the world's political and financial elites, with little public and academic debate. To this date the events of 1971 are little known, little understood and seldom studied. One of the few academics to have explored these events in depth is Eric Helleiner, whose book, *States and the Reemergence of Global Finance* is essential reading.

The US defaults on its debts: 1971

The story, summarized briefly, began thus. By the late 1960s, the US had become the world's biggest creditor, and had used its position to displace the UK as a super-power. However it had begun to build up a deficit, as a direct result of military spending on the Vietnam War. The UK too had earlier built up a massive deficit as a result of war, the war against Hitler, and had appealed to the US for assistance and for debt relief. However, both during, and at the end of World War II, the US had been merciless in its treatment of its old colonial master, and demanded of Britain that it pay its debts by selling off gold reserves and international investments. This considerably weakened Britain's position as a world power.

By the 1960s when the US found itself in a similar predicament, it was unwilling to abide by such rules itself (Hudson, 2003).

Instead, on 13 August 1971 at Camp David, President Nixon made an electrifying policy reversal and announced unilaterally that the US would no longer conform to the Bretton Woods system. Nixon made clear that the dollar would no longer be linked to gold, nor would payments be made in gold. Nor would the US sell its gold or international investments to raise funds to pay for imports or to pay off debts (van der Wee, 1983).

In other words, the US declared that it would unilaterally default on its foreign obligations to repay debts in the form it had contracted to do so. This represented, at the time, the biggest-ever default by a sovereign government.

As Herman van der Wee has written:

> ... such a fundamental decision as the abolition of the gold-dollar standard, taken unilaterally by the United States and without any prior consultation with the rest of the world, was regarded as an arrogant expression of the American policy of domination. (Van der Wee, 1983)

Instead of paying its debts by selling exports and earning gold, with which to repay its creditors, the US offered something much less tangible: bank money in the form of US debt – US Treasury Bills. In other words it was suggested to creditors that they might want to hold new loans to the US as a form of collateral for the debts they were owed!

At the same time, US policy-makers invited the IMF to design a new international financial system. An effort was made; some insist that the effort was serious, but that it came to nothing. Instead, and by default, the dollar became the global reserve currency; and US debt – low-cost loans to the US – formed the basis of all international reserves. Central banks would no longer hold gold, as evidence of their reserves and to pay for foreign purchases; as evidence of the general health of their economy. Instead they would hold US debt – IOUs of the US's Federal Reserve Bank printed on paper.

It is important to note that this new financial system was not the result of considered, planned and co-ordinated action by the international community of world leaders. That while the Bretton Woods system worked well overall, there were clearly strains, and it had become necessary to make changes and improvements, in particular to the exchange rate system. But these changes were not then made as a result of careful deliberation by wise scholars, responsible leaders and their expert advisers. Instead they were made in reaction to the unilateral default on its foreign obligations by the US government in 1971.

The effect of these new arrangements was to dramatically transform the international financial system. First, by dismantling a cornerstone of the Bretton Woods system, the link of the reserve currency to gold, the removal of controls over the movement of capital, in particular US capital, began.

The US could expect to borrow money in the currency it printed. By revaluing or devaluing that currency the US could, therefore, increase or lower the value of its foreign debts. Furthermore, because there was no longer any benchmark (i.e. gold) against which its currency would be measured, or indeed any constraints against which its balances (imports/exports) would be assessed, the US need never again be obliged to *structurally adjust* its economy to restore it to balance (a requirement regularly made, since the 1980s, of poor, debtor nations). This meant that the US could now borrow limitless amounts of money on the international capital markets without restraint, and use these resources to pursue apparently endless consumption.

That is not to say that constraints to international borrowing were all removed instantaneously. Potential creditor countries still maintained capital controls, which made it difficult for money to be transferred to the US in the form of a loan. The US, supported by the finance sector and the UK government, then began a sustained campaign to discredit and lift international *capital or exchange controls* – a campaign that succeeded with the elections of Margaret Thatcher as British Prime Minister and Ronald Reagan as US President in 1979.

Today, instead of holding gold reserves, all countries mainly hold low-cost loans to the US (Treasury Bills) as reserves. These huge holdings of reserves represent staggeringly large loans to the US, at very low real interest rates. (Poor countries that need to borrow on international capital markets pay much higher rates of interest.) Rich and poor countries alike hold these Treasury Bills in their central banks, as evidence of their creditworthiness, and of the health of their economies. Larry Summers, until recently the US's Treasury Secretary or finance minister, has noted that:

> The largest international flow of fixed-income debt today takes the form of borrowing by the world's richest nations at (probably) negative real interest rates from countries with very large numbers of poor. (*Business Times*, 9 March 2004)

The silent, revolutionary changes to the international financial system began the process that was to remove the stabilizers which had ensured that international trade remained balanced, without countries accumulating deficits or surpluses.

The result, after more than 25 years is the build-up of substantial imbalances. The US today imports half as much again as it exports. Not only does it have the biggest deficit run by a G7 economy in the past 30 years, at approximately 7% of national output, but it needs to raise from abroad an approximate $1 trillion a year, about $3 billion a day. As a share of America's economy, this external deficit has more than doubled since 1999 (IMF, 2005). Meanwhile, US net international investment – the broadest measure of US external debt – is currently estimated at $3.2 trillion (Setser, May 2006). This is equivalent to more than 25% of GDP. The US is not the only country to build up trade deficits: Britain's trade deficit has recently hit record levels.

Somewhat alarmingly for the central banks and private lenders that have lent money to the US, American policy-makers have indicated that the US could use its power to cancel its own debts, by printing more dollars and lowering the value of the reserve currency. A speech in 2002 by the new governor of the Federal Reserve, Mr Bernard Bernanke, caused considerable controversy, but is illuminating:

> Like gold, U.S. dollars have value only to the extent that they are strictly limited in supply. But the U.S. government has a technology, called a printing press (or, today, its electronic equivalent) that allows it to produce as many U.S. dollars as it wishes at essentially no cost. By increasing the number of U.S. dollars in circulation, or even by credibly threatening to do so, the U.S. government can also reduce the value of a dollar in terms of goods and services, which is equivalent to raising the prices in dollars of those goods and services. (Bernanke, 2002)

Mr Bernanke has helped ensure that the reproduction of bank money, by means of a mechanical or digital printing press, will remain at the centre of the debate about international finance. Above all he has demonstrated that the US has extraordinary powers to manipulate the global economy.

The US's ability to use its financial assets to obtain, cheaply, additional resources; its ability to leverage its political hegemony to hoover up assets from poor countries; the absence of any form of international framework to discipline the US (and other sovereign) policy-makers: all these issues raise profound ethical questions about the unjust edifice that is today's international financial architecture.

President Nixon's unilateral actions in 1971 granted the United States powers and rights to embark on a path of sustained and unchecked consumption. As a result, the US has massively increased consumption, and has moved from being the world's biggest creditor, to the world's biggest debtor.

When deficits become surpluses

American policy-makers, including the new governor of the Federal Reserve Mr Bernard Bernanke, are fond of turning this story upside down, and blaming the deficit on foreigners. It's not, they argue, that Americans are consuming more than they earn; it's just that the Chinese and other countries are exporting too many goods into the US. In other words, without US consumption, the global economy would falter. While it is true that US consumption has stimulated exports and growth in other parts of the world, and in particular in China, the question of who is pushing and who is pulling is easily answered: US consumption has stimulated growth in exports elsewhere, it has resulted in imbalances – with the US consuming more than it can pay for; and another (China) generating economic growth through one leg of its economy – exports. These imbalances must unwind, and when they do it is unlikely that the unwinding will result in what economists like to refer to as a soft landing.

Orwellian Chutzpah and Doublespeak in the Economic Report of the President

... the latest example of this Orwellian doublespeak is the Economic Report of the President (ERP) published today by the White House Council of Economic Advisers. Its chapter on international macro issues is titled '*The U.S. Capital Account Surplus*' when the more appropriate and honest title would have been '*The U.S. Current Account Deficit*'.

Roubini (2006)

Another argument put forward by US policy-makers is that there is a foreign savings glut and foreigners are dumping this glut on the US! As *The Economist* (22 September 2005) noted, this self-serving argument 'conveniently deflects attention from monetary and fiscal decisions made by American policymakers'. In any case, the rate of global saving as a proportion of global output has been falling over the past 30 years.

Foreigners are lending money to the US largely because the international financial architecture obliges them to do so.

There are of course other economic reasons for the transfer of these funds from relatively poor countries to very rich countries. The holding of US debt, or Treasury Bills was until recently the only way in which central banks expected to hold their reserves, as noted earlier.

Second, in the absence of any management or co-ordination of currencies by the US government or the G8, the value of the dollar could fall if funds were to flow out of the US. This would increase US competitiveness vis-à-vis exporters like China and Japan, not because the US was more efficient, but because of the fall in the value of her currency. Asian and other central banks are determined to prevent a) the dollar from devaluing and b) the competitive devaluation of other currencies, which in turn would exacerbate beggar-my-neighbour policies and trade wars.

Until recently, loans to the US held as US Treasury Bills were regarded as the world's safest investment; the US could always be relied upon to pay its debts. But as the US deficit ballooned, so between 2001 and 2004 foreign *private* investors lost confidence in the ability of the US to repay its debts. During 2003 and 2004 these commercial investors withdrew from the US Treasury Bill market, which partly explains the fall in the dollar during that period. As a result of the withdrawal of the private sector from this lending, the US's debts were and are largely financed by the *official* sector – central banks (backed by taxpayers). If they had not lent funds at low rates of interest to the US, a dollar collapse in 2003/04 would have been inevitable. Instead central banks sent $395 billion to the US in 2004 (Setser and Ramaswamy, 2006), and the dollar drifted downwards by only 14%.

Asian central banks have the largest holdings of US Treasury Bills, so that it is Asian taxpayers, mainly in Japan – which owns 16% of Treasuries, the highest ratio outside the US (Bloomberg, 10 April 2006) – but including the governments of India and China, who today effectively finance the US deficit (and thereby US consumption). In 2004 the gross reserves held by economies in South and East Asia and the Pacific (the majority accounted for by China and India) rose to an estimated $917 billion (World Bank, 2005). More than $1 trillion of foreign income, investment and the gains from Asian trade surpluses has been transferred to the US in the form of Treasury Bills (Bloomberg, 8 May 2006).

Trickling down becomes hoovering up

As the World Bank has noted, this means that today, in contradiction of orthodox neo-liberal economic theory, money often flows from where it is scarce (low-income countries like India and China with large numbers of poor) to where it is plentiful (high-income countries like the US and the UK).

> Americans in January 2006 are a fat and happy race. At home, there is no mirror that doesn't flatter them, no number that doesn't encourage them, no headline that doesn't praise them. Abroad, their warships range the seven seas. No sparrow is so small that it can fall without setting off sensors at the Pentagon. And no country is so poor that it cannot lend the United States of America money. (Bonner, 31 December 2005)

In other words, money flows from the poor to the rich. This is the very reverse of what orthodox economists teach in all our universities when they write of wealth trickling-down from rich to poor. Neo-liberal economists imply that the trickle-down effect is as natural a law of economics as gravity is a law of physics. Today's international financial system proves that it is not.

Wanna Buy a T-Bill, Sucker?
The foreign fools who are buying American bonds

Yesterday's trade deficit figures showed that Americans continue to hurl dollars overseas in exchange for cars, oil, televisions, you name it. In theory, that's bad news, since it means the money we earn isn't stimulating domestic demand.

The good news is that a lot of the dollars we export find their way back here. And while we Americans shrewdly use our greenbacks to get a lower price on things we need or desire like DVD players, many foreigners are using the cash we send them to buy stuff that Americans don't want to buy – government bonds. What a great deal! We underpay for their great electronics; they overpay for our mediocre bonds.

Dollars wash back to the United States in a variety of ways: A Japanese tourist splurges at Disney World, a German pension buys General Motors stock, a Dutch supermarket buys Oracle software, the Royal Bank of

▶

Scotland purchases Cleveland-based Charter Financial, or the Chinese central bank buys American Treasury bills.

It's this last type of transaction – Asian central banks and other foreign investors buying our government debt – that has been most important in recent months. The massive foreign purchases of U.S. government bonds have helped keep interest rates at or near historic lows, even as federal surpluses have turned into massive deficits. Just as we can't get enough of foreign manufactured goods, foreigners can't seem to get enough of American paper goods.

At the end of the first quarter, according to this Federal Reserve report [link], foreigners owned about 40 percent of outstanding Treasury securities, up from 30 percent in 2000. Foreigners own $1.65 trillion in Treasury securities, up from $1.03 trillion in 2000.

Foreign central banks are on a spending spree. As recently as 2001, central banks bought just $10.7 billion in Treasury securities on a net basis. But their net purchases have risen dramatically: to $43.1 billion in 2002 and $128.5 billion in 2003.

With each passing quarter, foreigners have become more significant consumers of U.S. government debt. In 2002, non-Americans accounted for about half of net purchases of Treasury securities. But in the first quarter of 2004 they accounted for *150 percent*! That is – the rest of the world bought a net $679.8 billion in Treasury securities while U.S. brokers and dealers *sold* a net $202.7 billion.

As interest rates rise, smart investors tend to flee bonds. But the foreigners are still buying despite rising rates.

In theory, there's something dangerous about this increased reliance on foreign creditors. They have a call on our national savings. And if the Japanese and Chinese central banks suddenly decide to stop buying – for political or economic reasons – we could be in for a nasty shock.

But it also works the other way around. The Asian central banks aren't buying U.S. government bonds for investment purposes; they're buying for mercantilist purposes. By buying dollars and dollar-denominated assets like Treasury bonds, they help keep their currencies relatively weaker and the dollar relatively stronger. And by providing a ready market for our government's chief product, they've helped keep U.S. interest rates low. That keeps politicians happy and enables American companies and consumers to do what they do best: borrow tons of money at favorable rates and spend it.

Jingoists can also take comfort in knowing that all these foreign buyers are going to turn out to be chumps. These huge purchases have all the signs of dumb money. The central banks and other foreign investors

▶

cycled into U.S. Treasuries – big time – as rates were hitting their lows. They apparently increased their purchases after rates bottomed – and as U.S. institutions were furiously dumping the bonds. Now interest rates are rising, pushed up by a bond market that is fearing inflation and anticipating an interest-rate hike in late June by the Fed. As a result, people who bought Treasury bonds in the past couple of years will be collecting meager interest payments compared to current buyers. And as rates rise, the value of the bonds they hold will fall.

In a way, then, the huge trade deficit is redounding to our benefit. Somebody's got to fund the gigantic federal budget deficits that have materialized over the past few years. Without foreign investors – and foreign central banks in particular – we'd have to stuff all these lousy bonds into the portfolios of American investors. Better them than us.

Daniel Gross, 17 June 2004
<www.slate.com/id/2102433/>

The US's paper money

In 2003–04 the US government tried to correct its deficit, not by cutting back at home, but by standing by and allowing the dollar to devalue. A lower dollar makes imports more expensive, and makes US exports cheaper in global markets. The US government hoped by this means to correct its massive and growing deficit, and to eliminate at least part of its foreign debts.

But a lower dollar performs another magic trick for the US, one that other debtor governments cannot pull off. It cuts the value of US debts – including all those Treasury Bills – denominated in dollars. In other words the US is able to write off its debts, just by standing by and allowing its currency, the dollar, to devalue. If Rwanda or Nigeria or Indonesia could cut their debts by a) repaying loans in their own currencies instead of having to pay in foreign currencies like the dollar, and b) write off those debts by devaluing their own currency – they could solve their debt crises overnight. The US has so far been able to do this, without apparently hurting her rating with foreign creditors. This is not a privilege which low-income, debtor countries enjoy. Sony Kapoor has calculated that India lost $12 billion in 2003, as the lower dollar eroded the value of its US Treasury Bill reserves – money which could have been better spent on the development of its people (Kapoor, 2005).

Why do Asian governments and their conservative, prudent central bankers behave in this way? Why do they continue to finance the US deficit, by making low-interest loans to the US? Until recently, they had little or no choice. There was no other international asset which could replace US Treasury Bills as a reserve asset, and which would give confidence to the finance sector. Today that is changing as the euro develops as a competitor to the dollar. Instead of making low-income loans to the US, poor countries can now make low interest loans to the European Central Bank, and hold these as reserves.

Asian governments and central bankers are also attempting, often single-handedly, to stabilize a volatile global economy. Their conduct has been in stark contrast to that of world leaders. Meetings of the G8 these last few years have been grand jamborees involving rock stars, protesters and any number of international political figures and civil servants. What they have not been are forums in which world leaders gather to co-ordinate and guide the global economy. This stoic refusal to intervene in the global economy to guarantee stability, is viewed by some as irresponsible and poses a threat not only to economic stability, but also to global political stability. However, it is typical of the attitudes of adherents to the ideology of the invisible hand. Harry Dexter White, the chief US negotiator at the Bretton Woods Conference, warned in 1944:

> The absence of a high degree of economic collaboration among the leading nations will ... inevitably result in economic warfare that will be but the prelude and instigator of military warfare on an even vaster scale. (White, 1944)

The poor are financing the rich

Because central banks operate under conditions of great secrecy, these facts are not widely known to the citizens of poor countries – or indeed of rich countries like Japan, the US's biggest creditor. However, they explain in part why the World Bank, in its Global Development Finance reports in 2003 and 2004, expressed concern that, since 2001, low-income countries have become *net lenders* to high-income countries. This means low-income countries' earnings from exports (creating current account surpluses), and from financial inflows, have been used to build up reserves of US Treasury Bills, i.e. to make cheap loans to the US, rather than to undertake domestic spending to reduce levels of poverty.

The dramatic current account surpluses chalked up in the past few years have been used primarily to accumulate foreign exchange reserves, rather than to finance productive domestic investments. (World Bank, 2005)

These flows from South to North, from the poor to rich, are not just taken up by the flow of foreign investment or loans to finance US consumption. Poor countries are also transferring debt payments. Each year low-income countries pay hundreds of billions of dollars in repayment of interest and principal on loans to high-income countries.

To exacerbate matters, the absence of controls over the movement of capital means that international corporations are free to remit the profits they make in low-income countries back to rich countries. Of course they choose to remit these profits, not in local currency, but in hard currency – invariably the dollar. This means that in order to remit their profits, they have to make a claim on the hard currency stored in the central banks of poor countries.

Poor countries find it tough accumulating reserves of hard currency, because they earn so little from their exports, and have such large debts to repay. So each time a big corporation taps the central bank for hard currency, reserves are run down, and transferred to a rich country.

The trade policies of rich countries further exacerbate these transfers. By forcing low-income countries to adopt US-style patent and copyright laws, rich countries can extract rent from low-income countries in the form of royalties and licensing fees, which in turn will lead to outflows from poor to rich. At the same time, low-income countries pay over the odds for imports from rich countries.

Finally, loose regulation of capital flows ensures that capital flight takes place. Rich elites in low-income countries regularly export their wealth to banks in London, New York and Zurich, rather than investing it back home.

The hoover effect

As a result, the flimsy, unstable international financial system created by President Nixon in 1971 and consolidated since, acts as a hoover – scooping up wealth from the poorest countries and transferring it to the richest.

And it is not just doing so at an inter-governmental level. The hoover effect works *within* liberalized economies where the rich, those who own assets, have watched those assets become enormously inflated as a share of GDP (despite the anti-inflationary protestations of orthodox economists and central bankers); while the rest of society, workers, farmers and shopkeepers included, have found their wages, commodities and other prices falling, or deflating, as a share of the whole economy. But inequality between rich and poor is not only to do with the ownership of assets. US trade policy, as Dean Baker, co-director of the Center for Economic Policy Research, has noted, pits some workers (primarily manufacturing workers) into competition with workers in low-income countries. At the same time, the US government maintains protection for high-paid occupations like doctors, lawyers, journalists and even economists.

Today's liberalized international financial and trading system differs only in scale from the divisive and unstable international system of the gold standard. Globalization is a system characterized by high real rates of interest, low investment, high unemployment, low wages and high rates of debt. It is a system which has generated an embarrassment of riches for the rich, and which shrinks the share of the global economic cake allocated to workers, and those who do not own assets. Above all it is a system that prioritizes the interests of international creditors – as it did under the gold standard.

The contrast between economic conditions today and the low rates of interest, the high levels of investment, employment and wages of the Bretton Woods era could not be greater. Low rates of interest are anathema to money-lenders; but are vital to all those who engage in productive work; those who undertake vital research, and develop new medicines and other products. Full employment and good wages are vital to social and political stability; they nurture a sense of stability and well-being in society, and give us the confidence and assurance to do more than just pursue money, profit and consumption.

Globalization's effects are everywhere to be seen. The poor are getting poorer, and the rich, richer. Worse, the poor are becoming more indebted. *Real* interest rates on long-term loans (as opposed to the rate set by the central banks) are high in most countries, deterring investment in research and development. As a result investment in productive industry is low, manufacturing is failing, and shrinking as a share of GDP in a number of OECD countries. Real unemployment is as high in parts of the rich world as it was during the 1930s; and in many developing countries unemployment is far worse than in the 1930s.

Mega-mergers leading to the establishment of giant oligopolies now control our marketplaces. These oligopolies, aided by loose government regulation, eliminate competition. Ignoring the cheerful, blind ideology of free marketers, they force up prices for vital goods like drugs, and capture disproportionately high profits. As the *Financial Times* noted:

in a production system marked by extreme outsourcing, oligopoly does not result in the end of competition so much as the redirection of competition downwards, as lead companies capture more power to set supplier against supplier, community against community and worker against worker. (*Financial Times*, 14 February 2006)

Worse, such competitive pressure has raised tensions between trading nations, and led to a rise in nationalism and protectionism – just as it did during previous phases of globalization.

The failure to regulate trade and the flow of capital has been exploited and abused by international criminal gangs of drug-runners and money-launderers. The polarizing of wealth at an international level has led to a rise in insecurity, violence, terrorism and war; and the exponential exploitation of the earth's resources and sinks has made us all more vulnerable to climate change shocks.

Elected democratic governments have been weakened, and lack the powers, resources and institutions to protect their citizens and firms and to compensate citizens when shocks occur, for example to pension funds. In some countries the failure of government to afford protection to citizens is leading to disillusionment with spineless parliaments; and with leaders that have given away to invisible 'markets' key powers to allocate resources – for health, public sanitation, transport etc. These markets are failing to provide pensions, hospitals, railways, schools and culture to the satisfaction of their communities. As a result, there is growing disillusionment with the democratic process. Why vote for politicians, when they are not allocating resources for pensions, or public transport or health? Instead a culture of corruption now permeates most political systems as spectacular cases of fraud and corruption erupt periodically. Voters in many countries are turning to strong leaders in right-wing, populist and even fascist parties.

Globalization's prize legacy: debt

But perhaps the most striking characteristic of globalization is the rising level of personal, household, corporate and governmental debt. At the same time creators of that debt, members of the finance sector, are riding high; enjoying spectacular capital gains and bonuses.

Where will all this lead? Unfortunately, because of the ideological dominance of financiers and their grip on many of the world's most powerful politicians, it is difficult to imagine that leaders will emerge with sufficient grasp of the threats posed to all of us, including the finance sector, and with the courage to challenge the dominance of this sector. Should courageous politicians (or academics or journalists) have a proper grasp of the threat, they will almost certainly lack the massive political backing, and the resources needed to challenge the dominance of the finance sector.

Of course a financial crisis, resembling that of the 1930s, will clarify everything. But by then it will be too late, and many millions of people will have had their lives and livelihoods destroyed, and much of our ecosystem will have been irreparably damaged. That is why it is vital that citizens equip themselves with sufficient understanding, and begin to organize politically to once again ensure that the finance sector is subordinated to the needs of society and the ecosystem.

Above all we need to empower our political representatives and our government officials to regulate and manage the global economy democratically, in the interests of people, nations, elected governments and the ecosystem; and not in the interests of a tiny, arrogant and greedy financial elite.

Sources and suggested reading

Aldcroft, D.E., *From Versailles to Wall Street 1919–1929*, in W. Fischer and A. Lane (eds), *The History of the World Economy in the Twentieth Century*. Penguin Books, 1977.

Baker, D., *The Conservative Nanny State: How the Wealthy Use the Government to Stay Rich and Get Richer*. Center for Economic and Policy Research, May 2006.

Bank for International Settlements, 75th Annual Report, 27 June 2005. <www.bis.org/publ/annualreport.htm>.

Bernanke, B.S., *Deflation: Making Sure 'It' Doesn't Happen Here*. Remarks by Governor Ben S. Bernanke before the National Economists Club, Washington D.C., 21 November 2002. <www.federalreserve.gov/boarddocs/speeches/2002/20021121/default.htm>.

Block, F., 'Introduction' to the new edition of *The Great Transformation* by Karl Polanyi. Beacon Press, 2001.

Bloomberg, 8 May 2006, 'It's feeling like 1996 in Asia once again', by William Pesek Jr. Reproduced in *The Taiwan News*.

Bloomberg, 10 April 2006, *Treasuries May Extend Declines as Japanese Stay Away*.

Bonner, B., *Empire of Debt: the Rise of an Epic Financial Crisis*. John Wiley and Sons, 2005.

Bonner, B., 'Star-spangled Bumpkins'. *Spectator*, 31 December 2005.

Dalton, H., *High Tide and After: Memoirs 1945–60*. Muller, London, 1962.

Dalton, H., *Practical Socialism*. G. Routledge, 1935.

Daly, H., interview in the *Developing Ideas* series – 'Economics at the Crossroads', 8 February 1995. International Institute for Sustainable Development. <www.iisd.org/didigest/special/daly.htm>.

Economist, 22 September 2005, 'The Great Thrift Shift', by Zanny Minton Beddoes.

Eichengreen, B. and Lindert, P.H., *The International Debt Crisis in Historical Perspective*. MIT Press, 1991.

Financial Times, 14 February 2006, 'Wake up to the old-fashioned power of the new oligopolies', by Barry Lyon.

Fukuyama, F., 'Europeans Should Beware of Wishing for US Failure in Iraq'. *Guardian*, 21 March 2006.

Galbraith, J.K., *The Age of Uncertainty*. Houghton Mifflin Company, 1977.

Gilbert, M., *Churchill: A Life*. William Heinemann Ltd, 1991.

Greenhill, Romilly. 'Globalisation and its Consequences'. Chapter 2 in *Real World Economic Outlook*, ed. Ann Pettifor. Palgrave Macmillan, 2003.

Hardach, Gerd. 'The First World War 1914–1918'. *Pelican History of World Economy in the Twentieth Century*. Penguin Books, 1987. Translation first published by Allen Lane, 1977.

Helleiner, E., *States and the Reemergence of Global Finance, From Bretton Woods to the 1990s*. Cornell University Press, 1994.

Hudson, Michael. *Super Imperialism. The Origin and Fundamentals of US World Dominance*. Pluto Press, 2003.

International Monetary Fund (IMF), *A Remarkable Prospect: Opportunities and Challenges for the Modern Global Economy*. Lecture by Anne O. Krueger. First Deputy Managing Director, IMF McKenna Lecture at Claremont McKenna College Claremont, California, 2 May 2006.

International Monetary Fund (IMF), *World Economic Outlook: Globalisation and External Imbalances*. April 2005.

Kapoor, Sony, 'The Opportunity Cost of Reserves'. Unpublished paper for the new economics foundation, 2005.

Keynes, J.M, *The Collected Writings of John Maynard Keynes*, 30 Volumes. General editors: D.E. Moggridge and E.S. Johnson. Macmillan and Cambridge University Press for the Royal Economics Society, 1971–89.

Keynes, J.M., *The Originating Causes of World Unemployment*. First Harris Foundation lecture, June 1931.

Kindleberger, C.P. and Aliber, R., *Manias, Panics and Crashes – A History of Financial Crises* (fifth edition). Palgrave Macmillan 2005.

Milward, Alan S. 'War, Economy and Society, 1939–1945'. *The Pelican History of World Economy in the Twentieth Century*. Penguin Books, 1987. Translation first published by Allen Lane, 1977.

Pettifor, A., (ed.), *Real World Economic Outlook*. Palgrave Macmillan, 2003.

Polanyi, K., *The Great Transformation: The Political and Economic Origins of Our Time*. First published by Beacon Press, 1944.

Roosevelt, F.D., *First Inaugural Address*, Saturday, 4 March 1933. Reproduced at: <www.bartleby.com/124/pres49.html>.

Roubini, N., 'Orwellian Chutzpah and Doublespeak in the Economic Report of the President'. Global Economics Blog, 13 February 2006. RGE Monitor (by subscription). <www.rgemonitor.com/blog/roubini/117412>.

Setser, B., 'Muddle through until the end of 2008, and then it is someone else's problem'. Web log, *RGE Monitor*, 6 May 2006. <www.rgemonitor.com/blog/setser/126692/>.

Setser, B. and Ramaswamy, S., 'RGE Global Reserve Watch'. *RGE Monitor*, March 2006.

Summers, L., quoted in *The Business Times*, Singapore, 9 March 2004.

Tily, G. Private correspondence with the author, 2002. But see also 'Keynes's Theory of Liquidity Preference and his Debt Management and Monetary Policies', *Cambridge Journal of Economics*, 4 January 2006.

van der Wee, H., *Prosperity and Upheaval: The World Economy 1945–1980*. Pelikan Books, 1987. First published by Deutscher Taschenbuch Verlag GmbH & Co. KG in 1983. Translation published in Britain by Viking, 1986.

White, H.D., 1944. Quoted in Robert A. Pollard, *Economic Security and the Origins of the Cold War, 1945–1950*. Columbia University Press, 1985.

World Bank, 'Global Development Finance 2005: Mobilizing Finance and Managing Vulnerability'. World Bank, 2005.

2
Costless Money and Costly Credit

The Colonel: I don't read no papers, and I don't listen to radios either. I know the world's been shaved by a drunken barber, and I don't have to read it.

Long John Willoughby: Hey, stop worryin', Colonel, fifty bucks ain't gonna ruin me.

The Colonel: I've seen plenty of fellas start out with fifty bucks and wind up with a *bank* account!

Beany: Hey, what's wrong with a bank account, anyway?

The Colonel: And let me tell you, Long John, when you become a guy with a bank account, they gotcha! Yes sir, they gotcha!

Beany: Who's got him?

The Colonel: The helots!

From the film *Meet John Doe* (1941). Directed by Frank Capra.
Writing credits Richard Connell and Robert Presnell Sr.

Money and debt-creation

Money and its link to debt-creation is not well understood. However, the link is firmly established. By creating money at virtually no cost, charging high real rates of interest on loaned money, and then adding additional 'charges', banks and creditors:

- extract assets from the productive sector in a manner that can fairly be described as parasitic;
- transfer assets from those without, to those with assets;
- make a claim on the future;
- build up exponentially rising levels of debt, which are unlikely to be repaid in full.

The debt becomes ultimately unpayable because the rate of interest, or the rate of return on this privately created credit, exceeds the rate at which society (broadly Industry and Labour) and the ecosystem can be renewed, can generate *additional* resources, and can repay.

This would be bad enough, but Costly Credit is a crime against society and against nature for another reason: it demands exponential rates of return on an asset, money, which is costless to create. This chapter sets out to explain simply, how costly, debt-creating money is generated by private banks; and how all but short-term interest rates are determined by the private sector.

But first I must acknowledge my own debts. This chapter draws on the work of John Maynard Keynes, and in particular on his monetary policies. I am beholden to Dr Geoff Tily (Tily, 2005) and Professor Victoria Chick (Chick, 1983) for drawing my attention to these policies and helping me unravel some important confusions – not only about Keynesian theory, but also about money; confusions shared by most mainstream economists and repeated in textbooks.

Money defined

Money is all things to all people. It can be made up of beads or shells, coins or notes; cigarettes or sweets; cheques, credit cards or digital information.

It emerged, so the historians and anthropologists tell us, because of the limitations to barter. When women going to market to swap their chickens found there was nothing they fancied to *exchange* for the chickens, business would come to a grinding halt. It then proved useful to invent a metal token, to which both the chicken-farmer and others in the market gave a value. Using this metal token meant that the chicken-farmer, having sold one speckled hen, but failed to exchange a product to show for it, nevertheless came away from market with a token in her pocket. This represented the value of her hen. She could defer her purchase, until, say, a tinker visited the village, offering something she really wanted (like a leather purse) which she could buy with the metal token.

Economists argue that this metal token, or money performs three functions: it acts as a *store of value*; as a *standard of value* (which everyone accepts, e.g. determines that one hen is worth the same as two rabbits); and as a *medium of exchange* – i.e. it helps make an exchange at an exact price.

So money's great benefit is that it facilitates exchanges. Furthermore as Keynes noted, it can do that without 'ever coming into the picture a substantive object' (Keynes, *Collected Writings*, Volume XIV). In oth words we can get paid our wages/salaries or can pay taxes without not or coins – substantive monetary objects – ever being required.

Money's other great virtue is generally said to be its worth as a store of value. The villager may not have the hen, but she has a metal token safely tucked into her pocket, or piggy-bank, equivalent to the value of the hen.

But there is a great problem with this notion of money as a store of value. Why? Because the token in her pocket is a static, barren *asset*. It remains a small, cold metal token. The hen, a live procreative animal, is, in contrast, probably already laying eggs for her new mistress, from which new chickens are hatching – thereby adding considerable interest or value to the newly-acquired *asset* that is the hen.

In other words, the live hen, is multiplying itself. Money, also an asset, is barren and cannot multiply itself. Instead, for money to be multiplied, *interest* must be added. A hen can generate a form of interest, i.e. can increase herself, by laying eggs and producing chickens. But money cannot increase itself. Interest on money *must come from some other source or process*.

This is, for holders or borrowers of money, one of its great flaws. But for those who lend money, it is one of its great and truly magical powers. Under older banking systems, a lender of money could expect not just the return of his metal token equivalent, say, to a hen; but some additional asset(s) obtained from, say, another hen. A borrower, though, must return not just the metal token equivalent to the hen; but some additional asset.

So for example, if, in our mythical village of the past, a villager *borrowed a hen* for a week, he could expect to pay interest on the loan of the hen by offering a few of the eggs she lays or perhaps one of the ten chickens that she hatches. That would represent payment (interest) for the loan of the hen.

If, instead the villager *borrowed money* (equivalent to the value of a hen) he would have to capture a few eggs or a hatched chick from a *second* hen, to pay interest on the money. In other words, if you borrow a productive asset, the asset itself generates the interest; if you borrow an unproductive asset, like money, you have to draw on a separate asset which is productive to generate the interest.

By this magical means does the invention of metal money enable lenders to use debt to extract *additional* assets from borrowers and from the planet.

Bank money: what you get is not what you see

Of course money today enjoys much greater sophistication than it did in our mythical village of the past. Even then, it was a significant innovation and evolution over a system of exchanges based on barter.

If our chicken-farmer were around today, she would have the benefit both of her metal tokens, known as coins; but also of paper money, known as banknotes. In addition she and her community would benefit from another form of money: *bank money*.

For over time money has evolved. The original token money (including the bank note) was, at the first stage of its evolution, based on a commodity – a bead, or shell or metal, and then a precious metal, silver or gold. During the second stage of money's evolution commodity money was changed into *bank money*, based not on a tangible object but on something more ephemeral: trust and confidence.

In today's economy, most transactions no longer involve *cash* (i.e. notes and coins) but entries in a ledger or account – that is, *bank money*. If our chicken-farmer were active today, and set up a small business selling hens, then her taxes would not be paid in tokens, coins or notes; instead they would be paid by bank transfers from her business bank account to government. If she has employees, she would be paying salaries and making PAYE transfers with bank money. She would pay for her new hen-house by direct debit, or credit card; and would pay the company selling chicken-feed by bank transfer. She would pay for everyday *consumption* (clothes, food, magazines, entertainment) both through *bank money* (using credit, debit cards and cheques) and *cash*.

Bank money, unlike commodity money, is *intangible* – you never see or hold it. The amounts held by economic actors at any point in time are simply figures entered into a ledger or a computer, printed occasionally on a bank statement. Of course you could choose to withdraw the amount on the ledger of your bank account and hold it as notes and coins, in which case bank money is turned into 'real' money, but generally people do not do this – they keep their money in the bank and spend a large part of it in transactions which do not involve cash. As Geoff Tily notes:

> there is no tangible quantity corresponding to the aggregate of bank money in an economy at any point in time. Such a tangible quantity/

quality is not a necessary characteristic of money. The acceptability and hence validity of bank money is due to its being able to facilitate... transactions. (Tily, 2005)

In understanding bank money we need to understand that money held in banks does not necessarily correspond to what we understand as income. Nor does it correspond to savings. It does not necessarily correspond to any economic activity. The one-to-one link that existed between our chicken-farmer and her metal token, back in the Middle Ages, does not exist in today's banking system.

Understanding bank money

Bank money does not exist *as a result* of economic activity. Instead, bank money *creates* economic activity.

As long as 50 years ago, the economist Joseph Schumpeter noted that

it proved extraordinarily difficult for economists to recognise that bank loans and bank investments do create deposits ... And even in 1930, when the large majority had been converted and accepted the doctrine as a matter of course, Keynes rightly felt it necessary to re-expound and to defend the doctrine at some length ... and some of the most important aspects cannot be said to be fully understood even now. (Schumpeter, 1954)

Things have not changed much since 1954. The quotation below, from a recent Question and Answer session with members of the UK's House of Lords (about a report by James Robertson of the New Economics Foundation on creating new money) demonstrates that it is still extraordinarily difficult for economists, officials and ministers to recognise that bank lending does not depend on the receipt of deposits; that loans create deposits.

Contrary to the report of the New Economics Foundation, banks are not provided with a hidden subsidy. Funds loaned out to customers must either be obtained from depositors or the sterling money markets, both of which usually require the payment of interest. (Lord McIntosh of Haringey, UK Government minister, 2001)

Like Lord McIntosh, many of us still assume that bank loans represent a gift from someone who, unlike ourselves, has taken the trouble to deny themselves a portion of their income and to deposit this in a piggy-bank or savings account. Most mainstream economists still believe that banks have 'savings' – either theirs, or those of others – and extend these savings to others as credit – charging interest. This is not the case. *The money for a bank loan does not exist until we, the customers, apply for credit.*

In other words, far from the bank starting with a deposit, and then lending out money, the bank starts with our application for a loan, the asset against which we guarantee repayment, such as our house, and the promise we make to repay with interest. A clerk then enters the number into a ledger.

> It is well enough that people of the nation do not understand our banking and monetary system, for if they did, I believe there would be a revolution before tomorrow morning.
>
> Henry Ford, American industrialist and pioneer
> of assembly-line production method

Having agreed the loan, the commercial bank then applies to the central bank which provides – on demand – the necessary cash element of the loan. This cash element (notes and coins) is the small proportion of the loan that will be tangible to the borrower. The rest is bank money, which is intangible. Once the commercial bank has obtained the cash from the central bank, we the borrowers then obligingly re-deposit both the bank money (the undrawn part of the loan) and the cash, which together make up the sum of the loan, in either our own or in other banks – *creating deposits*. Even if we spend the cash, the recipient of our cash will deposit it.

The central bank, in issuing the cash, charges a rate of interest to the commercial bank. The commercial bank pays this in due course, adds its own interest, and passes both charges on to the borrower.

Cash on demand

While an increasing amount of transactions can be carried out without cash, there are many that still depend on cash, like coins for parking meters; so we, bank customers, want to hold a portion, albeit (in the UK) only a small proportion, of our money as cash. A bank is therefore obliged to offer cash to its customers according to *demand*, depending on their credit standing or overdraft limit. As a consequence banks have to hold a ratio of deposits in the bank, as cash. This is known as the *cash ratio* or 'reserve requirement'. This tends to be a small fraction of total deposits. In any case, as noted above, any cash issued and spent (mostly in retail transactions) very quickly returns to the banking system as deposits. If our farmer were to go to a 'hole in the wall' and draw out £100 in cash to spend at her local coffee shop, newsagent or cinema – this money would quickly be re-deposited in banks.

This being the case, a popular illusion nevertheless persists: that banks can only lend on the basis of reserve requirements. In other words, to lend £1,000, banks need a reserve requirement of £100 in their vaults. The reality is exactly the opposite. *Reserves are created to support lending.* The Bank of England (for example) provides cash to British commercial banks, *based on public demand for that cash.* Cash is created by the central bank only once borrowers apply for loans from the banks, and central banks place no limit on the cash made available to banks. *Because the central bank provides cash on demand, there is therefore no limit to the cash, bank money or credit that can be created by commercial banks.*

However, there is a cost to commercial banks in applying for cash (as I explain below); they pay interest to the central bank for this cash (and promptly pass on the cost to the customer). There is, however, no cost in the creation of bank money, or free money – the proportion of the loan that is intangible, that is not cash.

The decline of cash and the rise of credit

In the UK in 1982 the ratio of coins and notes to bank deposits was 1:14. At the end of 2005 the ratio had more than doubled, to 1:34. Put differently, in 1982 there was about £10.5 billion in circulation as notes and coins. Retail and wholesale deposits amounted to almost 14 times as much: £144 billion. By 2005 there was only £38 billion circulating in notes and coins, and almost 34 times as much – £1,289 billion – held in banks as retail and wholesale deposits (Office for National Statistics, May 2006). So for every £1 circulating in cash in 2005, £34 took the intangible form of bank deposits.

These historic numbers demonstrate that the ratio of cash to bank money is not a constant: cash declines over time as confidence in bank money grows, and we make ever-greater use of credit cards, bank transfers and internet banking, for example.

Today in the UK and US (but not in many countries in Africa, for example) a larger, and ever increasing proportion of transactions will be carried out as simple account transfers that do not involve coins and notes. The increased use of credit cards and of internet banking are two of the most visible examples of this non-cash bank money.

Fixing the price of money: interest as a social construct

The rate of interest is effectively, the price of bank money. The basis for this price is set by the central bank, for example the Bank of England (BoE) or the Federal Reserve.

How is this done? Remember, the central bank enjoys the sole power to issue notes and coins. No other private bank can issue notes or coins. In the past, publicly-controlled central banks would have had the power to create, or regulate the creation of, bank money, and therefore credit. Today, the *private* banking sector has the power to create unlimited volumes of credit – and does so through the creation of intangible, costless, bank money.

However, it is this sole power to issue notes and coins that provides such institutions as the Bank of England with the mechanism for setting the official, base rate of interest. The central bank does this by providing cash on demand, i.e. without limit to a commercial bank, in exchange for collateral (assets, e.g. Treasury bills or bonds).

To give a practical example, if Citibank UK intended to make a loan of say £6,600 to Josephine Bloggs, the bank could demand £300 of that loan from the Bank of England in cash (the amount that Josephine is likely to draw in cash. Bear in mind that the cash to bank money ratio in the UK in 2004 was 1:22). In return Citibank would offer an asset of £300 to the Bank of England. The central bank holds this 'collateral' or asset for a period, say two weeks, and then returns it to Citibank at a *discount* of its value, retaining say 5% of the asset, or £15.

The difference between the original value of the asset and the new value – i.e. 5% – is the rate of interest (an arrangement known as a repurchase agreement or 'repo') on a specified date. In other words, the central bank takes its cut, and returns the assets to the commercial bank. The rate at which these assets are discounted is the rate set by (in the case of the Bank of England) the Monetary Policy Committee, and is known to us as the Bank rate of interest.

It is important to note at this point that the rate of interest is a *social construct*. The Bank of England arrives at its decision as a result of consultation between members of the Monetary Policy Committee and the Governor of the MPC – all of whose members are there by political appointment of the UK's finance minister, the Chancellor of the Exchequer. The rate of interest is fixed bearing in mind the various interests within the economy, broadly represented by Finance, Labour and Industry. The rate of interest is *not* set according to the demand for money.

The cash withdrawn from the central bank by the commercial bank is only a small proportion of the total that the commercial bank loans out: £1 in cash for every £22 in bank money lent out. So if the commercial bank demands £300 from the central bank in cash, it is proposing to make a loan of £6,600. Remember too that while the commercial bank may pay the rate of interest to the central bank on £300 of cash, it is not doing so on the balance of free bank money – £6,300. The borrower, however, will be paying an interest rate above the official rate of 5% – possibly 8% – on the whole amount of £6,600.

The less cash there is in the economy, the more free money the banks create. This might illuminate the intention behind an advertising campaign run by the Maestro credit card company in the UK, in May 2006.

> 'Cash is oh-so-last-millennium.'
> 'Cash stinks.'
> *Maestro*: 'the new cash'.

It gets worse. Not only do banks charge interest on this free money, they add a range of unnecessary charges that in the UK brings in about £3 billion ($6 billion) a year in additional revenue (*Daily Mail*, 10 May 2006). These include charges for overdrawing on authorized overdrafts; arrangement fees for loans; charges for 'premium' account holders (which ensure that telephone calls are answered!) etc. This rate of interest is central to the functioning of the economy as a whole, and is thus vitally important to all who have to borrow to finance investment or consumption: individuals, home-owners, small-business people, big-business people; and of course governments that have to borrow to finance investment.

Money is a free good

So how much can banks lend given that they do not need to find money/ deposits in the first place? The answer is that there are no limits to the creation of bank money and therefore of credit, and like other free goods, the price (or interest) should be very low.

The cost to a bank or finance company of entering numbers into a ledger is ludicrously low, or non-existent. Note too, that the cost of obtaining cash from the central bank is passed on to the borrower. If pushed, bankers would explain that their costs involve an infinitesimally small share of the cost of the ledger, of the pen or computer; of the wage of the member of staff that enters the number; and of the rental costs of the building. With the development of technology, and with the growth of credit, these fixed costs disappear.

> The modern banking system manufactures money out of nothing. The process is perhaps the most astounding piece of sleight-of-hand that was ever invented. Banking was conceived in inequity and born in sin ... But if you want to continue to be slaves of the bankers and pay the cost of your own slavery, then let the bankers continue to create money and control credit.
>
> Josiah Charles Stamp (1880–1941), English economist,
> President of the Bank of England in the 1920s
> and the second richest man in Great Britain

Given these very low costs, and given that there is no limit to the volume of credit/debt that can be created, then credit is essentially *a free good*. Prices in free markets are supposed to rise for scarce resources. There is (as yet) for example, no price for the air we breathe, because there is no (apparent) limit to it; and it is not scarce. In the same way, there is no scarcity of credit; no limit to its creation.

To understand how the cost of an almost free good can be multiplied, it might be useful to compare the interest charged by commercial banks on 'free' bank money, to the rates paid for the use of 'wi-fi' wireless networks in hotels, airports, restaurants etc. Like bank money, the cost of generating wireless is very low for the provider, so in the US public authorities like libraries offer free access to the radio frequencies needed to transmit data. But by capturing and controlling access to this essentially free good, private sector providers are able to charge a rent on units of time-use of radio frequencies, and to make extraordinary capital gains from this rent.

This is pretty much how commercial banks make their money.

Keynes understood that money was essentially a free good. In his *Treatise on Money*, he wrote:

> Why then ... if banks can create credit, should they refuse any reasonable request for it? And why should they charge a fee for what costs them little or nothing? (Keynes, 1930)

The answer of course is that if the bank is a publicly-owned bank, a bank answerable to the citizens of a nation, then there is no reason why it should charge a fee, or interest, for what costs little or nothing. There is no reason why it should not create debt-free (i.e. non-interest bearing) money for public works. If publicly-owned banks, or the government, exercised the power to create credit, citizens would be saved a great deal in taxation. President Lincoln, Henry Ford and Thomas Alva Edison (the latter were both brilliant engineers) all argued for governments to exercise such powers. Ford and Edison made the case in an extended debate about the financing of a dam, in the *New York Times* in December 1921. Ford wrote:

> Army engineers say it will take $40,000,000 to complete that big dam (Muscle Shoals dam). But Congress...is not in the mood to raise the money by taxation. The customary alternative is thirty-year bonds at four per cent. The United States, the greatest Government in the world, wishing $40,000,000 to complete a great public benefit *is forced to go to the money sellers to buy its own money.* [Emphasis added]. At the end of thirty years the Government not only has to pay back the $40,000,000 but it has to pay 120 per cent interest, literally, has to pay $88,000,000 for the use of $40,000,000 for thirty years ... Think of it. Could anything be more childish, more unbusinesslike?
>
> ... whenever the Government needs money for a great public improvement, instead of thinking of bonds with heavy interest charges, think of redeemable non-interest bearing currency... Do you appreciate that 80 cents of every dollar raised by taxation is spent in the payment of interest? ... Here is a way to get the improvements without increasing the debt.
>
> The interest load is breaking down our whole financial system.
>
> It is simply a case of thinking and calculating in terms different than those laid down to us by the international banking group to which we have grown so accustomed that we think there is no other desirable standard. ... The only difference between the currency plan and the bond plan is that there is no interest to be paid and the Wall Street money merchants, who do nothing to build the dam and deserve nothing, will get nothing ...
>
> The function of the money-seller will have disappeared. (Quoted in Boyle, 2002)

Bank money: the democratization of lending and borrowing

This is not the place to delve into the fascinating history of how bank money was invented. (But I do recommend that interested readers explore the life of one John Law, the 'reckless, and unbalanced but most fascinating genius' (Marshall, 1923) who played a key role in the invention of bank money. Janet Gleeson's biography *Millionaire* (1999) would be a good start.)

Instead I want to focus on bank money's great virtues, but also its flaws.

The fundamental reasons for its virtue are twofold. The first is this: if in our mythical medieval village, the chicken-farmer was ambitious and wanted to expand her business, she would need 'capital', i.e. some savings which would allow her to build more hen-coops; to buy more chicken-feed and to breed more chickens. Furthermore, as she herself explored nearby villages for new buyers, she might need to employ someone to feed and care for the chickens while she was away. If she had money to do all this, her output would expand, employment would rise, and with it economic growth for her community.

To raise this money in olden times, either she would have had to try and save money over time, or she would have had to approach a member of her local elite; a powerful landlord or warlord who had accumulated assets and savings (by no doubt, brutal and dubious means). She would probably only have been able to obtain a share of his savings after much genuflection and obeisance; and at great cost. Not only would she have been expected to pay interest; but the local lord of the manor would have demanded other favours too.

The invention of bank money – money that did not depend on existing economic activity, but *created* economic activity – meant that borrowers could end their dependency on those who were *already-rich*. Bank money provided a mechanism for lending that precisely did not depend on the generosity or meanness of individuals holding savings, towards those who did not have savings. Bank money was not the result of economic activity; bank money created economic activity.

As a result, bank money widened and democratized the allocation of credit.

After the invention of bank money, to the astonishment and delight of many, money was no longer a scarce resource. *Once banks are able to create credit, investment is no longer constrained by saving* (Chick, 1983; Davidson, 1986; Thirlwall, 1999; and Studart, 1995. All in Tily, 2005).

Economic activity was no longer bound up with and dependent on the already-rich. This was indeed a liberating and great social advance.

However, for bank money to be sustainable, it had to be loaned at rates of interest compatible with human society's priorities; and with the limits of the ecosystem. For governments, the money, as Henry Ford argued, should be interest-free. For others, it had to be *cheap money*. Cheap money makes most economic activity possible. Cheap money makes it possible, for example, to research, design and build long-term, whether it be vacuum cleaners, homes or alternative energy sources.

James Dyson, the manufacturer of products that have achieved sales of £3 billion world-wide, put it succinctly in his Dimbleby Lecture of 8 December 2004.

> We need to encourage manufacturing investors. And to make them think long term. ... Banks and venture capitalists are not going to invest long term unless we give them an incentive.
>
> To do that we need two things. Tax breaks on long-term manufacturing investment. *And lower interest rates. Permanently.* [Emphasis added]
>
> High interest rates ... hamper investment. And high exchange rates create the double whammy of less revenue from exports and more competition from cheaper imports. We should set low targets for interest and exchange rates. That will encourage investment in manufacturing and R&D.
>
> We need to encourage more people to become engineers and scientists. (Remarks reported by BBC News, Friday, 10 December 2004)

Sadly, Dyson's appeal for low interest rates on long-term investments went unnoticed by the finance sector, who offer entrepreneurs like Dyson Costly Money; money which is allocated by the private sector on the basis of existing *assets*; and for the purpose of the private gain of 'money-sellers', not public benefit.

Keynes was aware of the great virtues of bank money; of how it could be used to end poverty; and of how short-sighted is the 'financial calculation' of the private sector – those who argue we cannot *afford* homes for the poor, or money for the arts, or the money needed to protect endangered species. In the midst of the Great Depression, brought on by the recklessness of the finance sector, Keynes wrote:

> We have to live in hovels, not because we cannot build palaces, but because we cannot 'afford' them. The same rule of self-destructive financial calculation governs every walk of life. We destroy the beauty of the countryside because the unappropriated splendours of nature have not economic value. We are capable of shutting off the sun and the stars because they do not pay a dividend. London is one of the richest cities in the history of civilisation, but it cannot 'afford' the

highest standards of achievement of which its own living citizens are capable, because they do not 'pay'.

If I had the power today, I would surely set out to endow our capital cities with all the appurtenances of art and civilization on the highest standards...convinced that what I could create I could afford ... Once we allow ourselves to be disobedient to the test of an accountant's profit, we have begun to change our civilization. (Keynes, 1933)

Bank money and the power to set interest rates

This leads us to bank money's second great advantage, the very thing that had motivated its invention: lower interest rates. Karl Marx was fully aware that bank money took place 'as a reaction against usury':

the development of the credit system takes place as a reaction against usury ... this violent fight against usury ... robs usurer's capital of its monopoly by concentrating all fallow money reserves and throwing them on the money-market ... (Marx, 1894)

The invention of bank money, enabled the lowering of the rate of interest to sustainable levels. It also removed control over lending from the privileged few who insisted on unsustainable rates of return.

Instead, under a system of bank money, public banks could both increase the supply of money, and lower its price: the rate of interest. This led almost directly to the industrial revolution, as entrepreneurs and industrialists were freed from the shackles of the powerful few that hoarded wealth, and could borrow bank money for investment in new inventions *at very low rates of interest.*

Throughout the whole of the eighteenth century, the discount rate at the Bank of England was five per cent. Interest rates on long-term government bonds were broadly between three and four percent except during the Napoleonic wars (at the start of the nineteenth century) and between 1885 and 1900 when it fell from three to close to two per cent. (Tily, 2005)

Which is why bank money, regulated properly, and with proper constraints, can be a very good thing. By making money available to those who want to use it productively, and by keeping the rate of interest low, bank money facilitated what we have come to regard as progress. (Of course there are many today who question whether we have put this money to good use, but that requires another book altogether.) The development of modern technology (e.g. the light bulb and the steam engine) would not have taken place if brilliant entrepreneurs had not had their research and development funded by *low-cost finance* made available by bank money. Trade was made possible with bank money. The welfare state was made possible by bank money. And financial crises were averted by the issuance of bank money. These are just some of the great advantages of a system based on *cheap* bank money, and not on the savings and insatiable demands for returns by the already-rich.

As Abraham Lincoln clearly understood, a private bank, by contrast, insists on extracting rent and additional assets from the loans that have been created out of nothing; and will multiply the rent on units of money loaned out. The motivation here is not the financing of investment and development, the maintenance of full employment, the treatment of AIDS; the development of the Arts, or environmental sustainability. The motivation is a great deal more narrow-minded and mercenary.

Whatever the motivation, the result of privately created bank money is credit and debt – 'vast as space'.

Interest is man-made

It is important to note that the Bank rate, the official rate set by the central bank, or the rate of interest, is, first, not the only rate of interest. It is not the rate of interest on medium- or long-term loans, which in economies like that of the UK, the US, Australia etc. are determined by the private sector, although underpinned by the Bank rate.

Second, interest is not a form of magic; it does not occur naturally and as a result of supply and demand. It is not a function of the amount of savings in the economy, nor even of the amount of credit, for, as we have noted, there is no limit to the supply of credit.

No, the rate of interest, as set by the central bank, is a social construct. It is something man-made and as such can always be varied – by rational choice. While it may be the case that procedures for fixing the Bank rate have evolved differently in different banking systems, the underlying principle remains the same: the central bank of any country can control the price of credit, the rate of interest, through its powers (explained above) to issue coins and notes in exchange for certain assets, and by issuing bonds.

From the point of society as a whole, high interest rates benefit *finance capital.* Low interest rates benefit *industry* (which includes agriculture) and *labour.* Low interest rates, or even better, interest-free money creation by the government, benefits taxpayers, society and ultimately, the ecosystem.

Those who earn money from money and other assets prefer high real rates of interest. Those who earn money from productive activity, including investment in land and labour (in the broadest sense) prefer low real rates of interest. Those who care about the ecosystem know that we cannot extract the earth's assets at rates that cannot readily be replaced.

However, as noted above, the Bank rate is just one part of the interest rate story, because it is only one of a *spectrum* of rates, which differ according to *time* – the term of the loan – and the *risk* attached to the loan. The longer the term of the loan, the higher tends to be the rate of interest; the greater the risk the higher the rate of interest.

Keynes' great practical contribution to economics and to the British economy in the 1930s and 1940s was in explaining the relation between these rates (through his theory of liquidity preference) and through this theory the recognition that Britain's authorities, including the central bank and the Treasury, could determine both the short-term 'repo' rate and longer-term rates. Keynes encouraged Britain's monetary authorities to deal in all the (time and risk) spectrum of loans, in other words in bond issues and debts of all maturities. By so doing, Britain's authorities could determine rates of interest across the spectrum of loans; by making a direct link between the quantity of money in the economy and the rate of interest.

> Perhaps a complex offer by the central bank to buy and sell at stated prices gilt-edged bonds of all maturities, in place of the single bank rate for short-term bills, is the most important practical improvement which can be made in the technique of monetary management. (Keynes, *Collected Writings*, Volume VII)

The rate of interest and the movement of capital

Unfortunately, the ability to manage money within a national economy, and to lower interest rates in the way that Keynes proposed is compromised if the owners of money in say, the UK, move their funds abroad and invest them in countries where interest rates are higher. In other words, the control of interest rates can only be achieved if money stays at home – in the economy in which the authorities are trying to lower interest rates. The removal of controls over the movement of money, removes a powerful lever over control of interest rates, and therefore control over a national economy by the central bank and other financial authorities.

Keynes argued that it was very unwise to assume that the rate of interest that suited an economy like Australia, would be appropriate for an economy like the UK. In just the same way, critics of the European monetary system argue that it is inappropriate for interest rates to be set across a range of economies, when the interest rate appropriate to Portugal, say, is not appropriate for say, Germany. He warned that if interest rates were higher in Australia, for example, then British savers would export their savings to Australia.

> Freedom of capital movements ... assumes that it is right and desirable to have an equalization of interest rates in all parts of the world. It assumes, that is to say that if the rate of interest that promotes full-employment in Great Britain is lower than the appropriate rate in Australia, there is no reason why this should not be allowed to lead to a situation in which the whole of British savings are invested in Australia, subject only to different estimations of risk, until the equilibrium rate in Australia has been brought down to the British rate. In my view the whole management of the domestic economy depends upon being free to have the appropriate interest rate without reference to the rates prevailing in the rest of the world. Capital controls is a corollary to this. (Keynes, *Collected Writings*, Volume XXV)

How capital should be controlled and regulated, especially in a world of electronic money, is a challenge that will be met by central bank officials and their advisers. In the final chapter of this book, I explore possible mechanisms. However, for central bank officials to succeed, they will need to be backed by broad-based political will. This can only be generated if society at large understands why it is vital to control the movement of money, and defends this control against the demands of the finance sector; and in the interests of society as a whole.

The rate of interest and democracy

In a democratic society, citizens, and in particular those who work in ways that can broadly be defined as 'Industry' or 'Labour', will want to determine economic policies appropriate to their conditions and circumstances. That, after all, is what democracy is about. The removal of controls over capital strips citizens and their elected representatives of this control over a vital lever for adjusting the economy – the rate of interest – and transfers this power to invisible, unaccountable players in international capital markets – the Big Brothers of the financial system. *These financiers never deign to stand for election.*

Today, the defenders or promoters of globalization once again argue that it is right and desirable to have, for example, the same rate of interest for Portugal as for Germany; and that a rate of interest that might be inimical to economic development in Argentina, should nevertheless be equalized to an interest rate more appropriate to say, the US. By these means do the 'invisible hands' of the global capital markets determine the rate of interest to be applied to national economies like those of Britain or Australia.

The freedom of capital to move, without regulation, across the globe means that those who have a surplus of capital – including oil-producers of the Middle East, governments like Japan, Germany and China – can affect interest rates around the world by the way in which they deploy this surplus capital. Because Japan, India and China choose to invest their surplus by making low-cost loans to the US (see Chapter 1) money has flowed to the US, helping to lower interest rates there. Not even the most powerful central banker in the world at the time, Alan Greenspan, had the power in 2003–05 to counter the lowering of interest rates by this flood of money. Instead he had to stand by and watch as US consumers used this low-interest money on longer-term loans to borrow more, re-finance old loans and pour this money into more purchases of property – further fuelling the property bubble.

The rate of interest, politics and autonomy

While most ordinary members of the public may be unaware that interest rates are effectively set by invisible players in the international markets, nevertheless, they are aware of the importance of interest rates. They are particularly aware of interest rates when, in a deflationary environment, the real rate of interest rises so high as to cripple activity in, say, a small business or a farm – or make repayments on a mortgage painfully difficult. The consequent awareness that nothing can be done by local politicians or national authorities to correct such high rates of interest is very likely to lead to disillusionment in both political and official processes. It is not impossible that in these circumstances ordinary voters will turn to politicians and populists who promise to restore some national control, through protectionist, nationalist and even fascist policies.

This is only one of the grave dangers of allowing the invisible hand to render democratic politics futile, and to exercise powerful control over the lives and livelihoods of millions of people.

Readers interested in Keynes' theory of liquidity preference are referred to the work of Tily and Chick, cited at the end of this chapter. However, it suffices here to point out that Keynes, at a time of international financial crisis, encouraged the public authorities, the Treasury and the Bank of England, to intervene in the capital markets; regulate the flow of capital in and out of the country; and adopt a Cheap Money policy by issuing a range of bonds, at a range of low interest rates, while at the same time regulating the availability of credit. These policies would guarantee the availability of money or loans at reasonable rates of interest to all the distressed companies and individuals seeking to recover from crisis. Such policies also subordinated the *private* finance sector to the interests of the nation as a whole. Today the very reverse occurs: national interests are on the whole subordinated to the interests of the finance sector.

The Bank of England and the Treasury adopted Keynes' policies, and, largely as a result, Britain was able to begin the recovery from the devastating crisis of the 1930s, and then to finance and produce the armaments, food and other goods needed to conduct a major war against fascism. *In other words, at a time when demand for money was very high, interest rates were extremely low.*

In facing the crisis of the 1930s and 1940s, Britain faced no shortage of money for domestic production and for paying wages – thanks to Keynesian monetary policies, which ensured that economic activity was financed by very low rates, including a Bank rate which was 2% between 1932 and 1951. On the home front, money was not a barrier to research, innovation and the production of resources needed to fight a terrible war; and to pay the wages of those at home, and at the front.

Keynes' eclipse: money privatized

After the war Keynesian policies for the management of interest rates were gradually abandoned, under great pressure from the finance sector. Capital controls were maintained, but even these were abandoned by the late 1970s. The result: high and sustained rates of interest (adjusted for inflation/deflation) which while hugely beneficial to the finance sector, have hurt and undermined the productive sectors of both high-income and low-income economies. While the Federal Funds or Bank of England rate might sometimes seem low (although never as low as Keynes' 2%) the *real* rate paid by credit card holders, businesses seeking to invest and entrepreneurs taking risks, has for a long period been much, much higher.

Orthodox economics accepts that central banks should set short rates, but sees long rates as determined by 'natural forces'. As a result, these long rates, vital to home-owners and entrepreneurs, are beyond the control of government policy. Some even question whether short rates, for example, in the US, are still within the control of government policy. Indeed, although it is not quite the same thing, the governors of the Bank of England and of the Federal Reserve tend to judge the success of a policy on whether it is anticipated and accepted by the market.

Freddie Laker: entrepreneur vs the finance sector

Freddie Laker was a bold entrepreneur, who in the late 1970s and early 1980s challenged the monopoly of big airlines, and won the approval of Mrs Thatcher, then Conservative Prime Minister. In fact so proud was she of his achievements in denting the profits of big airline companies that she knighted him in 1978.

The pinnacle of Sir Freddie Laker's achievement came with the launch of the Laker Skytrain in 1977 – the first low-cost transatlantic operation.

In January 1978 the Bank of England's Minimum Lending Rate was 6.6%. In 1979, capital controls were lifted, and the Bank began to lose control over the setting of interest rates. By November 1979 the Bank rate was 15.6%. By July 1980 the rate was at 16%; in November, 1981, it was 14.7% (source: Bank of England). Like many businessmen and women, Sir Freddy had cash flow problems, and had an overdraft of £9 million, even though his business always made a profit (*The Australian*, 21 February 2006). At the beginning of August 1982, the year in which Freddie Laker's business went bust, interest rates had declined, but were still at a whopping 12.2%.

1982 was a year of economic turmoil, with rising oil prices, recession (caused in part by high real rates of interest) and a falling pound (which had to be supported by hiking up interest rates). In addition to this, Sir Freddie's business was constantly under attack from his competitors. Nevertheless, there can be no doubt that high real rates of interest played a big part in the destruction of a bold business venture.

As for Mrs Thatcher, she had shown her true colours: knighthoods for entrepreneurs in the productive sector; de-regulation and massive capital gains for the private finance sector.

Real rates of interest since money was privatized

The *Oxford Review of Economic Policy* examined in its 1999 edition the 'large and sustained rise in real interest rates in the late 1970s and early 1980s' – but found no sensible explanation for these 'high real rates since 1980' (Tily, 2005). Like many in the academic sphere, the *Oxford Review* has a blind spot for the finance sector, and is indifferent to Keynes' achievement in bringing down UK interest rates.

The 2004 UK Pensions Commission report, *Pensions: Challenges and Choices*, provided useful figures revealing the long-term trend of the real cost of borrowing to governments and corporations. *Real* returns on UK gilts (i.e. a measure of the interest that governments pay on borrowing) over five-year periods from 1899 to 2003 show that the average rate over the whole period was 1.4%. But after 1977 it was 7.0%. *Real* returns on US Treasuries over five-year periods, between 1925 and 2003, show that the average over the whole period was 2.2%; but the average rate after 1977 was 6.8%.

Stocks and shares, or equities, pay a dividend on investments. *Real* returns for UK equities over five-year periods from 1899 to 2003 (i.e. a measure of interest that corporations are paying on their borrowings) show that the average over the whole period is 5.7%. But after 1977 it was 10.4%. *Real* returns for US equities over the period 1925–2003 show that the average rate for the whole period was 7.1%; but the average rate since 1977 has been 10% (UK Pensions Commission, 2004).

These figures explain a great deal about the impact of de-regulation on interest rates and the adverse affect on entrepreneurs, on corporations, governments. Above all, these rates explain their growing mountains of debt. The average rate of return on productive investment is 3–5%. Any borrowing above that rate presents repayment difficulties for most investors.

So how have companies been able to pay for investments, with such high real rates of interest? The answer is that they have either collapsed and gone bust; corruptly tried to stay afloat (as in the case of Enron and other corporations); or else have gone deeply into debt.

Interest rates for ordinary consumers can in many cases be described as usurious. A 2006 report from the UK's Competition Commission noted that annual percentage rates (APRs) of interest for store cards 'have been some 10% to 20% above what they would have been had they reflected providers' costs across the sector'. The UK's General Electric Consumer Finance routinely charge interest rates of more than 25% on credit raised through store cards.

Rates of interest on store cards in the UK

B&Q (hardware and home furnishing). Card provided by General Electric Consumer Finance at an annual interest rate of *26.8%*.

Miss Selfridge (women's clothing). Card provided by GE Consumer Finance at an annual interest rate of *29.9%*.

Laura Ashley (women's clothing and home furnishing). Card provided by GE Consumer Finance at an annual interest rate of *29.9%*.

IKEA (home furnishings). Card provided by Ikano at an annual interest rate of *12.9%*.

French Connection (women's clothing). Card provided by Style at an annual interest rate of *26.8%*.

UK Competition Commission, March 2006

Tremendous capital gains have been made by those who control the rate of interest. By those private sector organizations that have made loans to governments, corporations or individuals, and thereby extracted additional assets and even greater wealth.

De-regulation of credit creation

Government de-regulation of credit and the banking and finance sector has removed controls over lending and borrowing, and has allowed new financial organizations to enter the money-lending business. This de-regulation largely took place in the UK between 1979 and 1989, during the tenures of two Conservative finance ministers, Geoffrey Howe and Nigel Lawson. They oversaw the abolition of all controls over consumer credit together with the total de-regulation of housing finance. This led to a massive growth in lending, which in turn fuelled the Lawson housing boom of the 1980s. This housing bubble crashed, with painful consequences for millions of home-owners, in the early 1990s.

Earlier, government licensing processes limited and constrained the business of money-lending. No longer. Today, businesses like supermarkets and privatized post offices are permitted to provide banking services. As this book goes to press, WalMart, the giant US retailer, was applying to a US Federal Agency for a licence to open an industrial loan company. If granted, it would join General Motors, General Electric and Target (another retailer) in offering banking services.

Governments and free-marketeers have argued that by broadening the number of money-lenders in the market, competition is intensified,

---

Falling credit standards in the US

Anecdotal evidence suggests that falling credit standards have played a role in pushing housing prices higher. Of home buyers who financed their home purchases in the first six months of 2005, more than 38 percent made down payments of 5 percent or less of the purchase price. In 2000, a little over 30 percent purchased their homes with so little down. Similarly, the percentage of buyers paying 20 percent down declined from 39.1 percent in 2000 to 33.7 percent in the first six months of 2005.

Papadimitriou et al. (January 2006)

---

and the cost of lending falls. Many question this rationale, noting that banks are merging and acquiring other banks, and this consolidation is leading to oligopolies, if not monopolies, in the sector. These in turn lead to high rates of interest, with apparent collusion between different banks and finance companies.

In the past too, regulations placed limits on the amount that could be borrowed in relation to, for example, incomes. In some countries regulation still prevents money being borrowed against the *current* value of an asset, but instead requires borrowing against the average value over 30 years. However, in countries where de-regulation of credit is the norm, such inhibitions on lending and borrowing have been lifted.

Credit and the inflation of assets – not goods or wages

There is a positive correlation between household borrowing and increases in the prices of assets. Papadimitriou (et al., 2006) of the Levy Institute has shown that since 1970 peaks in housing prices are nearly matched by peaks in household borrowing. Similarly, the troughs in real home prices are nearly matched by troughs in household borrowing. The late 1970s experienced rapid growth in both real home prices and borrowing. Lower household borrowing followed falling housing prices in the early 1980s.

When credit is used to inflate the value of assets, as happens now in economies like that of the US, the UK, Spain and Iceland, then even the limits imposed on borrowing by the value of assets evaporate, like bubbles. This is because unregulated credit offered to borrowers on the basis of an asset rising in price, will rise in line with the inflating asset. (In other words, if our chicken-farmer's English estate agent informs her that the value of her house has appreciated dramatically, this immediately increases her capacity to borrow against that asset. She sells up, at the higher price, and uses her larger borrowing to pour money into another house – further fuelling the property and credit bubbles.) This process helps explain why over the last decade we have witnessed the quite extraordinary and credit-fuelled inflation of assets, in particular property, in economies like that of the UK, the US, Spain, New Zealand and Iceland (to name but a few).

Property bubbles from Chile to Namibia

About two years ago, driving toward the Vineyard area outside Santiago, Chile, the sight of, literally, miles of residential construction astounded us. The Chileno accompanying us averred that this was a new, expanding development in the country. As he said: 'Only the rich used to be able to buy houses; now we have banks (he particularly mentioned the local entity of Citibank) that lend to everybody with these mortgages.' A year or so later, on the Cape Town waterfront, we saw condo development rivaling the now well reported current excesses in Miami. Again, the same story, the banks were open door on residential lending. Up the coast a country in Namibia, there are villas going up aplenty in the little town of Swakopmund on the beach. (Nice beach but the water stays in the 40–50 degree range). Again, the lenders have come to town and the South Africans and Europeans love the fishing. Although the diving is great, the infrastructure and amenities of Providenciales in the Turks and Caicos are no Cannes. Thousands upon thousands of condominiums are under construction or for sale (with a lot of empty ones standing around). On the uninhabited (until now) island of West Caicos, an enormous condo development is under way. No airport, no roads, no town and until the developer completes it, no port but what an opportunity (For Investment?).

McCarthy, 17 October 2005

All this borrowing has led to excessive credit chasing a limited number of assets (property, classic cars, works of art) which in turn has led to the inflation in value of these assets. These assets have then been used to raise even more credit. As noted earlier, the rich on the whole own assets, and therefore excessive credit has enabled the rich to effortlessly increase the value of their assets. This is an inflationary bubble that the US Federal Reserve's chairman, Mr Alan Greenspan, made no effort to deflate during his term of office. On the contrary, the policies of the Federal Reserve under his helm helped exacerbate the inflation of assets; in other words, actively inflated the value of assets held by the *already-rich*.

Compare the average *incomes* of everyone on earth between 1982 and 2004 to the increase over that period in the *assets* known as stocks, bonds and derivatives (a sophisticated financial instrument). The *average* income of everyone on earth between 1982 and 2004 has risen three times in a period of 22 years; from $2,147 per person to approximately $6,440 (source: World Bank and Hahn, 2006). The rise in the total value of all stocks, bonds and derivatives in the world during this time rose from $1,920 per person to $61,443 (Hahn, 2006). In other words, the value of these assets rose by 32 times over this period – 29 times more than incomes. That represents a growth rate of more than ten times faster than the average annual growth rate of income.

It turns out that working for a living over this period was most unrewarding. Earning rent on assets, by contrast, was immensely rewarding. For this state of affairs the owners of assets, the rich, have neo-liberal economists, central bankers and politicians to thank. Working people, on the other hand, have every reason to resent a system created by economists, central bankers and politicians that enriches the already rich.

Asset-price inflation: further examples

The *Financial Times* (24 March 2006) reviewed inflation in the value of a select range of assets over the last ten years:

Classic cars: Ferrari 250 GT Lusso. This was worth £300,000 in 1996. Christies sold one in 2006 for £950,000.

Rock memorabilia: Handwritten 'All You Need is Love' lyrics from the Our World broadcast in 1967 – the Beatles' final live television performance. Worth £20,000 in 1996. Sold for £690,000 at auction in 2005.

Chinese art – Ming bowl: A blue and white ceramic Chenghua palace bowl dating back to the Ming emperor Chengua, who ruled between 1465 and 1487. In 1996 it was worth £300,000 to £400,000. By 2006 its value was estimated at £1,000,000, based on its sale for £820,000 in 2002.

Stocks – Canadian company: Niko Resources, a Canadian oil and gas exploration company. In 1996 a share was worth C$0.34. By 2006 a share was worth C$49.50.

Cartier bracelet: A 'tutti frutti' bracelet from Cartier. The circa 1930 Art Deco piece, consisting of emeralds, rubies, sapphires and diamonds, sold at auction in 1996 for $540,000. In November 2005 it sold for $1,093,000.

Once the horse has bolted ...

When credit bubbles result in high levels of debt and an economic shambles, as happened in Japan in 1990 and in the US in 2001 (after the stock market crash), then central banks invariably seek to deal with the *symptoms* of the debt crisis by lowering the rate of interest, thereby *increasing* lending! In Japan rates were lowered to negative levels after the 1987 international financial crisis, which in turn led to an even greater expansion of credit, or liquidity. Because there are few restrictions on the movement of capital, these lower rates attract more borrowers/ lenders/investors (known as the 'carry trade') who borrow cheap in say, Japan and lend dear in say, Iceland. Under the de-regulated conditions of globalization, low rates, in a world of restless money flows and easy credit, thus encourages the growth, at an international level, of even more reckless borrowing. This was the background to the very low long-term rates that prevailed in the US between 2002 and 2006, and encouraged the great mortgage re-financing spree of that period.

In a global economy in which credit is privately created, and lightly regulated, and in which interest rates are determined as a result of the random or herd instincts of gamblers, speculators and investors in the international capital markets, this expansion of credit is very difficult to control. As a result, today's global economy is awash with liquidity – i.e credit, and its corollary, debt.

Conclusion

Bank money, as Abraham Lincoln, Henry Ford and John Maynard Keynes argued, can be a powerful tool in the right hands: that is, if its exclusive monopoly is controlled by democratic governments, accountable to the people as a whole. Liberalized and under the control of a minority – private bankers and financiers – bank money can lead to unpayable mountains of debt, and massive transfers of wealth from poor to rich; from those without assets to those with assets; from debtors to creditors.

Citizens of countries around the world live, work and borrow in ignorance of how bank money is created, and of the parasitic way in which bankers and financiers use bank money and debt to extract wealth from individuals, businesses and governments. Sir Frederick Soddy (1877–1956), the Nobel Prize-winning chemist, was outraged when he came to understand how banks create money, even attempting to take the Bank of England to court. He argued that banks have 'usurped supreme power over the State, and are now the effective rulers of the world'. And he correctly warned: 'this hold-up of the flow of wealth is the prime cause of war' because 'it renders nations naked and exposed to external monetary domination, universal, unsuspected and supreme' (Boyle, 2002).

The most dangerous feature of the system of private money creation – of Costly Credit, de-regulated credit – is that it generates debt that cannot be repaid, which in turns precipitates crises. These crises are generalized, and while they may hurt the rich, impact most disastrously on the poor, those innocent of a role in the creation of the crisis, and bereft of the capital gains made during a period in which assets were deliberately inflated.

The debt cannot be repaid because it is based on future real income that will not be generated; investments that have failed to yield what was expected; consumer borrowing based on salary increases and employment prospects that will dry up; government borrowing based on a scale of economic activity that may not happen. Ultimately this debt hits the buffers of human tolerance or the limits of the ecosystem.

The only sustainable way for societies to avoid high levels of debt, the obscene polarization of wealth between rich and poor, and the crises that follow, is through policies that regulate control over the movement of capital, and the creation of credit. Above all, to function well (and without usury or war) societies and the ecosystem need policies for debt-free government money; cheap commercial money and regulated credit creation. Policies for lending that will generate future income in line with the ecosystem's limits; investments that will yield sustainable results; and consumer borrowing that will not lead to over-consumption, debt, a slump and then unemployment.

Such cheap money policies can only be implemented within the democratic sphere: by accountable governments that have subordinated the private finance sector to the interests of society and the ecosystem as a whole.

Sources and suggested reading

The Australian, 21 February 2006, 'The Father of No-Frills Flying', by Iain MacIntosh.

Bank of England, *Statistical Interactive Database* – interest and exchange rates data at <www.bankofengland.co.uk/statistics/index.htm>.

Boyle, D., *The Money Changers: Currency Reform from Aristotle to e-cash*. Earthscan Publications Ltd, 2002.

Chick, V., *Macroeconomics after Keynes*, MIT Press, 1983.

Daily Mail, 10 May 2006, 'Banks in the Dock: These men grab £3 billion a year for your mistakes', by James Coney.

Davidson, Paul, 'Finance, funding, saving and investment'. *Journal of Post Keynesian Economics*, Fall 1986, 9(1) pp. 101–10.

Financial Times, 24 March 2006, 'Ten Great Ways to Get Rich', by Ming Liu.

Ford, H., 'Muscle Shoals and the end of war', 1921. Interview published in the *New York Times* on 4 December 1921 and quoted in *The Social Creditor* vol. 77, no. 3, May/June 1998. In D. Boyle, *The Money Changers: currency reform from Aristotle to e-cash*. Earthscan Publications Ltd, 2002.

Ford, H., *Henry Ford*, Wikipedia. <http://en.wikipedia.org/wiki/Henry_Ford#Quotations>.

Gleeson, J., *Millionaire: The Philanderer, Gambler and Duelist who Invented Modern Finance*. Simon and Schuster, 1999.

Hahn, Wilfred, *Money Changers in the Temple: Then and Now*. Midnight Call, January 2006. <www.eternalvalue.com/MCM/MET_0601.pdf>.

Keynes, J.M, *The Collected Writings of John Maynard Keynes*, 30 Volumes. General editors: D.E. Moggridge and E.S. Johnson. Macmillan and Cambridge University Press for the Royal Economics Society, 1971–89.

Keynes, J.M., 'National Self Sufficiency'. *The Yale Review*, Volume 22(4), June 1933.

Keynes, J.M., *A Treatise on Money*. First published by Macmillan, 1930.

McCarthy, E., International Perspective: *James Jones and Global Finance*. PrudentBear.com, 17 October 2005. <www.prudentbear.com/archive_comm_article.asp?category=International+Perspective&content_idx=47703>.

Lord Mackintosh, UK Government minister, Lord McIntosh of Haringey, in answer to a question from Lord Beaumont in 2001 in the British House of Lords.

Marshall, A., *Money, Credit and Commerce*. Macmillan & Co., 1923.

Marx, K., *Capital: A Critique of Political Economy, Volume III: The Process of Capitalist Production as a Whole*. Charles H. Kerr and Company, 1909. First published in 1894.

Office for National Statistics, time series data: <www.statistics.gov.uk/statbase/TSDTimezone.asp>.

Papadimitriou, D.B.; Chilcote, E. and Zezza, G., *Strategic Analysis: Are Housing Prices, Household Debt and Growth Sustainable?* The Levy Economics Institute of Bard College, January 2006.

Schumpeter, J.A., *A History of Economic Analysis*. Oxford University Press, 1954.

Stamp, J.C., *Josiah Charles Stamp Quotes*, Thinkexist.com <http://en.thinkexist.com/quotes/josiah_charles_stamp/>.

Studart, Rogerio, *Investment Finance in Economic Development*. Routledge, 1995.

Thirlwall, Anthony P., *Growth and Development*. 6th edition. Macmillan, 1999.

Tily, G., *Keynes's General Theory, the Rate of Interest and 'Keynesian Economics': Keynes Betrayed*. University of London PhD thesis, 2005.

UK Competition Commission, *Store Cards Market Investigation*. 7 March 2006. <www.competition-commission.org.uk/rep_pub/reports/2006/509storecards.htm>.

UK Pensions Commission report, *Pensions: Challenges and Choices*. 2004. <www.pensionscommission.org.uk/publications/2004/annrep/appendices-all.pdf>.

3
Easy Credit: Costly Debts

> However fruitful have been the mines of Mexico and Peru ... there is yet a discovery more precious for humanity, and which has already produced more wealth than that for America; that is the discovery of Credit; a world altogether imaginary, but vast as space, as inexhaustible as the resources of the mind.
>
> M. Gustave de Puynode, quoted in Dunning Macleod (1879)

In April 2006 a story exploded on the sports pages of newspapers around the world. It was alleged that Wayne Rooney, Manchester United's footballing star, had built up debts of £700,000 ($1.2 million) from gambling. According to the London *Times*, the young star (18 years old at the time) had started placing these bets by phone or text message with a bookmaker. He was given unusually large credit and allowed to accrue huge losses. 'I would think twice about giving someone that much credit, no matter who he was', one established bookmaker is quoted as saying (*The Times*, 11 April 2006).

Rooney is a victim of unregulated bank money run riot. Bank money, which as noted in the previous chapter can be a stimulus to the economy, can ensure that there is no shortage of money for new inventions, for business start-ups, for environmental conservation, hospitals, schools, AIDS medication, or for the Arts. But while bank money can be a great servant to the economy if regulated by a state informed by the interests of the majority, it can be a monstrous master in the hands of unregulated profiteering, greedy casino-owners and money-lenders – as Wayne Rooney and many millions have learned to their cost.

Fortunately Rooney and his advisers were jolted by the wake-up call of a media-driven scandal, and had enough ready money to quickly pay off these debts. But many millions of ordinary borrowers and gamblers are not, and will not be, so lucky. They will not be members of a high-paid, if risky profession. They might very well be in far more insecure jobs, dependent on the whims of tourists and the weather; in fashion, dependent on vagaries in the tastes of high-street shoppers; or in industries made redundant by competition from low-pay countries in Eastern Europe and China. All they might have in common with Wayne Rooney would be a willingness to gamble to stave off boredom and depression, and a susceptibility to the charms and overtures of those touting easy money. Indeed if they are poor, without access to low-cost housing provided by the state, or to affordable healthcare, they are likely to be desperate and far more susceptible to the overtures of bank-money lenders and gamblers than Rooney.

Debt – the opium of the masses

But Wayne Rooney's story does not just shine a light on the way in which millions of ordinary borrowers have been, almost unconsciously, lured into indebtedness by the siren voices of creditors. (Texting a bet is just one way of detaching oneself from the messy reality of spiralling debts; talking to a voice at the end of a telephone line to set up a credit card, or agree a home loan, is another.) Rooney's experience shines a light on the nature of the global economy – or globalization. For in the same week that his debt repayment story reverberated around the world, the London *Guardian* reported that Anurag Dikshit had become one of the ten richest Asians in Britain because of his stake in PartyGaming – an internet gambling site. By making a lot of money from unregulated money (and from the bored and depressed) Mr Dikshit is said to enjoy a fortune of £1.7 billion (about $3 billion) at the tender age of 34 (*Guardian*, 18 April 2006).

Men like Rooney and Dikshit are the poster children of a global economy constructed on the basis that mountains of wealth can effortlessly be made from the sterile asset that is money. All one has to do, it is suggested, is fiddle with predictive text on a mobile phone or sit, helplessly mesmerized, at a computer, to make money from that token first invented by our ancestors. Like Rooney, gamblers and debtors are almost hypnotized by the process. Doped by the opium of debt, they remain convinced that wealth, happiness, companionship, love and fancy goods can be achieved at little personal cost and with little effort; and at no cost to the rest of humanity or the earth.

US gambling revenues (including casino betting and lotteries) are soaring (Hahn, 2006). Between 1990 and the end of 2003, gaming revenues world-wide rose from $24.7 billion to $72.8 billion (American Gaming Association) – almost twice as fast as average income. 'These figures do not measure the actual money wagered, which is approximately 10 times the amount spent (money actually lost) – or greater than $600 billion per annum' (Hahn, 2006). Online sports betting had already surged to $5.7 billion per annum in 2003, and is projected to more than triple to $18.7 billion by 2010.

Total lottery ticket sales in the US during 2004 reached a peak of $45 billion. According to the World Lottery Association combined annual revenues are now in excess of US$120 billion (Hahn, 2006).

Those in the driving seat of the globalization juggernaut – financiers, hedge fund managers, international investment bankers, gamblers, speculators, central bankers and finance ministers – believe that we can continue to enrich the rich, and extract additional assets from the earth and from people like Wayne Rooney, without any social or political cost, or indeed without any ecological cost – forever. This is what keeps them going. They live in a world in which making money from money is like baking an enormous, yeasty cake which can be expected to rise exponentially and inexorably. All it needs is, for example, access to the markets of billions of Chinese, Indian or Russian borrowers, gamblers and speculators. These markets have not yet, it is argued, been deeply mined for capital gains. Creditors and gambling men are confident of finding hundreds of millions of Wayne Rooneys out there – beyond those 'new' frontiers. The potential to exploit both land and humanity for additional assets appears infinitesimally vast – vast as space – and with this vision do they deride those of us who are sceptical.

It is a far, far better thing to have a firm anchor in nonsense than to put out on the troubled seas of thought.

Galbraith (1977)

But the global cake being cooked up by these international financial bakers already represents the debts and liabilities of hundreds of millions of ordinary people, of corporations, governments and of nations. When the oven door opens and the cold air of reality deflates the cake, there will be an unholy mess – financial, economic, political, social and ecological – that will inflict great pain on the poorest and most vulnerable and will be comparable only to the economic catastrophe that followed the credit-fuelled collapse of the US stock market in 1929, and the bond market crash of 1987 (which in turn led to Japan's economic implosion and ultimately to the 1997/98 international financial crisis). To understand

hy such a collapse would be so destructive we need to explore and
nderstand:

- deflation;
- that deflation increases the cost of debt;
- the importance of cash in a deflationary environment;
- that interest rates can never fall below zero; but prices and wages
  can.

Inflation transfers assets *from* creditors to debtors. Inflation will erode
the real value of any debt, meaning that the debtor pays back less in real
terms. Conversely deflation – where prices are falling – increases the real
value of debts. The combination of consumer price deflation and asset
price inflation is every wealth-holder's dream. Under deflation, the costs
of wages, commodities, and other inputs fall, while asset price inflation
means that capital gains steadily rise and are not eroded in real terms.
Lowering costs can make higher profits. Capital gains can be recycled
into further capital purchases leading to yet more capital gains. So the
rich make money from money while those reliant for their income on
current wages, and not from capital gains, receive a smaller and smaller
share of national income.

Real World Economic Outlook 2003

Inflation and deflation

Ask any woman on the street to define 'deflation', and one would probably
get a blank look. By contrast, 'inflation' – *rising prices and wages, which
help cut the cost of mortgages* – is much better understood. Our high-street
shopper would not be alone. I have come across economic textbooks
that have extensive definitions and long-winded chapters on the grave
threat of inflation, but fail to explain or define deflation or 'disinflation'
as it is sometimes described. The most senior economists in the world,
backed by the most powerful bankers, are mesmerized by the threat of
inflation – even though it has for several decades been absent from most
economies.

If our high-street shopper does have some understanding, she would
probably define deflation as *falling prices* – and add: *a jolly good thing too*.
But there are dangers lurking in falling prices – for those who make and
sell goods, services and their labour: producers, professionals, shopkeepers,
and their workers. However, there are even greater dangers in deflation
for debtors.

First, let's explore what is happening to prices in an economy tha in the spring of 2006, is booming: the UK. David Smith, a respecte economist, points out that while the prices of essential items like oil, ga and hairdressing are rising, we are living through a period of dramati falls in the prices of *goods*.

Haircuts aren't a snip – even with low inflation

Hairdressing prices, according to official figures, have gone up by 3.8% over the past year and by an impressive 57% since the start of 1997. That compares with a rise of 2% in the consumer prices index (CPI) in the past 12 months, and a surprisingly small increase of just 13.9% since 1997. Haircuts, in other words, have risen at more than four times the rate of prices in general.

Gas prices ... have gone up by more for domestic users in the past 12 months – 14.5% – than the consumer prices index has in nine years. Other spectacular increases include liquid fuels (heating oil), up 42.1%, water bills 13.6%, and electricity 10.7%.

Not so dramatic but still increasing much more rapidly than inflation are household repair bills, up 5.2%, bus fares 6.4%, and train fares 4.3%.

... But how, people ask, can you have inflation of 2%, and an index that has risen by less than 14% in nine years, when so many things are going up much faster? ... the National Statistics website ... shows that while many things are indeed going up, many others are falling. Cameras are down 24% in a year, clothing 4.5%, shoes 5.7%, sports equipment 4.1%, computers 14.2%, and so on.

In general, goods prices are stable or falling – 'things' costs no more now on average than in 1997 – while anything involving people and services is rising fast ... It all adds up to low inflation, even though there is huge volatility within an index that is stable overall.

Smith, 16 April 2006, <www.economicsuk.com/blog/000323.html>

What David Smith demonstrates is that energy prices in the UK are rising thanks largely to global insecurity and instability (conflict in the Middle East and Nigeria), increased demand from China, and the dawning realization that both gas and oil are finite resources. In contrast, the prices of other goods are falling, which is why in the week this was written, inflation in the UK fell, from 2% in the month before, to 1.8%. Core inflation, which excludes energy, food, alcohol and tobacco, remained unchanged at 1.3% (BBC News, 16 May 2006).

While energy and commodity prices may *appear* high in the UK, these numbers (taken in isolation) can be misleading. The United Nations Conference on Trade and Development (UNCTAD) points out that today's price hikes in commodities follow severe price falls over a sustained period. In the case of coffee, for instance, rising prices have still not caught up with pre-1997 levels, despite the fact that the price of a cappuccino for our high-street shopper has risen dramatically over the same period. *Real* dollar prices for the exports and commodities of poor countries over the longer term are even less impressive, with such prices still about one-third lower than the average for 1975–85 (UNCTAD, 8 March 2006).

So in the UK and at a global level, prices of key commodities are still low in real terms, and compared to 30 years ago, while prices of many goods are falling. In other words, while we may not be living through a period of deflation, we are certainly living in a deflationary environment. Countries like Japan are haltingly emerging from more than ten years of, first, disinflation, and then deflation.

Now deflation can be a good thing for ordinary consumers – but especially for the already-rich, as the above quotation from the *Real World Economic Outlook* notes. Lower prices for labour, commodities and goods leads to lower wages, inputs and costs which can lead to lower prices for consumers and higher profits for producers. These profits can be used to reinvest in, and make more capital gains from, assets (e.g. property, the stock market or a business).

However, the flipside of this good news is that falling prices can also lead to tighter margins and falling profits for producers and retailers, and then lower wages for workers and prices for entrepreneurs. While lower prices for labour and commodities can increase prices and therefore profits, in a competitive environment in which trade is not regulated, and low-paid workers in rich countries are forced to compete with even lower-paid workers in poor countries; *prices* of goods and services fall, and this can squeeze profits. *50% off* and *spring/summer/autumn/winter/ clearance sales; last day of special offer!; special discount; unique promotion* – these high-street slogans are all sure signs of falling prices and of the pressures facing producers and retailers in white goods, computers, auto manufacturing, and clothing industries, to name but a few.

Big global conglomerates invariably push this squeeze lower down the supply chain, and make their suppliers take the pain – but the pain itself cannot be avoided. Tighter margins and falling profits lead producers and retailers to cut back on costs, including labour costs, by lowering wages in real terms, or by laying off staff, increasing unemployment.

Doctors and dishwashers

The United States government has designed trade policy to put some workers (primarily manufacturing workers) into competition with workers in developing countries. It has maintained or increased protections for many high-paid occupations like doctors, lawyers, journalists and economists. While proponents of this path for trade policy might prefer that it appear to be the outcome of an inevitable process of globalization, this is not so.

... the conservative nanny state allows many less-skilled workers into the country to fill jobs at lower wages than employers would be forced to pay the native born population ... placing downward pressure on the wages and compensation of workers without college degrees more generally.

Baker (2006)

One-legged economies and the double bind

Financially liberalized economies are increasingly dependent on borrowing and debt to boost consumption; consumption in turn is the only leg of the economy increasing output, and therefore boosting economic growth, and jobs. These economies are therefore one-legged, largely dependent on private consumption – and not say, government spending or business investment – to boost growth. (Note that in both the US and the UK, government spending has risen since 2001, adding another leg to economic growth, and helping to avoid a recession.)

In order to maintain the economic growth needed to, for example, raise the money to repay debts that grow inexorably, this consumption, and the borrowing needed to finance it, has had to grow – exponentially.

Which presents governments and central banks with a double bind: if they try and curtail borrowing or lending, to prevent a debt crisis, they will simultaneously cut back, or cut off, an important leg holding up the economy – personal consumption. If, on the other hand, personal consumption keeps growing, borrowing to finance it will keep rising, stockpiling problems for the future.

Consumers and citizens face the double bind too. If they stop borrowing, stop buying houses and shopping for goods, and instead start saving – that will help *precipitate* the crisis – because the economy is now so dependent on their consumption. However, if they go on borrowing, shopping and *not* saving – they will just store up bigger trouble for themselves and make the crisis worse when it does finally break.

This truly is a lose-lose world for millions of consumers and home-owners in economies following the Anglo-American economic model of financial and credit liberalization.

When lending or borrowing fall, consumption and output fall, leading to job losses and rising unemployment. In other words, a crisis may not be precipitated by unpayable debts; it might be precipitated simply by a fall in lending, leading to a fall in output, and then unemployment and recession.

Because most debtors repay their debts, not by selling an asset like their home, but out of income earned from employment, unemployment has a disastrous impact on the ability of debtors to service debts. Those who lose their jobs will be the very consumers that have heroically propped up economies over the last decade. (Note that bankers and economists frequently assess whether debts are payable by comparing the debt to the value of the debtors' assets; or by comparing it to their income. But debtors don't normally repay their debts by selling their assets, which often includes their home. They pay debts out of income, which is fine – until they lose their income.)

The magic of compound interest

Things will get worse for those debtors who lose their jobs and have not secured their borrowing against an asset. They invariably end up consolidating their debts; i.e. borrowing more to pay off debts. In this way debts begin to spiral. If debtors simply default, i.e. suspend debt service payments altogether, then the lender will add compound interest to the outstanding payments. This compounding of debt is commonly referred to as a form of 'magic' and causes debts to rise exponentially.

Deflation and cash

Spiralling debts, compounded by interest, will be exacerbated in a deflationary environment. There are a number of features of deflation that are not well understood, including the impact on cash, and on interest rates.

In a deflationary environment, where the prices of goods, services and wages are falling, the value of *cash* increases. This is because, when prices are falling, it is possible to buy *more* goods, say in a month's time, with the *same* amount of cash. $100 tomorrow will buy more than $100 today. So holding cash in a deflationary environment becomes sensible

Compound interest

This is interest computed on the accumulated and rising *unpaid* interest added on to the original principal.

The rate of interest is calculated as a proportion of the principal amount borrowed, e.g. 5%. It is calculated and paid not once, but, in this case, at 5% per year for every year, with interest depending on how much has been paid off. For example: if the original loan is £1,000, and the borrower agrees to repay £250 a year:

- Interest payment at end year 1 = 5% × £1,000 = £50
- Interest payment at end year 2 = 5% × £750 = £37.50
- Interest payment at end year 3 = 5% × £500 = £25
- Interest payment at end year 4 = 5% × £250 = £12.50

Now, say, at the end of year 2, the borrower defaults. She will have £750 of the principal outstanding, and in addition owes £37.50 in interest for year 2. This interest amount is added to the principal, which leaps to £787.50. Interest is now calculated on the new, expanded sum. This means in year 3, the borrower owes interest equivalent to 5% of £787.50 = £39.38. If unpaid this interest is added to the principal, bringing it to a total of £826. If the borrower continues to default, interest in the next year will be calculated at 5% of the bigger sum: £826.88 = £41.44.

Default, or delay ensures that the debt grows exponentially, thanks to the 'magic' of compound interest.

It gets worse. A borrower in default may be liable for a penalty as well, which could be added to the ballooning debt each year; causing the debt to rise faster.

Nigeria provides a good example of the blight caused by compounding interest on debt. The government borrowed a total of $17 billion from rich countries from 1964. But by 2005, after six years of no borrowing, this had ballooned to a liability of $31 billion – because the creditors compounded debt and added penalties when Nigeria failed to meet its scheduled payments of principal and interest.

and wise. (Holding debt, which becomes more expensive in a deflationary environment, is most unwise.)

Many consumers have borrowed large sums of money and set the borrowing against their assets, meaning that most of their wealth is tied up in these assets. That is, it exists in the form of equity, not cash. When the price of assets (e.g. property) starts to fall, so does the wealth tied up in the assets. But because in a generalized crash everyone's asset is falling in value, property-owners rush to sell. It quickly becomes difficult to sell assets fast enough to obtain a good price, repay debts or mortgages, and realize the cash.

What will happen to equity when US house prices crash?

At the end of the third quarter of 2005, U.S. household real estate was estimated to be worth $19.11 trillion, while mortgage debt stood at $8.19 trillion, leaving total equity at $10.92 trillion ...

A 5 percent drop would lead to a $960 billion dollar loss in equity. A 10 percent drop would reduce it by $1.91 trillion dollars. A 20 percent drop would eliminate $3.82 trillion dollars in equity, representing a 35 percent loss. This suggests that given the highly leveraged position of households, even a modest drop in housing prices would reduce their wealth considerably.

Papadimitriou et al. (January 2006)

If, in a housing crash, many indebted home-owners are either unable to sell, or sell at a value lower than the outstanding debt; and if at the same time unemployment rises, a real shortage of cash develops. It is at this point in a generalized financial crisis that *cash becomes king*.

In previous debt-deflationary crises, those holding large amounts of cash (like the Kennedy clan in the 1930s) have made a killing buying up assets sold cheaply by desperate debtors, and holding these in preparation for the next economic upturn.

Interest rates don't fall like prices

Now all this would be bad enough for debtors if it were not for one additional concern: prices of goods and wages can fall below zero, but interest rates cannot.

In other words, it is quite possible that our proverbial chicken-farmer could be forced to sell her chickens and eggs in the marketplace at prices *below* the cost of producing those chickens and eggs. (Even though she might be selling below cost, she is probably desperate to raise *some* cash – perhaps to pay off debts, including her mortgage, as well as to buy basic foodstuffs etc.) Once she starts selling at prices below cost, it will then be inevitable that she lays off workers, because she will just not be raising enough to pay wages. If our farmer has fixed costs (her mortgage, water and electricity) her income can become negative, i.e. fall below zero – as she probably has to borrow to pay for these essentials. Her workers could be in the same position.

However, interest rates cannot fall below zero – or else no-one would ever lend. If interest rates fell below zero (in real terms, taking into account inflation) lenders would be paying borrowers to borrow – an unlikely event, and only known to happen in economies where the state fixes interest rates.

If interest rates were to fall to zero, say, and the prices of chickens and eggs fell by 10% *below* zero or the cost, *then the real rate of interest for our farmer would be 10%, not zero.* In other words, in a deflationary environment *real* interest rates *rise* relative to prices.

I believe that very few of the millions of young people recklessly borrowing or paying for groceries on credit cards, taking out loans for holidays, or the millions of home-owners increasing or re-financing their mortgages, are aware that in a deflationary environment the cost of debt rises. Surely they would cease to borrow so much if they did understand?

In a deflationary environment our chicken-farmer will do what you or I would do: she would sell the farm to raise some cash and get out from under her debts. Her workers would be obliged to sell their homes (if they were lucky enough to own homes) to pay off debts that would not just be high relative to their non-existent incomes, but would be *rising* in real terms. However, as falling prices affect a large number of small businesses and workers, and as more and more cut back on spending, and put their assets on the market for sale, so the prices of the goods they are selling falls; and the prices of their assets (property etc.) begin to fall too – exacerbating and deepening what is known as a debt-deflationary spiral.

Which is why deflation in an economy mired by debts can be so destructive and terrifying; much more so than inflation. Inflation hurts creditors, but not the population in general, if prices and wages remain in line. However, deflation can hurt the population in general, while protecting the value of the assets (loans) of creditors. The exception of course is a generalized and catastrophic crisis.

At the time of writing, April 2006, central bankers and finance ministers in rich countries continue to be obsessed by the concerns of creditors; to compulsively focus on, and control, the very low inflation of goods and wages; and to do little about the inflation of assets.

In the US in March 2006, producer prices rose by only 0.5%, with core inflation rising 0.1%. On a year-over-year basis, consumer prices rose by

4.3% and core inflation by 2.8% (Baker, 19 April 2006). Given the margin of error in calculating inflation, these levels are very low indeed.

Irresponsibly, in my view, central bankers and finance ministers pay scant attention to the threat of deflation both in the UK and in the global economy. The cost of this blinkered obsession with the interests of creditors and with inflation, in economies heavily laden with debt, will be borne by hundreds of millions of debtors when bubbles in property, stock market and other assets burst, as some are already beginning to do. The pain and anguish will be intense, in many cases unendurable. There will be suicides, health breakdowns, family break-ups and divorces, as there already are in poor countries caught up in a debt-deflationary spiral. There will be social unrest and massive economic dislocation as creditors go after debtors and demand that they give up more and more of their existing assets, to repay debts. Exploitation of both labour and land will intensify. History shows that such exploitation, pain and dislocation often acts as the trigger for war.

The 'nanny state' steps in

When the crisis breaks, of one thing we can be sure: politicians, creditors, financiers, pension funds and other loss-makers will quite quickly abandon the widespread distaste for big government. Instead they will turn to the 'nanny state' and demand compensation from taxpayers. Taxpayers, having been denied the benefit of *gains* made by the private finance sector will nevertheless be expected to finance this sector's *losses*. Paying compensation of this kind through taxation will increase the cost of a financial crisis to innocent and often ignorant taxpayers.

BT says state is liable for £28bn of pension fund
BT Group revealed earlier this month that a large part of its £38bn of gross pension liabilities under IAS19 are backed, in extremis, by the state. The commitment appears to apply to civil servants employed before the company's privatisation in 1984 ...

... The Department of Trade and Industry is challenging BT claims that, if the company becomes insolvent, the government will pay the pension liabilities for all of the workers on its payroll when it was privatised in 1984 as well as those previously employed by BT.

Financial Times (24 April 2006)

Blaming the victims

Worse, in a financial crisis, creditors, bankers and the finance sector will blame the victims – individuals, taxpayers, families, small businesses, even governments – persuaded to build up large debts by creditors responsible both for lending itself, but also for encouraging the de-regulation policies that facilitated massive lending. As noted above, this will be particularly ironic for the millions of indebted consumers, heroic individuals that have, like Atlas, been keeping the global economy afloat by borrowing and spending over this last decade.

Sadly, victims might very well blame themselves; or their neighbours; or black/Eastern European/Jewish immigrants/Chinese/Japanese workers. In a financial crisis there will undoubtedly be a rise in racism and anti-semitism. In the 1930s Hitler exploited the pain and despair of Germans grievously hurt by the aftermath of World War I; Germany's long period of indebtedness; and the Great Depression. He used these conditions to fuel anti-semitism and world war. He and his fellow-travellers, including Oswald Moseley, stirred up rhetoric against the finance sector; but they did little either to challenge those responsible for the crisis, or to transform the international financial system. On the contrary, Hitler made good use of the system to finance a terrible war.

Ignorance will prevent victims from understanding the true cause of their troubles; will allow the real perpetrators to escape judgement; and will delay the process of re-regulating and stabilizing the global economy.

This is the context in which below I give some idea of the scale of debts that have been run up by individuals, households, corporations and governments in a select group of countries: the UK; the US; France; Australia; South Korea; and Iceland.

UK debt: consuming more than can be paid for

The UK is one of the most open and liberalized economies in the world. Like citizens of the US, Britons have become used to living well beyond their means, as a nation, and to have their excess spending on foreign goods, and their failure to produce and export goods to pay for these – covered by financing from foreigners. In this respect the UK differs from its main competitor in Europe, Germany, which enjoys a surplus on its balance of payments; and France, which for more than a decade has had a balance of payments surplus. Unlike the UK, Germany and France are not dependent on foreign borrowings to finance their trade deficits.

Growing trade deficit 'sustainable'

The large and growing trade deficit should be sustainable, as long as British investments abroad earn more than foreign investments in Britain, according to Stephen Nickell, one of the external members of the Bank of England's monetary policy committee.

Financial Times (26 April 2006)

The UK has had a trade deficit for 30 years now, since the early 1970s (with a brief positive balance in the early 1980s). The deficit in goods and services widened in 2005 to its worst level in 16 years, at 3.9% of national income, as imports of goods continued to be sucked in and Britain's share of world exports continued to fall. While this is the highest on record in cash terms, the deficit as a share of GDP in the mid-1970s and late 1980s was much higher. There is widespread confidence in Britain that foreigners will continue to finance this deficit by pouring funds into the UK, as the quote above from a Bank of England governor demonstrates. We hope this confidence is well founded.

The UK government's debt (both the annual budget deficit and the total) is often exaggerated by UK commentators. It is equivalent to 3.6% of GDP (£43.7 billion) just slightly above the severely low target set by the monetarist Maastricht Treaty, which by law requires European governments to incur deficits of no more than 3% of GDP. General government UK debt was £526 billion in 2005, equivalent to 42.8% of GDP, again lower than the cautious limit set for the countries of the euro, which is 60% of GDP (Office for National Statistics, 31 March 2006).

Debt a 'way of life' for the EU's biggest borrowers

It is in the area of *personal* and household debts that Britons outstrip their European counterparts. Britons, leaders in financial liberalization, are much more indebted than most Europeans. According to Credit Action, the UK's credit card debt (£56.35 billion) accounts for fully two-thirds of total credit card debt in the EU (Credit Action, 2006).

In early 2006, UK individuals and households owed £1,174 billion (Credit Action) – almost exactly equivalent to total UK income or GDP: £1,210 billion. In other words, every UK adult owed on average £25,200, more than median annual earnings, which in 2004/05 were only £22,900 (Office for National Statistics Time Series Data).

A 2006 survey for debt consultants found that about 1 in 20 young people in the UK – more than 200,000 18–24-year-olds – owed at least £10,000 (BBC News, 17 April 2006). The number of 18–24-year-olds seeking advice on how to manage debt had doubled since 2002. Young people had become 'desensitized' to debt, because according to Malcolm Hurlston, Chairman of Consumer Credit Counselling Service, 'credit cards have blurred the distinction between borrowing and spending, and for many young people, student loans have made borrowing normal' (BBC News, 13 September 2005).

Research for the UK government in 2006 showed that students in their final year were predicted to have an average debt of £7,918; but that students from poor homes owed on average £9,842, £2,000 more than those from better-off families (*This Is Money*, 30 March 2006).

The US: debts worth '28 Eiffel towers, made out of pure gold'

The US has built up mountainous debts at international, governmental and personal/household levels.

The US's foreign debts pose a grave threat to the global economy because a point will arise when creditors lose confidence in the ability of the US to repay its debts. They will then begin to withdraw the money that is currently financing the debts, which will in turn lead to a collapse of the dollar. This process might begin slowly, but it will soon accelerate as the herd panics, and joins in. A lower dollar will increase the cost of imports for American consumers, who will cut back on consumption. At this point banks will likely stop lending so aggressively, which will exacerbate the effects of cuts in consumption and investment caused by the falling dollar. Cuts in consumption will sharply reduce imports, and hurt economies exporting into the US. Because the dollar is the world's reserve currency, and because its collapse has dire implications for the global economy as a whole, such a crisis would engulf most of the world in a severe recession and generate grave political tensions, perhaps even war.

On 28 March 2006, the US Congress raised America's national government debt ceiling to $9 trillion or $9,000,000,000,000. In 2001, the national debt had been just $5.7 trillion. Congress's latest increase to the limit is the fourth since George Bush took office.

The US's national debt is the *total* debt outstanding and owed by the government. It should not be confused with the US government's budget deficit – which is the *annual* build-up of government debt. Nor should it be confused with the trade deficit, which is the difference between US exports and imports.

The US's annual budget deficit has been worsened by the *war against terrorism*, the war in Iraq, and by Mr Bush's tax cuts for the rich, which have helped lower tax revenues.

There is widespread concern in the US that much of the debt is owed to foreigners. One notable critic, Warren Buffett, 'the greatest stock market investor of modern times' (Kanter, 1999) and worth at least $36 billion, has not minced his words about the threat to political, social and economic stability that this deficit poses (see Box).

The Sage of Omaha, Warren Buffett, writing to investors in 2005

The US as a 'sharecropper's society'

The underlying factors affecting the U.S. current account deficit continue to worsen, and no letup is in sight. Not only did our trade deficit – the largest and most familiar item in the current account – hit an all-time high in 2005, but we also can expect a second item – the balance of investment income – to soon turn negative. As foreigners increase their ownership of U.S. assets (or of claims against us) relative to U.S. investments abroad, these investors will begin earning more on their holdings than we do on ours.

The U.S., it should be emphasized, is extraordinarily rich and will get richer. As a result, the huge imbalances in its current account may continue for a long time without their having noticeable deleterious effects on the U.S. economy or on markets. I doubt, however, that the situation will forever remain benign.

Either Americans address the problem soon in a way we select, or at some point the problem will likely address us in an unpleasant way of its own.

Mr. Buffett was quoted by the London *Guardian* (7 March 2005) as saying:

This force-feeding of American wealth to the rest of the world is now proceeding at the rate of $1.8bn daily ... in the last 10 years foreign powers and their citizens had accrued about $3 trillion worth of US debt and assets such as equities and real estate.

At current rates, he predicted that in another 10 years' time the net ownership of the US by outsiders would amount to $11 trillion.

This annual royalty paid [to] the world would undoubtedly produce significant political unrest in the US. Americans ... would chafe at the idea of perpetually paying tribute to their creditors and owners abroad. A country that is now aspiring to an 'ownership society' will not find happiness in – and I'll use hyperbole here for emphasis – a 'sharecropper's society'.

<www.berkshirehathaway.com/letters/2005ltr.pdf>

Japan is the US's biggest creditor and has lent $640 billion. China has lent $321 billion (both figures refer to holdings of US Treasuries as at March 2006) (US Department of the Treasury, May 2006). Many other, much poorer countries have lent money to the US and now own US assets – both public and private.

Tim Reid of the London *Times* (17 March 2006) has estimated that the US's National Debt

- would build 28 Eiffel Towers, made out of pure gold;
- is equal to $1,500 for every man, woman and child in the world;
- would buy all the tea in China – in fact it would buy all the tea in the world for the next 2,000 years;
- is enough to solve the Palestinian crisis by rehousing every Israeli and Palestinian family in a £1.5 million detached house in Henley-on-Thames (a rich London suburb).

US Personal/household debt

In 2005 total US household debt, including mortgages was $11,497 billion. This compares with US income or GDP in 2005 of around $12,410 billion (Federal Reserve, 9 March 2006). Household debt as a share of disposable income remained below 70% until 1985. Then it grew at a compound annual rate of 1.25%, until the end of the 1990s, when it was still below 95%. Since 2000, the growth rate of debt has increased at a compound rate in excess of 5%. Today, the ratio of debt to income for US households is near 122% (Papadimitriou et al., January 2006).

In 2004, the household sector borrowed $1.01 trillion. In the first three quarters of 2005, the household sector borrowed $831 billion. This contrasts with the period prior to 2000, during which the household sector never borrowed more than $487.5 billion in a year (Papadimitriou et al., January 2006).

As with the UK, this build-up of debt is largely due to loose regulation and lending standards and increased cash-out refinancing – encouraged by recent, very low interest rates for long-term loans. In the US, the private sector balance, which is the excess of private sector savings over investment, was positive in every year between 1952 and 1997. However, by the first quarter of 2005, the private sector balance was –2.2%. This is around 4% below its long-term average mainly because of the housing boom financed by exceptional levels of borrowing (Godley, May 2005). Lending to the personal sector has added up to 15% to the disposable income of households, and this of course has encouraged consumption.

These days Americans make a living by selling each other houses, paid for with money borrowed from China.

Krugman (29 August 2005)

Alan Greenspan, until 2006 Governor of the Federal Reserve, argued in October 2004 that the financial stress facing households was *'not worrisome'* (Papadimitriou et al., January 2006). Greenspan, again like many others, is assuming that because assets (i.e. property) in the US continue to rise in value, that households are not likely to experience stress. However, I reiterate: debts are not paid for on the whole by selling home and hearth; they are paid out of income. And when wages fall, and jobs are lost, the income for repayment dries up. When unemployment spreads, there will likely be a fire sale of assets – and sale values falling too low to cover principal and debt service payments.

The average debt owed by every US adult is a staggering $52,000. This compares with the mean annual wages in the US of $37,440 (as at 2004 – Bureau of Labor Statistics). The economist Wynne Godley argues that these trends are not sustainable; that household spending relative to income cannot grow indefinitely. He notes in passing that while interest rates are low, the burden of servicing this debt has reached new heights (Godley et al., September 2005). Debt payments as a percentage of disposable income have been well above 12% since 2000. In the third quarter of 2005 it rose to a record 13.55%. Household liabilities have risen more rapidly than household income (Papadimitriou et al., January 2006).

France

The level of indebtedness in France is very low compared with the US, UK and Germany and is growing less rapidly than in Spain and Italy. This is largely due to regulation: a prudent system prevails where credit card credit is severely restricted and instalment credit is closely linked to the goods and services it finances. Payment cards, where all credit is consolidated through the overdraft credit on the consumer's bank account, is the most typical form of consumer credit (responsible-credit.net).

At the end of February 2006, French household debt stood at €737.6 billion, non-financial business debt stood at €1,224.2 billion, and general government debt stood at €1,119.4 billion. With France's GDP in 2005 estimated at €1,671.5 billion, household debt is equivalent to around 44% of GDP (compared with 100% in the UK and 93% in the US);

non-financial business debt 73%, and general government debt 67% of national income – much higher than in the UK (Banque de France, spring 2006).

Loans from credit institutions to households outstanding at the end of February 2006 were €716 billion. Of this amount, €126 billion were consumer loans and €509 billion were mortgages (Banque de France, spring 2006).

Australia

Remarkably, all Australian government debt had been eliminated by 21 April 2006. However, levels of private debt – both household debts owed by Australians, and the foreign debts owed by Australian companies, have rocketed. Australia's foreign debt increased dramatically after the liberalization of the early 1980s. In 1990 foreign debt was equivalent to 46% of GDP and by 2005 it had grown to the equivalent of 79% of GDP (Reserve Bank of Australia, April 2006).

Whereas in the 1980s Australian households had low levels of debt relative to income, personal debt levels are now in the same league as the US and UK. The average debt of households is now around 150% of annual income. This is double the ratio of a decade ago. In addition, the ratio of debt *repayments* to income has risen to almost 11% from an average of 6% in the 1990s (*The Age*, 6 May 2006).

On 21 April 2006, the Australian Treasurer, Peter Costello, declared that Australia was free of government debt – one of only seven industrialized countries to be so. This was achieved by building up budget surpluses and selling off public assets. But Australia's private sector foreign debt continues to swell. Net foreign debt hit a record A\$472.8 billion in Q4 2005, up A\$22.4 billion from Q3 (Reserve Bank of Australia, 18 May 2006). Meanwhile the current account deficit (i.e. the trade deficit) is expected to reach A\$56.25 billion or 6% of GDP in 2005/06 (National Nine News, 9 May 2006). Foreign liabilities have grown to 130% of GDP from 70% 15 years ago and most of that is debt (Reserve Bank of Australia, April 2006). Even though these are private foreign liabilities they represent a risk to the government. This is because they have to be repaid in hard currency (dollars, sterling or yen) stored by the central bank as reserves. If there are insufficient reserves to finance these debt payments, there will be a run on the Australian dollar, which will cause wider economic dislocation.

South Korea

The South Korean economy was one of the victims of the crisis of 1997 – a crisis exacerbated by debt, which had been generated by financial de-regulation and financial excess, and which quickly led to financial collapse. Most of the conventional and unregulated banks had borrowed short-term, and lent on (at higher rates of course) to corporations that used the borrowing for highly speculative investments, in assets. Because of the ties between state and private sector in South Korea, there was an implicit assumption that the government (i.e. taxpayers) would guarantee this reckless lending and borrowing. The circular process of credit fuelling the prices of assets, pushed up the prices of property and other assets, just as today in the Anglo-American bubble economies. When the bubble burst, the economic, social and personal pain was indescribably intense.

The IMF was called in and, in return for its loans, offered a menu of austerity measures to protect the assets of foreign creditors; and return the economy to balance.

After 1997 South Korea relied on consumer spending to act as the engine of recovery and economic growth, and actively encouraged payment through credit cards in order to spur consumption. It did this by, for example, introducing tax deductions for purchases made by credit card. Credit card spending rose from $53 billion in 1998 to $519 billion in 2002 and household debt which had been 18% of GDP in 1999 exploded to 62% of GDP by 2001 (*Monthly Review*, 15 August 2005).

In the five years since the 1997 corporate debt crisis, household debt has nearly doubled, reaching $326 billion in 2002. As a result, this debt as a share of national income increased from 50% in 1999 to 73% in 2002 (*New York Times*, 3 December 2002). This report commented that:

> Card issuers were so eager to sign up new customers that they set up folding tables at busy intersections, handing out cards to passers-by who gave nothing more than a home address – no one asked nosy questions about assets or income. Today, credit card horror stories are staples of office water cooler gossip. (*New York Times*, 3 December 2002)

A report in *Business Week* in September 2004 noted that after a borrowing spree, some 10% of Koreans age 15 and older were at least three months delinquent in their debt repayments.

In 2003, the government finally took steps to contain credit card spending. This had the predicted effect: cuts in consumption led to recession, but did not diminish the debts. Indeed increased unemployment has exacerbated the situation of heavily indebted individuals.

In 2004 a Korean Broadcasting System survey found that 'more than half of South Koreans feel that the current economic situation is worse than it was in late 1997 when the financial crisis shook the nation' (*Monthly Review*, 15 August 2005).

Iceland

In recent years Iceland has been an economic success story according to conventional economic wisdom. She opened up her financial markets and international investors swept in to benefit from high interest rates. This helped finance a boom which has seen Icelandic business interests expand throughout Scandinavia and asset prices inflate dramatically. Iceland's stock market at only 20 years old was the best-performing western market for four years in succession. At the same time, however, massive inflows of funds helped Iceland's corporate and household debt to triple and double respectively since 1990 to 350% of GDP.

A report by Danish Danske Bank in March 2006 flashed strong warning lights. The report predicted recession in Iceland in 2006/07 and substantial risk of a financial crisis:

Iceland looks worse on almost all measures than Thailand did before its crisis in 1997, and only moderately more healthy than Turkey before its 2001 crisis.

On the state of indebtedness in Iceland the report commented that:

There has been a stunning expansion of debt, leverage and risk-taking that is almost without precedent anywhere in the world. External debt is now nearly 300% of GDP while short-term debt is just short of 55% of GDP. (Danske Bank, 21 March 2006)

In April 2006, investors, including hedge funds, withdrew money from Iceland. This precipitated a fall in the main stock index of 18% and a weakening of the currency. Analysts feared that other investors would follow suit, leading to a downward spiral.

This was bad enough for Iceland, which at the least faces economic slowdown, but the real fear amongst commentators was that these events could create the conditions for contagion to other similarly structured economies such as Turkey, Hungary, Spain, New Zealand, Australia – and the US. Why? Because all these economies have similar macroeconomic patterns, including a property price bubble, increased consumption and decreased savings, strong credit expansion, high levels of external (foreign-currency denominated) debt and large current account deficits (*International Herald Tribune*, 15 April 2006).

Conclusion

This brief outline of indebtedness in just a select group of countries is the backdrop to a global economy that appears to be booming; a global economy celebrated by financiers, politicians, orthodox and neo-liberal economists. There is little understanding of the threat posed to these debts by recession and deflation, and there have been very few attempts to learn from the Japanese crisis which began in 1989, and from the Asian crisis of 1997.

Instead debtors, their bankers and their governments appear to be sleepwalking into the coming First World debt crisis.

Sources and suggested reading

The Age, 'The hip-pocket under attack', by Marc Moncreif, 6 May 2006. <www.theage.com.au/news/business/the-hippocket-under-attack/2006/05/05/11463 35926527.html?page=4>.

Baker, D., *The Conservative Nanny State: How the wealthy Use the Government to Stay Rich and Get Richer*. Center for Economic Policy Research, forthcoming in 2006. <www.cepr.net.rom>.

Baker, D., *Prices Byte: Higher Rents Drive Core Inflation in March*. Center for Economic Policy Research, 19 April 2006.

Banque de France, *Quarterly Selection of Articles, Statistics*, spring 2006. <www.banque-france.fr/gb/publications/telnomot/bulletin/qsa3.pdf>.

BBC News, 'UK Inflation Rises to 2% Target', 16 May 2006. <http://news.bbc.co.uk/1/hi/business/4985300.stm>.

BBC News, 'Many in UK "have £10,000 debts"', 17 April 2006. <http://news.bbc.co.uk/1/hi/business/4914830.stm>.

BBC News, 'Debt "way of life" for under-25s', 13 September 2005. <http://news.bbc.co.uk/1/hi/business/4240906.stm>.

Buffett, W., 'To the Shareholders of Berkshire Hathaway Inc'. 28 February 2006. <www.berkshirehathaway.com/letters/2005ltr.pdf>.

Bureau of Labor Statistics, <www.bls.gov/>.

Business Week, 'South Korea: Debt-Laden – And Facing Slower Exports', September 2004. <www.businessweek.com/magazine/content/04_37/b3899034_mz010.htm?campaign_id=search>.

CIA, *The World Factbook: South Korea*. <www.cia.gov/cia/publications/factbook/geos/ks.html#Econ>.

Credit Action, 'Debt Facts and Figures – Compiled 4th May 2006. Total UK personal debt'. <www.creditaction.org.uk/debtstats.htm>.

Danske Bank, 'Iceland: Geyser Crisis', 21 March 2006. <http://danskeresearch. danskebank.com/link/FokusAndreIceland21032006/$file/GeyserCrises.pdf>.

Dunning Macleod, H., *The Theory and Practice of Banking*, Chapter IV: 'The Theory of Credit'. Longmans, London, 1879.

Federal Reserve, *Flow of Funds Accounts*. 9 March 2006. <www.federalreserve.gov/ releases/z1/current/z1.pdf>.

Financial Times, 'BT says state is liable for £28bn of pension fund', 24 April 2006.

Financial Times, 'Growing trade deficit "sustainable"', 26 April 2006, by Chris Giles.

Galbraith, J.K., *The Age of Uncertainty*. Houghton Mifflin Company, 1977.

Godley, W., *Some Unpleasant American Arithmetic*, The Levy Economics Institute of Bard College, May 2005.

Godley, W.; Papadimitriou, D.B.; Dos Santos, C.H. and Zezza, G., *The United States and her Creditors: Can the Symbiosis Last?* The Levy Economics Institute of Bard College, September 2005.

Guardian, 'Web gaming propels founder on to Asian Rich List', 18 April 2006, by Dan Milmo.

Hahn, Wilfred, *Money Changers in the Temple: Then and Now*. Midnight Call, January, 2006. <www.eternalvalue.com/MCM/MET_0601.pdf>.

International Herald Tribune, 'Iceland cools, raising worry of wider chill', 15 April 2006, by Heather Timmons.

Kanter, L., *Warren Buffet*. Brilliant Careers Salon, 31 August 1999. <www.salon. com/people/bc/1999/08/31/buffett/>.

Krugman, P., 'Greenspan and the Bubble', *New York Times*, 29 August 2005.

Krugman, P., 'What happened to Asia?', 16 January 1998. <www.hartford-hwp. com/archives/50/010.html>.

Monthly Review, MRzine, 'South Korea: The Unraveling of an Economy', 15 August 2005, by Martin Hart-Landsberg. <http://mrzine.monthlyreview.org/ hartlandsberg150805.html>.

National Nine News, 'Current account deficit to widen: govt', 9 May 2006. <http:// news.ninemsn.com.au/article.aspx?id=99511>.

New York Times, 'South Korea's Bane, in One Word: Plastic', 3 December 2002, by James Brooke. <www2.gol.com/users/coynerhm/koreas_bane_in_one_word_ plastic.htm>.

Office for National Statistics, Time Series Data: <www.statistics.gov.uk/statbase/ tsdintro.asp>.

Office for National Statistics, *UK Government Debt and Deficit*. 31 March 2006. <www.statistics.gov.uk/CCI/nugget.asp?ID=277>.

Papadimitriou, D.B.; Chilcote, E. and Zezza, G., *Strategic Analysis: Are Housing Prices, Household Debt and Growth Sustainable?* The Levy Economics Institute of Bard College, January 2006.

Pettifor, A. (ed.), *Real World Economic Outlook*. Palgrave Macmillan, 2003.

Reserve Bank of Australia, 'Australia's Foreign Debt – Liabilities and Assets', 18 May 2006. <www.rba.gov.au/Statistics/Bulletin/H06hist.xls>.

Reserve Bank of Australia, *Reserve Bank Bulletin: The Growth in Australia's Foreign Assets and Liabilities*, April 2006. <www.rba.gov.au/PublicationsAndResearch/ Bulletin/bu_apr06/growth_aus_foreign_assets_liabilities.html>.

Responsible-credit.net <www.responsible-credit.net/media.php?id=1790>.

Smith, D., 'Haircuts aren't a snip – even with low inflation'. David Smith's EconomicsUK.com, 16 April 2006. <www.economicsuk.com/blog/000323.html>.

The Times, 'Rooney denies rift with Owen over gambling debt', 11 April 2006. By Ashling O'Connor.

The Times, 'US spends its way to 28 Eiffel towers: made out of pure gold', 17 March 2006. By Tim Reid.

This is Money, 'Student debt soars', 30 March 2006. <www.thisismoney.co.uk/saving-and-banking/student-finance/article.html?in_article_id=407958&in_page_id=52>.

UK Government News Network, Insolvency Service, 'Statistics Release: Insolvencies in the First Quarter 2006'. 5 May 2006. <www.gnn.gov.uk/Content/Detail.asp?ReleaseID=199374&NewsAreaID=2>.

United Nations Conference on Trade and Development (UNCTAD), 'A pivotal year for commodity prices?' 8 March 2006. <www.unctad.org/Templates/Page.asp?intItemID=3732&lang=1>.

US Department of the Treasury, 'Major Foreign Holders of Treasury Securities', 15 May 2006. <www.treasury.gov/tic/mfh.txt>.

4
Poor Country Debt Crises: Causes and Parallels

There are striking parallels and differences behind the events dominating today's headlines in western nations – and those that led to the debt crisis that exploded with Mexico's default on its debts in August 1982.

The first is the effect of a falling dollar (and general currency volatility) on the revenues from commodities denominated in international markets in dollars, notably oil. In the 1960s and 1970s, the value of the dollar declined. This was important for countries that produce oil, as the price of oil is generally denominated in dollars. A fall in the dollar led to a fall in the value of their oil revenues. To compensate, oil-producing countries pushed up the price of oil (Stambuli, 1998).

The 1970s US deficit

Then as now, the fall in the value of the dollar was related to the US deficit. Then, the late 1960s, the US had built up a deficit partly as a result of the Vietnam War, and against Bretton Woods rules for balancing imports and exports. When creditors demanded that dollars be exchanged for gold as payment for imports, the US found its reserves of gold (which represented its surplus) run down. To deal with this problem President Nixon's administration took the unilateral decision in 1971 to abandon the Bretton Woods 'adjustable peg' system for fixing exchange rates to gold. From then on, the US would pay for its debts in bank money – dollars or bonds (US Treasury Bills) (Helleiner, 1994).

This decision ensured that the US could continue to borrow and consume, without undertaking the necessary 'structural adjustment' to its economy that would have been required if it had been obliged to restore balance to its external account by cutting back on consumption and imports, and building up a surplus of gold, earned from its exports. Furthermore, the US has been able to borrow and depend on the savings of others without losing *policy autonomy* – the right to determine its own destiny – to foreign creditors. This has not been true for poor, indebted nations.

While the abandonment of the Bretton Woods 'adjustable peg' system for currencies enabled the US to grow and consume by borrowing from the rest of the world, the lower dollar had a severe impact on the oil-producing countries.

Oil price hikes

Revenues earned (in dollars) by producer countries now purchased less in international markets. So in response, oil producers, organized in a cartel (OPEC), dramatically raised the price of oil in 1973.

This was the start of a decade of successive shocks. Rocketing prices for a vital resource, oil, placed a huge burden on poor countries. At the same time, massive earnings from Middle Eastern oil sales flooded into western banks and institutions. Banks in most of the developed world were reporting net average annual growth rates of deposits of between 25–30% (Stambuli, 1998).

Inflation threat: low-income countries to the rescue

While these monies from oil-producing countries were welcome, they also posed a substantial threat to the stability of western economies: that of runaway inflation. To deal with this threat, finance ministers, bankers and officials of the IMF and World Bank actively encouraged the disbursement of the excess funds to low-income countries, in the form of loans.

Many argue, correctly in my view, that low-income countries, by borrowing, rescued industrial countries from the crisis of runaway inflation in the 1970s and 1980s (Thirlwall, 1999).

In the autumn of 1981, Sir Geoffrey Howe, Britain's finance minister, praised the virtues of private banks in recycling funds to low-income countries. He described lending to these countries as

... the best form of recycling

because external loans

... enabled [low-income countries] to finance their external payments and to raise their living standards.

In March 1980, just 18 months before Mexico's default, Mr Paul Volcker, chairman of the Federal Reserve Bank of the USA, also endorsed the rise in low-income country bank lending. He dismissed fears of a debt crisis with comments like this:

> The impression I get from the data I have received is that the recycling process has not yet pushed exposure of either borrowers or lenders to an unsustainable point in the aggregate. (Stambulil, 1998)

Negative real interest rates – at first

The oil-price hike injected huge sums of money into the international financial system, which in turn caused the price of money – interest rates – to fall, until they effectively became negative. In real terms, banks were paying people and sovereign governments to take their money – to borrow. Then as now, the world engaged in a binge of lending and borrowing. The OECD, the club of high-income countries, blamed central banks for the massive expansion of credit:

> One of the reasons for the debt build up from $260 billion in 1975 to $1,265 billion in 1984 was the administrative complacency among monetary authorities that turned a blind eye to the unprecedented expansion of credit to the low income countries. (OECD, 1984, quoted in Stambuli, 2002)

The advent of the syndicated loan – a large loan in which a group of banks work together to provide funds for a borrower – led to the belief among financial institutions that they could minimize their credit risk by spreading loans to a variety of countries across the world among several banks, in such a way that the exposure of each bank was minimal. The lending proved to be profitable – but risk had not been avoided.

To quote Walter Bagehot again: 'All people are most credulous when they are most happy' (Galbraith,1954).

Debtors: emerging from colonialism

The need to stabilize western economies, and protect them from the threat of inflation, coincided with the need of low-income countries for development finance. Zambia was a prime example. At the time of independence in 1964, Zambia, a land-locked country, was wholly dependent on one commodity, copper; had one major road for transporting copper to the nearest port; a handful of citizens with university degrees; very few schools and no adequate health system.

When IMF staff encouraged the newly-elected Zambian President Kenneth Kaunda to borrow funds (at what were, effectively, negative interest rates) for development, Zambia's politicians were quick to sign loan contracts. They were assured by IMF staff that there would always be demand for copper, and the price would never fall so low as to prevent Zambia earning the revenues needed to repay these low-cost debts. These confident predictions were to be proved flawed.

Some countries, like Mexico and Venezuela, took out loans to repay previous debts. But for others, this was the first time they had borrowed from *commercial* banks. Many intended to use the money to improve standards of living in their countries. However, in the end, little of the money borrowed benefited the poor. Across the range, about a fifth of it went on arms, often to shore up oppressive regimes. Many governments started large-scale development projects, some of which proved of little value. All too often the money found its way into private bank accounts in rich countries. The poor were the losers.

Then the shock: a commodity price collapse worse than the Great Depression

By the early 1980s, low-income countries had begun to build up debts. To obtain short- or long-term loans to finance their debts and imports, these debtor governments were required to adopt 'structural adjustment policies' designed by their creditors (high-income country institutions or governments). The 'structural adjustment' that had to be made was the re-orientation of debtor economies towards the interests of foreign creditors, and away from domestic development. In other words, economies had to be 'adjusted' to generate hard currency for debt repayments. Policies for privatization generated assets for foreign creditors to 'cherry-pick' as compensation for unpaid debts. These assets included airports and airlines, electricity generators, telephone companies, copper and diamond mines, etc.

However, re-orientation of the economy towards the interests of creditors was most often achieved by promoting exports, which earn foreign currency.

Re-orienting a *range* of debtor economies towards exports meant, naturally, that the exports they produced in common – coffee, cocoa, copper, sugar, tea, tin – increased in supply. Increased supplies of these commodities on world markets then, predictably, caused prices to fall.

The fall in commodity prices meant that export revenues fell; which meant that low-income countries could not earn enough to repay debts. Commodity-dependent economies had fallen into the 'commodity trap' which in turn became a 'debt trap' and a 'poverty trap' (UNCTAD, 2004). These commodity price declines translated into falling farmers' incomes, lower wages, and debt (Greenfield, 2004).

> The falls in prices showed a drastic downward trend with relatively small annual fluctuations ... suggesting that the general commodity terms of trade fell as much as 35% between 1978–80 and 1986–88. This led to a recession that was more severe for low-income countries, and considerably more prolonged than that of the Great Depression of the 1930s (Maizels, 1992).

It is this commodity crisis that explains most conclusively the protracted debt crises that befell commodity-dependent, low-income countries from the 1980s onwards. As poor countries struggled to raise money for debt repayments, creditors regarded the situation as temporary. As a result they kept offering new loans to pay off old loans; re-scheduling debts, i.e. extending the terms of repayment, pushing the debts down the line, so to speak, into the future. This has been described as *defensive* lending, so that at least their existing claims were paid on a regular basis. Creditors imposed 'structural adjustment policies' believing that these could arrest the crisis. Debtor countries accepted these policies, in order to attract aid and new money; but their debt crises continued to get worse, 'giving rise to the serious question as to whether the debtor countries were facing a solvency crisis rather than a liquidity crisis' (Nissanke and Ferrarini, 2004).

However, it was not just low-income countries that were to be the victims of commodity price volatility, the inflationary impact of oil revenues and the accumulation of foreign debts.

Tightening the noose: higher interest rates

By the late 1970s, the inflationary pressures that were the result of the liquidity pumped into the global economy by oil producers, led to action by western governments. In an attempt to curb wage price inflation at home, western governments began to raise interest rates. As a result, total outflows of dividends, profits and interest payments (from developing countries) rose from \$15 billion in 1978 to \$44 billion in 1981 (Lever and Huhne, 1986).

UNCTAD has calculated that between 1976–79 and 1980–82, *the rise in interest rates alone* added $41 billion to the stock of low-income countries' debt (Inter-American Development Bank, 1985, quoted in Stambuli, 1998).

Meanwhile oil prices rose again.

Loosening the grip: de-regulated capital flows

But perhaps the most dangerous policies of this period were still to be adopted by leading western governments: the liberalization of capital flows. Led by Prime Minister Thatcher and President Reagan, and supported by central bankers and academic economists, controls over the movement of international capital flows were lifted in the late 1970s and early 1980s. Middle-income countries like Chile, Uruguay and Argentina followed their leaders – and lifted controls too.

As a result the elites in these countries promptly exported their capital to banks in high-income countries, leading to a surge in financial outflows. The trap was sprung.

Low-income countries were earning less than ever for their exports and paying more than ever on their loans and on oil – a vital import.

Low-income countries were in deep trouble. Their governments *had* to borrow – just to stay afloat.

The crisis breaks

The 1982 Mexican debt crisis occurred because a steep rise in US interest rates led to an appreciation of the dollar, which in turn magnified the cost of debt repayments in dollars (Edwards, 1996). In August 1982 Mexico announced to its creditors that it could not repay its debts. The announcement was made after Mexico had failed to raise a large enough loan to repay external debts that were falling due.

Between 1975 and 1980 four countries had to postpone the repayment of principal on loans while servicing interest only. By 1983 the number of countries defaulting on their repayments reached 21 and some low-income countries had instituted state criminal proceedings against public figures on account of alleged negligence and mishandling of public money (Stambuli, 1998).

This pattern was repeated over and over in the following years as other countries found themselves in similar situations to Mexico's. But their debts continued to rise, and new loans added to the burden.

Essentially, the poorest countries had become insolvent.

Enter the troubleshooters ...

When Mexico defaulted on its debt repayments in 1982 the global international financial system was threatened. Mexico owed huge sums of money to banks in the US and Europe, and they didn't want to lose it. So they clubbed together and with the support of the International Monetary Fund (IMF) developed a scheme that would spread out or reschedule the debts.

This was known as the Baker Plan. In 1985, as President Reagan's second Treasury Secretary, James Baker launched his plan, the first of several attempts by the US government to tackle the exploding Latin American debt problem. It was managed day-to-day by Baker's close associate, former Undersecretary of the Treasury Dr David C. Mulford, who later became chairman of Credit Suisse First Boston's International Group, and in 2003 was designated by President Bush II as the new US ambassador to India.

The Baker Plan relied heavily on a combination of tougher IMF/World Bank conditions in exchange for a modest amount of new loans from the multilateral agencies, and wrongly assumed that with the right policies, low-income countries could grow themselves out of their excessive debts.

Another creditor plan: Brady

By 1989 debts to commercial banks were no longer worth their value on paper because the banks had written off large chunks of them in theory, assuming they would never be repaid. US Treasury Secretary Brady argued that the banks should reduce the actual value of the remaining debt for larger debtor countries, so that they had less to pay. These would then be restructured into 'liquid, tradable and safe securities' the repayment of which would be secured against US Treasury bonds, that were to be held in a trust until the restructured bonds matured (World Bank, 2004). Debt service on these new, restructured debts were lowered to levels already being paid, so no actual benefit accrued to the debtor country.

In terms of total debt stock this plan did not help debtor countries. As commercial debts fell, debts owed to multilateral institutions like the IMF and World Bank rose. What the Brady plan did was to lay the foundations for today's era of low-income countries' access to international bond markets. Although bond issuance by developing countries dates back to the early 1800s, its importance in the 1980s was minimal, averaging only $3 billion per year. Bond issuance increased from $4 billion in 1990 to a peak of $99 billion in 1997.

This massive expansion of debt came to an abrupt end with the financial crises beginning with Thailand in 1997, followed by the Russian Federation (1998), Brazil (1999), Turkey (2000) and Argentina (2001).

Furthermore, the economic conditions imposed on countries during this period provoked bloody riots (Venezuela, 1989) and debt moratoria (Brazil, 1987; Argentina, 1988). And by the year 2000, the real level of low-income country debt was 150% higher than it had been in 1985.

Trinidad/Naples Terms

Nigel Lawson and then John Major, both British finance ministers, originally proposed (through Paris Club negotiations) that creditor countries cancel half the debt owed to them by the lowest-income countries, while rescheduling the rest. This could have resulted in debt relief worth £18 billion to the poorest countries.

Later Major went further and proposed two-thirds debt remission. In the end, 67% cancellation was agreed at the G7 Summit in Naples, in 1994.

However, in practice, this level of reduction was only applied to a small proportion of poor countries' debts – the 'eligible debt' – with eligibility defined arbitrarily by creditors. Creditors remained very reluctant to offer substantial debt relief, to return poor countries to solvency, or sustainability. Countries had to keep to stringent structural adjustment programmes to get debt relief, new loans and aid and were not exempt from any repayments to the IMF or World Bank.

Heavily Indebted Poor Country Initiative (HIPC 1)

In October 1996, largely as a result of pressure from NGOs in the South as well as the North, a major shift by G8 finance ministers, the IMF and the World Bank resulted in a debt relief initiative which contemplated for the first time in their 50-year history, the cancellation of debts. The agreement also recommended a strategy to enable countries to exit from unsustainable debt burdens. The initiative proposed 80% debt relief by the key creditor governments only after countries had fulfilled two 3-year stages of structural adjustment conditions. The World Bank announced the establishment of a Trust Fund to finance the initiative.

In reality, the initiative proved to be completely ineffective. Uganda and Bolivia received debt cancellation in April 1998 and September 1998 respectively – but within a year they were back where they started with unsustainable debt burdens. They had fallen victim to falling commodity prices and impossibly optimistic forecasts (made by creditors through the World Bank and IMF as the rationale to lower levels of debt relief) for their future export and economic growth. Mozambique, after treatment under HIPC 1, ended up only paying 1% less in debt payments than before HIPC. As a result no money was released for spending on health and education. Growing pressure from debt campaign groups, under the Jubilee 2000 umbrella, forced the creditors to admit that the initiative was failing to deliver. In May 1998, 70,000–100,000 protesters gathered at the UK G8 Summit in Birmingham; formed a human chain around world leaders Blair, Clinton, Kohl and Yeltsin, and demanded that the debts of the poorest countries be cancelled. 'Drop the Debt' soon became a world-wide slogan, as the campaign spread like wildfire. In January 1999, Chancellor Schröder of Germany announced that 'radical and bold' steps were needed on debt relief, prompting other G8 creditors to support calls for an 'enhanced' HIPC Initiative. This was launched at the Cologne G8 Summit, as once again, thousands gathered to form a human chain around the Summit to call for the 'chains of debt' to be broken.

Cologne Debt Initiative/HIPC 2

HIPC 2 was launched at the Cologne G8 Summit in June 1999 to great fanfares of publicity. Creditors promised to provide 'broader, faster and deeper' debt relief, and an improved link with poverty reduction. G8 leaders talked of a headline figure of $100 billion of 'debt relief' for HIPC countries which included $25 billion of additional relief in the 'enhanced' initiative.

By the end of the year 2000, 22 countries had received some relief on debt service payments and a total of $12 billion had been cancelled – but only Uganda had reached completion point, the final stage in the HIPC process. In some countries, debt relief has made a tangible difference. For example in Mozambique, $60 million was released through debt relief into various areas, all vital to sustaining development. The budgets for health, education, agriculture, infrastructure and employment training have all benefited.

However, overall the level of debt relief failed to deliver the necessary resources to tackle the HIPC countries' deep-rooted social and economic problems – built up and entrenched through the debt crises of the 1980s.

Haiti is not eligible for debt relief under the initiative even though it is the poorest country in the western hemisphere and nearly half of the debt was contracted under the Duvalier dictatorship. It will receive no debt cancellation even though it has 50% adult illiteracy, 70% unemployment and infant mortality is more than double the Latin America and Caribbean average.

In 1999, after pressure from the international Jubilee 2000 campaign, the HIPC Initiative was 'enhanced' and given a new, expanded set of objectives: to deliver a 'permanent exit' from debt rescheduling; to promote growth; and to release resources for higher social spending in debtor countries (World Bank, 2003).

What way forward for debtor countries?

At the time of going to press, the Heavily Indebted Poor Country Initiative had, according to the World Bank, approved *nominal* debt service relief of more than US$59 billion for 29 countries, reducing their Net Present Value of external debt by approximately two-thirds. Of these countries, 19 have reached the completion point of the various hoops and hurdles imposed by the HIPC Initiative, and 'have been granted unconditional debt service relief of over US$37 billion' (World Bank, 2006).

However, an Independent Evaluation Group appointed by the World Bank itself, concluded in April 2006 that in half of the 19 countries that had completed the debt relief process under HIPC, debt had climbed back to where it was before HIPC was launched. Nevertheless, net transfers (inflows vs outflows) to HIPC countries have doubled from $8.8 billion in 1999 to $17.5 billion in 2004, in contrast to other low-income countries, where transfers have only grown by a third.

A Global Jubilee

While these low-income countries have had their debts ameliorated very reluctantly by short-sighted and grudging creditors, their people remain trapped in a cycle of debt and under-development. This, sadly, will not change until rich, western creditors take responsibility for the crises that occurred after the trade and financial liberalization policies of the 1970s and 1980s – and offer outright debt cancellation – a Global Jubilee – to all the low-income countries affected by the debt and commodity crises of this period.

The western model

Second, development in these countries will not take place, until the people of these countries take responsibility for their own progress and development.

And what development model can low-income countries, including African countries follow? They could do no better than study the western model. These economies, as the great African thinker Abdul Rahman Babu (Rahman, 1994) once suggested in a lecture, are based on three pillars: agriculture, textiles and construction. These sectors enable any nation to feed, clothe and house its people. IMF and creditor-led policies undermine these sectors. They encourage low-income debtor nations to export raw materials, undermine subsistence agriculture and local businesses, and turn their societies into markets for imported food and irrelevant consumer goods. In the West these three key sectors – agriculture, textiles and construction – are still the three main pillars of economies, underpinning all other economic activity. All three sectors continue to be heavily protected.

Africa, and other low-income countries, should highlight the double-standards of western creditors; refuse to 'do as they say; but do as they do'.

And Africa should follow the model of Britain and other western nations, and not embark on further development until it has increased the capacity to save. On the eve of the industrial revolution (1760–80), British investment constituted little more than 5%, but certainly less than 10%, of GDP. In other words, after roughly 5,000 years of city civilization, it was still necessary for the (then) most advanced economy to devote *90%* of its economy to immediate consumption. Once the initial breakthrough was achieved, higher proportions of the economy were devoted to investment. Africa will have to do the same.

There are two arguments against this. First, Africa and other low-income countries have no savings capacity. This is not true. As Jacques B. Gelinas has shown in his book *Freedom from Debt*, the big state and international banks have failed the people of Africa. Africans are in bondage to foreign creditors, while there is a vacuum in the domestic financial savings sector. 'Finance, like nature, abhors a vacuum', says Gelinas, and so micro finance institutions have stepped in. Like the Tontines in Cameroon, and the Naam groups in Burkina Faso. They have done more than mobilize finance. They have mobilized women, the outcasts of the banking world.

Finally, western 'development experts' insist that Africa and other low-income countries have to 'catch up'. With whom and with what? Japan 'caught up' 150 years after Britain; Sweden 50 years after the rest of Europe. Needs are always relative. First, poor countries must escape from debt bondage. Then they need to feed, clothe, house, educate and provide health services to their people. Only then can they provide sustainable livelihoods for their people.

To achieve sustainable livelihoods, poor countries do not need foreign loans.

They do not need the West to give more. They need the West, and in particular western creditors, to take less.

Sources and suggested reading

Babu, Abdul Rahman Mohamed, *African Socialism or Socialist Africa?* African Books Collective, 1994.

Edwards, Sebastian, *A Tale of Two Crises: Chile and Mexico,* Working paper No 5794, Cambridge, Massachusetts, The NBER, October 1996.

Galbraith, J.K., *The Great Crash*. Mariner Books, 1954.

Gelinas, Jacques B., *Freedom from Debt*. Zed Books, 1998.

Greenfield, Gerrard, *Free Market Freefall: Declining Agricultural Commodity Prices and the 'Market Access' Myth*. Focus on the Global South. June 2004. <www.focusweb.org/content/view/306/29/>.

Helleiner, E., *States and the Reemergence of Global Finance, From Bretton Woods to the 1990s*. Cornell University Press, 1994.

Lever, Harold and Huhne, Christopher, *Debt and Danger: The World Financial Crisis*. Atlantic Monthly Press, 1986.

Maizels, A., *Commodities in Crisis*. Clarendon Press, 1992.

Nissanke, M. and Ferrarini, B., contribution to *Debt Relief for Poor Countries* edited by Tony Addison and Henrik Hansen, Palgrave 2004: 'Debt Dynamics and Contingency Financing: Theoretical Reappraisal of the HIPC Initiative'. p. 35.

Stambuli, P. Kalonga, 'Causes and Consequences of the 1982 Third World Debt Crisis', *International Finance*, 2002. Also pre-doctoral Research Paper, October 1998, Department of Economics, University of Surrey, Guildford, UK.

Thirlwall, Anthony P., *Growth and Development*. 6th edition, Macmillan, 1999.

UNCTAD, *Economic Development in Africa: Trade Performance and Commodity Dependence*, United Nations, 2003.

World Bank, *Global Development Finance*, April 2004, p. 49.

World Bank, *Debt Relief for the Poorest* – an OED Review of the HIPC Initiative, World Bank, 2003.

World Bank: Independent Evaluation Group. *Debt Relief for the Poorest: An Evaluation Update of the HIPC Initiative*. <www.worldbank.org/ieg/hipc/>.

5
Moneytheism and Lawless Finance

> And Jesus went into the temple of God, and cast out all them that
> sold and bought in the temple, and overthrew the tables of the
> moneychangers, and the seats of them that sold doves,
> And said unto them, It is written, My house shall be called the
> house of prayer; but ye have made it a den of thieves.
>
> Matthew 21: 12–13. King James Version

An ethical vacuum for finance

The economic system that dominates our world today – globalization,
financial liberalization, trade liberalization – did not evolve spontaneously.
It is the result of conscious decisions taken by men and women, many of
them elected and enjoying democratically-sourced power. They are, or
were influenced by their voters, by the media, by the organized religions
as well of course as by 'big business' and the finance sector.

And while this book suggests that the finance sector bears considerable
responsibility for the coming financial crisis, it would be wrong to suggest
that the finance sector, and money-lenders in particular, go about their
business in a moral and ethical vacuum; that those who work in the
finance sector are somehow less ethical than those who do not. Far from it.
Society, particularly western society, has provided the finance sector with
an implicit, if not explicit mandate to exploit humanity and the earth,
to extract maximum assets from both humanity and the earth, both now
and into the future. While it is always dangerous to generalize, I believe
it fair to say that western society has not, and does not question the
international system of debt-creation, usury, greed and the polarization of
wealth. The rich are, on the whole, too busy enjoying their extraordinary
gains; middle-incomers live in hope that they might one day be as rich;

and even many of the poor share in the delusion that the system, like a lottery, might deliver a lucky break. When questions have been raised and the system challenged it has been by those marginal to mainstream politics, economics and religion – anti-globalization protesters, left-wing political campaigners and fundamentalists. Representatives of Industry and Labour have complained from the sidelines, but have offered no real challenge to the finance sector. The major religions, with the exception of Islam, have on the whole acquiesced, focussing mainly on matters of private morality (gender and homosexual rights are a major obsession) and social affairs; not financial, economic or ecological issues. Islam itself is under pressure from the finance sector to dilute the condemnation of usury, and some of the fissures in Islamic society stem from this pressure. (See the discussion below.) And of course the economics profession has obliged the finance sector by focussing on everything *but* the role of the finance sector.

Westerners and the values they espouse are therefore co-responsible for any coming First World debt crisis, for its impact on the most vulnerably poor in rich nations; on the billions of vulnerable in poor nations; and for the impact of any crisis on the planet we temporarily inhabit.

If citizens of western societies are co-responsible for the coming crisis, not just passive victims, then (if it is not already too late) we can take action: first, to demand that governments act to ameliorate the crisis, and second, to radically alter the mandate given to the finance sector. But for that to happen, western society must set clear ethical and moral standards for not only the finance sector, but also the economy as a whole, recognising that the economy is but a subsidiary of the environment. In other words, citizens must act to reinvigorate ethics and moral standards in the economic sphere.

Ethical laxity of western economies

The ethical laxity of western societies in matters relating to credit and debt has had a profound impact on global economic life. It has freed private and public financiers from constraints on lending and borrowing. It absolves both official and private lenders from charging usurious rates of interest. It unleashes the far-reaching powers of official financial institutions, like the IMF and World Bank, to impose austere economic conditions on very poor sovereign borrowers, and continuously extract wealth from these poor countries.

In other words, the absence of clear ethical, legal and indeed ecological constraints gives permission to the powerful to extract and exploit physical and human assets as if these assets had no limits; and to exploit at a global level the weakest states at rates that probably have no precedent in history.

Barriers to an ethics of debt

Should we be concerned about the morality or ethics of the profits, or more accurately, the capital gains made by banking houses and financial institutions? Surely the benefits of these gains are spread widely, and have helped fuel rapid economic growth, and reduced poverty both in the Anglo-American economies, but also in China and India? While undoubtedly gains have been made, and these gains have been in the political sphere as well as the economic sphere, there is a debate about how economic gains have been distributed and shared (Wade, 2003). But that is not the key point. The major concern is that unregulated finance encourages excess, political and social instability, corruption – and the growth of unsustainable (i.e. unpayable) debts. As the Bank for International Settlements suggests in its 2005 report, unregulated finance has the ability to precipitate a systemic financial crisis. Such a crisis will be immensely destructive and prolonged, and will impact most cruelly on the poorest. These disadvantages alone require that finance be regulated.

However, regulation requires an ethical framework, and ethical benchmarks. The first ethical challenge concerns money: should money, which we have seen in Chapter 2 is essentially a free good, be regulated at all? If we accept the need for regulation, what would be the ethical basis of such regulation, at both national and international levels? Should there be limits on the power of the creditor to extract assets from a debtor? Should there be limits on the rate of interest? Should interest be charged at all? What of the ethics of the contract between debtor and creditor?

Developing ethical benchmarks in today's intellectual climate is challenging, given that public debate in high-income countries on the ethics and morality of lending and borrowing is seldom aired. This state of affairs is not accidental. Debate has effectively been suppressed by the economics, banking and finance sectors. Hudson defines these as the 'twin rentier interests – rent-takers and interest-takers – who have joined together to create and sustain a new orthodoxy' (Hudson 1994). An orthodoxy that is seldom challenged by western religions.

This orthodoxy, taught in all western universities, and echoed in economic journals and the financial media, applauds the accumulation of wealth, making no distinction between earned and unearned income, and is uncritical of limitless lending and borrowing. Herman Daly has noted that few colleges and universities teach economic history, because exploring this history, including the role played by excessive credit in the 1920s might expose the frailties and fallacies of economic assumptions that the profession likes to regard as universal and timeless. Mainstream economics, Daly argues, is mainly about the economic problem of efficient allocation of scarce resources among competing ends. However there are two other economic problems: *distributive justice* and *optimal scale* – and mainstream economics tends to ignore both.

As convenors of an international civil society campaign for the cancellation of poor country debts (Jubilee 2000) we found that few university economics departments understood, or took seriously, the issue of distributive justice in examining financial crises faced by sovereign debtors. Lecturers in the Economics Department at the London School of Economics (which attracts thousands of students from debtor countries) were particularly dismissive. Foreign students who tried to major on low-income country debt as part of their Masters or PhD degrees, reported to us that their proposals faced stiff opposition.

While activists in creditor countries argued that both creditors and debtors were co-responsible for debt crises, academics and politicians focussed on the supposed incompetence of debtor governments, and frequently blamed the crisis on corruption in poor countries. Blaming-the-victim is not an intellectually rigorous approach to a crisis in which it takes two to tango. Corruption linked to loans and the guaranteeing of loans is rife in rich countries, but such corruption is seldom publicly discussed.

These controversies were reflected in similar debates about individual and household debtors and creditors in the US. The US banking sector doggedly promoted changes to US bankruptcy law over a period of nine years (giving hundreds of millions of dollars of campaign cash to election candidates) and was rewarded when the Bankruptcy Abuse Prevention and Consumer Protection Act of 2005 was amongst the first legislative changes made by the second Bush administration. Spin-doctors for the finance sector ensured that public debate focussed largely on the feckless carelessness of credit card debtors; and not on aggressive lending practices by creditors. Creditors argued that debtors were abusing bankruptcy laws, but this was contradicted by evidence from Harvard researchers. This showed that 50% of bankruptcy filings in the US are a result of medical bills, with a further 40% due to divorce and job layoffs (Himmelstein et al., February 2005). Consumer advocates opposed the legislation, arguing it would be a gift to the credit card industry, which was expected to receive $1 billion or more from debtors as a result of the changes.

Overall the economics profession and the finance sector appear unconcerned about the impact on consumers, corporations, the broader economy and the ecosystem of high, real rates of interest set and controlled by unaccountable, private capital markets. Avoiding risk and making money from money is an increasingly lucrative activity, as demonstrated by the 'vintage year' that was 2005 when revenues of the world's investment banks rose by about 13% to $205 billion – beating profit records set during the internet bubble. Profits in the UK's financial services sector soared in 2005, with earnings at building societies, insurers and securities houses growing at their fastest rate since 1996.

When the economy appears buoyant, when 'times are good', society is invariably numbed into complacency about the ethics of debt. Such complacency is compounded when those with vested interests ensure that ethical debate is distorted, manipulated or marginalized. Having dampened debate on the ethics of debt, it should come as no surprise, therefore, that the finance sector at both national and international levels does not come under social and political pressure to behave more ethically.

Pressure is, however, building from below. Politicians are increasingly wary of the power of finance, and complain, especially during election campaigns. The deputy leader of Germany's SPD, Franz Muentefering, caused an uproar in international financial circles when he attacked hedge funds as 'locusts':

I fight against business people and people working in the international financial markets who act as if there are no rules. Some financial investors don't think about the people whose jobs they destroy. They remain anonymous, they don't have a face, like locusts they attack companies, devour them and move on. It is this form of capitalism we fight against. (Interview with *Bildzeitung*, 16 April 2005)

And the locust went up over all the land of Egypt, and rested in all the coasts of Egypt: very grievous were they; before them there were no such locusts as they, neither after them shall be such.

For they covered the face of the whole earth, so that the land was darkened; and they did eat every herb of the land, and all the fruit of the trees which the hail had left: and there remained not any green thing in the trees, or in the herbs of the field, through all the land of Egypt. (Exodus 10: 14 and 15)

Finance needs regulation; law needs ethics

Karl Polanyi, the great economic historian, argued (in his 1944 book *The Great Transformation*) that regulation of the conduct of human affairs by law is vital to the maintenance of civilized society, and to the market, because

> robbed of the protective covering of cultural institutions, human beings would perish from the effects of social exposure; they would die as the victims of acute social dislocation through vice, perversion, crime and starvation ... neighbourhoods and landscapes defiled, rivers polluted, military safety jeopardized, the power to produce food and raw materials destroyed. (Polanyi, 1957)

Law needs boundaries, ethical, political and geographical. Markets, in particular financial markets, *abhor boundaries*.

> Markets hate boundaries, but public policy, in the interest of community, requires them. Markets need policy and laws for their functioning; so indirectly, even markets ultimately require boundaries. (Daly, 2003)

Governments, or institutions making policy, or law, need boundaries, ethical boundaries as well as physical boundaries – in the interests of community. In the absence of ethical boundaries set by the community, what shapes the law? In the absence of physical boundaries, who is to enforce the law? In the absence of such boundaries, how are governments to punish criminals free to travel elsewhere? Or impose taxes? Or provide welfare? In the absence of boundaries, and in the absence of a democratically elected and accountable global government, there can be no international sphere of policy-making and law.

Such is the current state of the international financial system: ungoverned and virtually lawless. Where international financial law does exist, it cannot be said to apply equally or justly to relations between both parties in, for example, international lending and borrowing: creditors and sovereign debtors. New York and London serve as the jurisdictions for international bonds issued in those cities, and can be applied (often with little effect) to international *commercial* loans. However, these jurisdictions do not have relevance where loans are made by *official* institutions (e.g. the IMF, the World Bank or governments) to sovereign governments. By way of example we recount below the difficulties caused by this absence of law to one debtor.

Great Art as collateral for debt

In November 2005 the officers of the small Swiss canton of Valais on the Swiss–German border impounded a truck carrying priceless works of art belonging to Russia's Pushkin museum. They explained they were seizing the Pushkin's property, insured for more than $1 billion, in restitution of monies owed to a Swiss company, Noga, by the Russian government. The original loan of $70 million for a grain-for-oil deal had, with interest, mushroomed to $900 million, according to the London *Guardian* (*Guardian*, 29 November 2005). Although the Swiss Federal government quickly overruled the canton, grave damage had been done to the art world. The director of the National Gallery in Britain opined that 'it is more than mildly shocking that great works of art should be treated by commercial companies as collateral against debts incurred by a national government'. But, in the absence of protection for both creditors and debtors through the rule of law, lawlessness prevails in the international sphere of borrowing and lending.

Rules regarding *official* (i.e. governmental and inter-governmental) international lending through the Paris Club of international creditors are informal, and overwhelmingly dominated by high-income country creditors. In the absence of international law, relations between international creditors and sovereign debtors are based on the capricious imperiousness of political, military and economic power.

In nations with high levels of debt, with economies de-regulated and liberalized by foreign creditors, and suffering poor governance, millions of people die as the victims of 'acute social dislocation through vice, perversion, crime and starvation'. To ameliorate these debt crises, Prof. Kunibert Raffer of the University of Vienna proposes an international framework of law for governing relations between sovereign debtors and international creditors, based on Chapter 9 of the US legal code (Raffer, 1993).

> When it becomes necessary for a state to declare itself bankrupt, in the same manner as when it becomes necessary for an individual to do so, a fair, open, and avowed bankruptcy is always the measure which is both least dishonourable to the debtor, and least hurtful to the creditor. (Adam Smith, *Wealth of Nations*, 1776, quoted in Raffer, 1993)

A not dissimilar proposal for a 'sovereign debt restructuring mechanism' was mooted by European Central Bank governors, in particular Governor Mervyn King of the Bank of England, Gordon Brown and other G8 finance ministers, and finally the IMF in 2001. This was quickly 'kicked into the long grass' by the finance sector, in particular Wall Street, fearful lest a framework of law should limit the protection, hidden subsidies and lucrative capital gains to be made from lending to sovereign governments.

Usury, bankruptcy and money-creation

Given the need to redefine and reinvigorate the ethics underlying the regulation of lending and borrowing, what *are* the key ethical issues? I would contend that the main issue is usury; but that we also need to examine the ethics underlying bankruptcy; the need to periodically correct imbalances; and the ethics of money-creation itself. The following sections discuss these aspects, but also examine the different approaches of different faiths. I begin by briefly, and superficially, examining the way in which the ethics of debt and money has been treated by thinkers and faith organizations over the millennia. Readers interested in more scholarly approaches are referred to the reading list at the end of the chapter.

Ethics of debt in pre-urban societies

Ethics is defined as the body of obligations and duties that a particular society requires of its members. These obligations and duties are evaluated in light of moral principles. The moral principles underlying the ethics of debt have been at the centre of social struggles for millennia.

There is speculation and controversy about loans made in pre-urban and pre-money societies. It is presumed by some that these were made in seed grains and animals to farmers, a useful starting point for our discussion of ethics in this section. Since one seed grain could generate a new plant which would contain within itself many new seed grains, 'interest' could easily be repaid on the loan. Similarly the loan of a cow could potentially be repaid by sharing new calves born to the cow. The Sumerians (circa 3,000 BC) used the same word – *mas* – for both calves and interest, although scholars are divided over whether this association arose because calves were given as interest, or as rent on land.

Thus the payment of interest and debt was tied to the privatization and appropriation of land. Palaces and Temples handed over to middle-men the task of collecting rents from those living on collectively owned land. During Babylonian times, after about 2000 BC, the Middle Bronze Age,

conflicts between creditors and debtors over possession of the land, led to a deepening impoverishment of economies locked in a spiral of indebtedness mounting up in excess of the capacity to pay. Poverty became a systematic element of normal every day life as people were deprived of the ability to earn their bread. (Hudson, 2002)

Debtors sell their livelihoods

Today the power to use such indebtedness to appropriate land and extract assets is a systematic element of everyday life in both high- and low-income countries. One day during Niger's severe drought of 2005, the BBC reported that 'many people had to sell off their land to survive and now cannot produce enough food for the year ahead, while others borrowed and are now in debt'. A few days later another BBC report highlighted debt crises facing poor farmers in Kerala, India. The price of their commodity, coffee, had fallen, while costs and and the value of their debts had risen. To pay their debts they sell their livelihoods. Suicide is now common amongst these farmers.

Debt, and foreclosure on the land or assets of debtors has, over millennia, been the means whereby individuals, estates and nations have gained assets and property rights, and with those rights and advantages have used lending to further amass wealth and power. Today's empires were frequently yesterday's looters of the assets of colonized countries. Today such blatant colonial exploitation is frowned upon; instead the de-regulation of international lending is used by rich creditors to extract additional assets from countries less powerful.

Because orthodox economics does not take into account how property rights are obtained, this imbalance of power between the lender and the borrower is mostly ignored in discussions of the ethics of debt. Instead attention is focussed narrowly on the terms of the loan contract.

In the past, laws against usury imposed limits on the rate of exploitation of those without assets, by those who owned assets. Any well-developed ethics of debt would enquire into how wealth and power was accumulated; in this light consider the imbalance of power between those with wealth and those without; provide a framework of justice and set restraints or limits on the ability of the powerful and the already-rich to use credit and debt to extract further assets from the relatively powerless.

Ethics and the 'barrenness' of metal money

During the fourth millennium BC, as noted in Chapter 2, a major innovation took place, one whose impact was to be felt down the ages. In towns, loans began to be made on *metals*, allowing interest to be paid in more metal. This radical innovation transformed lending, for many reasons; but mainly because as Aristotle (384–322 BC) later noted, metals, unlike cows or seeds, are 'barren' and have no powers of generation. *Any interest paid in them must originate from some other source or process*. He wrote in 'Politics' that money made from money was 'very much disliked':

and the dislike is fully justified, for the gain arises out of currency itself, not as a product of that for which currency was provided. Currency was intended to be a means of exchange, whereas interest represents an increase in the currency itself. Hence its name Tokos (offspring) for each animal produces its like, and interest is currency born of currency. And so of all types of business, this is the most contrary to nature.

These views were much later echoed by Karl Polanyi, who argued that *money*, like *land* and *labour*, is a 'fictitious commodity', because 'the postulate that anything that is bought and sold must have been produced for sale is emphatically untrue in regard to them'. Today economists like James Roberston of the New Economics Foundation, London, and Herman Daly of the University of Maryland make the same point about the 'alchemical' nature of money.

The transmutation of paper into money remains fundamentally a 'chymical wedding' of mercurial, liquid imagination (imagining it to represent unmined gold still in the ground) and fiery, sulfurous impression (the impressive authority of the emperor's (or Duke's) signature on the note. (Daly, 2003)

Today 'confidence' is the 'sulphurous impression' that largely sustains the 'alchemy' of finance.

Calvin and capitalism: moving western ethical goalposts

When money is lent on a contract to receive not only the principal sum again, but also an increase by way of compensation for the use, the increase is called interest by those who think it lawful, and usury by those who do not.
Blackstone's Commentaries on the Laws of England, p. 1336

With time, as we have seen, Aristotle was overruled and discredited. Christians began to accept that the charging of interest on money was not unnatural; on the contrary, it could be a useful stimulus to trade. John Eck, supported by the Fugger banking family, in his book *Tractates contractu quinque de centum* (1515) defended 5% as an acceptable rate of interest as long as the borrower and lender mutually agreed to the loan.

Martin Luther took exception to this laxity, and raged against Christian acceptance of usury, arguing that

> heathens were able, by the light of reason, to conclude that a usurer is a double-dyed thief and murderer. We Christians however, hold them in such honour, that we fairly worship them for the sake of their money ... whoever eats up, robs, and steals the nourishment of another, that man commits as great a murder as he who starves a man ... Such does a usurer ... Meanwhile, we hang the small thieves ... Little thieves are put in the stocks, great thieves go flaunting in gold and silk... (Luther, quoted in Marx's *Capital*, 1971)

Luther's views were regarded as fanatical and were to be firmly displaced by the teachings of John Calvin (1509–1564) whose writings altered the status of the usurer in society. Instead of arguing in effect that loans should be 'natural' or sustainable, Calvin argued that 'interest is lawful, provided that it does not exceed an official maximum' (quoted in Tawney, 1984).

Calvin's commentaries on Psalm 15 explained that when Christ said 'lend hoping for nothing in return' it meant that we should help the poor freely. He dissected the two Hebrew definitions of the word usury – *neshek*, 'to bite', and *tarbit*, 'to take legitimate increase' – and argued that only 'biting' loans were forbidden. Thus, one could lend at interest to business people who would make a profit using the money (Calvin, Christian Classics Ethereal Library, 1999).

In what was to be an epic shift, the Christian goalposts had been moved; by Eck and then Calvin. Whereas Islam remained unwaveringly opposed to interest and usury, elites in Christian societies were given permission to decide on a rate of interest. Lenders could offer credit confident that a profit would be made from the money. Loans offered above this rate were from then on to be considered usurious, and Calvin was critical of such exploitation. The financier was not a pariah, but a useful member of society.

After Calvin the justification for charging interest on money loans was taken up enthusiastically in works promoting capitalism, notably by Francis Bacon in his essay on usury. Adam Smith too endorsed Calvin's definition of usury:

The interest or the use of money ... is the compensation which the borrower pays to the lender, for the profit which he has an opportunity of making by the use of the money. Part of that profit naturally belongs to the borrower who runs the risk and takes the trouble of employing it; and part to the lender, who affords him the opportunity of making this profit. (Smith, 1999)

But both Calvin and Smith err in their analysis: *they ignore the fact that lenders can make a profit, or a capital gain, even when the enterprise makes a loss. And while profits can rise or fall, the interest on the loan remains fixed.* The risk of losses falls largely therefore, on the borrower, not on the lender; and gains from interest remain fixed, regardless of the rate of profit. In other words, and again in contrast to Islam, Smith and most liberal economists since, extend co-responsibility only to gains, not losses.

This analysis is flawed. Loans should be considered ethical if they are evidently repayable; and lenders should be held co-responsible with the debtor for determining the repayability of a loan. In other words, lenders and borrowers should share in both gains and losses.

Calvin's legacy as applied today: usurious rates of interest

One of the economic characteristics of the period from 1980 to the present day is high rates of real interest (i.e. adjusted for inflation/deflation) paid by borrowers. By this we mean interest rates in the broadest sense: short, long, real, risky, safe. While the Federal Funds or Bank of England rate might seem low (often lowered by central banks and global capital markets as a way of influencing exchange rates, *increasing* lending and to avoid recession), the *real* rate paid by credit card holders, businesses seeking to invest and entrepreneurs taking risks, has for a long period, been much, much higher.

These high rates are not set according to the priorities of society; nor do they pay regard to ethical or moral guidelines. Nor are they determined through democratically accountable central banks or governments. Instead they are set by invisible and unaccountable banks and creditors operating in capital markets, and seeking to make capital gains from lending.

The average rate of return on investment is 3–5%. Any borrowing above that rate presents repayment difficulties for most investors. The post-1977 rates of interest, described in Chapter 2, can be described as usurious. Tremendous capital gains have been made by those who held assets, lent them on to governments, corporations or individuals, and thereby extracted even greater wealth. This is what has always been understood as usury.

Islam and interest-bearing money

> Those who consume interest shall not rise, except as he rises whom Satan by his touch prostrates [i.e one who is misled]; that is because they say: 'Trade is like interest'; whereas, Allah [God] has permitted trading but forbidden interest. Whosoever receives a warning from his/her Lord, he shall have his past gains and his affairs committed to Allah (God); but whosoever reverts (to devouring interest) those, they are the inhabitants of the fire, therein dwelling forever.
>
> Qur'an 2: 275

Islam prohibits the taking or giving of interest or *riba*, regardless of the purpose of the loan, or the rates at which interest is charged. As Wilfred Hahn notes, *riba* 'includes the whole notion of effortless profit or earnings that comes without work or value-addition production in commerce' (Hahn, 2006). In Islam money can only be used for facilitating trade and commerce – a crucial difference with the world's major Christian religions. This was because Islamic scholars were fully aware that debt-creating money can stratify wealth, and exacerbate exploitation, oppression and the enslavement of those who do not own assets. Because Arabs were the world's foremost mathematicians, having imported the decimal system invented by Hindus, and having later discovered the concept of zero – they fully understood the 'magical' qualities of compound interest, and its ability to multiply and magnify debts.

Riba is also forbidden because it is, according to Hahn,

> sometimes understood to infringe upon Allah's sovereignty. In this view, the charging of interest is said to guarantee a rate of return in the future. This is considered blasphemy since only Allah can guarantee or know the future. To set a fixed interest rate upon a loan is to put oneself in the place of Allah. Since the fate and security of mankind rests in the will of Allah, only an 'unbeliever' relies on the future obligations of mankind. (Hahn, 2006)

The Qur'an is unequivocal: in various revelations it asserts that those who disregard the prohibition of interest are at war with God and His Prophet. The prohibition of interest is also cited in no uncertain terms in the Hadith (sayings of the Prophet). The Prophet condemned not only those who take interest but also those who give interest and those who record or witness the transaction, saying that they are all alike in guilt (Barwa, 2005).

The Qur'anic ban on interest does not imply that capital or savings are without cost in an Islamic system. While Islam recognizes capital as a factor of production, it does not allow capital to make a claim on the productive surplus in the form of interest. Instead Islam views *profit-sharing* as permissible, and a viable alternative. The owner of capital can legitimately share in the gains made by the entrepreneur. *That implies that the owner of capital will also share in the losses.*

As Conrad Barwa writes,

investors in the Islamic order have no right to demand a fixed rate of return. *No one is entitled to any addition to the principal sum if he does not share in the risks involved.* The owner of capital (rabbul-mal) may 'invest' by allowing an entrepreneur with ideas and expertise to use the capital for productive purposes and he may share the profits, if any, with the entrepreneur-borrower (mudarib); losses, if any, however, will be borne wholly by the rabbul-mal. This mode of financing, termed *mudaraba* in the Islamic literature, was in practice even in the pre-Qur'anic days and, according to jurists was approved by the Prophet. (Barwa, 2005)

Another legitimate mode of financing recognized in Islam is based on equity participation (*musharaka*) in which partners use their capital jointly to generate a surplus. Profits or losses are shared between partners depending on the equity ratio.

Mudaraba and *musharaka* constitute, at least in principle if not in practice, the twin pillars of Islamic banking. The *musharaka* principle is invoked in the equity structure of Islamic banks and is similar to the modern concepts of partnership and joint stock ownership. In so far as the depositors are concerned, an Islamic bank acts as a *mudarib* which manages the funds of depositors to generate profits – subject to the rules outlined above.

By its very nature, Islamic banking is a risky business compared with conventional banking, for risk-sharing forms the very basis of all Islamic financial transactions. To minimize risks, however, Islamic banks have taken pains to distribute their eggs over many baskets and have established reserve funds out of past profits which they can fall back on in the event of any major loss (Barwa, 2005). Islamic banks operate, therefore, primarily as savings/investment institutions rather than commercial banks.

Global finance poses a profound threat to Islam. Because Islam expressly prohibits the concentration of wealth in the hands of the few – i.e. hoarding (*kenz*), waste (*tabthir*), extravagant consumption (*israf*) and miserliness (*bukhl*) – the excesses of global financial liberalization are in deep conflict with Muslim values (Hahn, 2006). Indeed, as Hahn stresses, 'it is not possible for Islam to ever have any financial power in the modern world of global capital. Islam recognizes this and is therefore prepared to endure holy hardship because of this' (Hahn, 2006).

> The Prophet has foretold us of a time when the spread of riba would be so overwhelming that it would be extremely difficult for the Muslim to avoid it. This situation calls for Muslims to be extra cautious before deciding on what money payment of financial methods to use in any personal or business transaction. (Riba According to Quran and Sunnah. Source: <http://muttaqun.com/riba.html>. Quoted in Hahn, 2006)

This is the context in which the *Financial Times* on 20 May 2006 reported that 'leading banks are scrambling to find Islamic experts who can issue religious edicts (fatwas) approving new financial products, such as "Islamic" bonds, hedge funds or loans'.

> At present, devout Muslims will only buy such instruments if a recognized sharia scholar, such as a mullah, has issued a fatwa to approve it. That is because many Muslims consider usury (riba) a sin – and will only invest in products structured to avoid interest payments.
>
> However, there are very few Islamic scholars who command enough religious respect to issue fatwas, understand the complexities of global structured financial products – and speak good enough English to read the necessary market documentation.
>
> That, coupled with the fact that investment bankers are rushing to expand their business in the Middle East amid an oil price boom, has triggered heated competition for shariah advice.
>
> The fees charged for shariah advice are a closely guarded secret, and much of what is received is reportedly paid to charity. However some investment banks say they have paid up to $500,000 for advice on large capital markets transactions, a dramatic increase from the levels seen a few years ago.
>
> Some banks such as HSBC and Citigroup have created fully-fledged, independent 'shariah advisory' boards of Islamic scholars to offer

advice, while others, such as Barclays Capital, hire scholars on an ad-hoc basis. (*Financial Times*, 20 May 2006)

While there can be no doubt that there are Muslims and mullahs willing to 'sell their souls' and values to HSBC, Barclays Capital, Citigroup and other international institutions for large sums of money, the fact is that Islam has successfully warded off attempts by the finance sector *to legitimize the institution of interest*. However, the struggle to resist the financial overtures of liberalized capital, is, in my view, at the heart of Islamic attacks on western values and western civilization.

Credit, debt and the ethics of usury today

> The love of money is root of all kinds of evil.
> 1 Timothy 6: 10

Usury is defined by the Oxford Dictionary as 'the fact, or practice of lending money at interest; esp. in later use, the practice of charging excessive or illegal rates of interest for money on loan'. I wish to argue that this is a definition too narrowly framed; that it is vital for society to broaden the definition of usury, making it clear and explicit. I will offer a revised definition to stimulate further debate:

> Usury is the practice of exalting money values over human and environmental values; of creating money at no cost and lending at rates of interest intended not to foster and maintain humanity or the ecosystem; but to
>
> a) accumulate reserves of unearned income;
> b) extract wealth from the productive sector in a manner that is parasitic;
> c) extract wealth from those who lack wealth (the asset-less) and to transfer this wealth to the already-rich (those with assets); and
> d) make a claim on the future.

Usury is first and foremost to be condemned for its promotion of money values: the 'love of money' as an *end*, not a means. For its role in corrupting moral values and therefore society; and for the immense *psycho-spiritual power* those with money, the already-rich, exercise over those without.

Second, usury must be condemned because it is *unearned income*; income gained without the expense of labour or risk on the part of the lender; or at least of the labour and risk undertaken by the entrepreneur. Of course lenders can lose their money when a debtor defaults; but lenders, unlike, say, entrepreneurs growing tomatoes, ensure that the state protects them from this risk (through tax breaks, bankruptcy laws) in a way that the state does not protect the entrepreneur. International lenders (including the World Bank, the International Monetary Fund and sovereign governments) use military force, economic conditionality, and a 'legal' framework that they have created, to protect them from the risk of sovereign debtor defaults. In other words they seek protection from 'bad debts' but deny protection to borrowers from 'bad loans'. Prof. Kunibert Raffer of the University of Vienna explains how the multilateral banks (banks owned by a range of governments) advocate free market policies which entail considerable risk; but are not prepared to take such risks with their lending:

> IFI decision making is not only delinked from financial responsibilities, their errors may even cause financial gains. This is a system absurdly at odds with the Western market system. At a time when riskless decision making by bureaucrats is abolished in the East, there is no reason why it should be preserved in the West. It is the most basic precondition for the functioning of the market mechanism that economic decisions must be accompanied by (co)responsibility: whoever takes economic decisions must also carry financial risks. If this link is severed – as it was in the Centrally Planned Economies of the former East – efficiency is severely disturbed. Bringing the market mechanism to multilateral institutions is therefore advisable. The striking contrast between free-market recommendations given by IFIs and their own protection from market forces must be abolished. (Raffer, 1993)

Islam permits trade yet forbids usury; because profits 'are the result of initiative, enterprise and efficiency. They result after a definite value-creating process' (Ahmad, 1958, quoted in Visser et al., 1998). The capital gains from interest, by contrast, require no labour; and no risk (except in the event of default) – as the price of lending, unlike the price of labour, goods or services, or the rate of profit, is fixed for the duration of the loan. Profits, by contrast, do not rise exponentially but are much more volatile, rising and falling. Unlike wages or profits, the gains from usury are fixed regardless of whether value has been added or losses made. Worse, capital gains can increase *exponentially* for the lender when losses are made by the borrower because payment arrears attract compound interest. The idea that compound interest is 'the greatest mathematical discovery of all time' and 'the eighth wonder of the world' is attributed to Albert Einstein. Whether or not he really said it matters not: the truth is that compound interest causes capital gains to rise exponentially.

For this reason the setting of interest rates, and control over the powerful force of credit-creation, should be in the hands of democratically accountable institutions. In other words, the benefits and power of bank money, essentially a social construct, should be shared more widely, not just allocated to a small money-creating and money-lending elite.

Third, usury must be condemned for the role it plays in *transferring* resources from those without assets, to those with assets; i.e. in transferring wealth from the poor to the already-rich. This is another reason Islam condemns usury because it contradicts the Principle of Distributive Equity which its political economy strives to enshrine: 'Interest in any amount acts in transferring wealth from the assetless section of the population' (Choudhury and Malik, 1992, p. 51, quoted in Visser et al., 1998).

Fourth, usury must be condemned because of the role it plays in using and usurping natural resources, now and into the future; and thereby causing a 'disjunction between financial and ecological economy' (Visser et al., 1988). This is achieved by the claims that usury (high real rates of interest) makes on the future – through rates or yields, that are fixed for years ahead. Underlying this assumption is the notion that somewhere in the future, there will always be limitless supplies of 'unmined gold' (Daly, 2003) that can be found to help repay debts. This assumption is in turn rooted in the notion that what we have today, has a higher value than it will have in the future; and second, that the earth's commodities will never be exhausted; that somehow the inventions of new technology will tackle, and overcome nature's limits.

'Barren money'

Any discussion of the ethics of lending must take up Aristotle's and Daly's challenge, and recognize that money, whether it be metal money, paper money, bank money or fiat money, is 'barren'. It does not itself generate the means of repayment, but its ability to increase exponentially places great strain on, and exploits, the other sources or processes which support repayment. The strain is particularly intense if these physical and human assets (i.e. land and labour in the broadest sense) are not reproduced, and cannot be exploited, at the same rate of exponential increase as money or credit. To quote Daly:

Money is by its nature an order for the future, for what one can buy in the future by spending it, or gain in the future, as yield or interest, by investing it. One can therefore virtually say 'money is future.' But since the economy is geared to money values, the future is lost again because the money value can only be secured through constant *additional* consumption of the world, for this money must be covered by real goods excavated from the mine of the world. The future is then threatened to the extent that the world is limited, that is, the world mine is exhausted. (Daly, 2003. Emphasis added)

The ethics of lending and borrowing should take into account the 'unnatural' or 'fictionalized' nature of money; strict limits should be placed on the use of money to burden individuals, corporations and nations with debt; and on the ability of money (or interest) to exponentially increase exploitation of both land and of labour, both now and into the future.

Usury was an excommunicable offence in the Catholic Church until relatively recently, with usurers denied the sacraments and burial in sacred ground. The perceived usury of a foreign power (Rome) in collecting tithes was at the heart of the German Peasants' Revolt of 1524 and fuelled the Protestant revolution led by Martin Luther.

One of the first tasks facing those wishing to challenge the finance sector's dominance, will be the reinvigoration of long-established ethical principles. This is a task for us all, but in particular for faith organizations. Condemnation of usury has a long history, stretching back 4,000 years. Today, thanks to centuries of active lobbying by landowners, bankers and financiers, usury as a sin has been diluted and modified, in particular by the pro-usury counter-movement of the Christian faith. If the finance sector is to be subordinated to the role of servant to the global economy, not master, then usury must be rescued from usurers and those who collude with usurers, and its denunciation actively revived.

The ethics of forgiveness

Forgive us our sins, for we ourselves forgive everyone indebted to us.

Luke 11: 4

The notion of 'forgiving' or 'redeeming' debts is fundamental to New Testament Christianity. (Note, I prefer the use of 'to redeem' when referring to debt cancellation, as 'to forgive' implies that the debtor has sinned; when both the lender and borrower are co-responsible for debt.) Yet we live in a world that makes it more and more difficult for debtors to emerge from under the yoke of creditors; for the periodic correction to imbalances; and for the restoration of balance after periods of disruption, external shocks or crisis.

One of civilization's great advances was the introduction of bankruptcy laws; laws which recognized that generalized economic crises, weather conditions and warehouse fires were shocks often beyond the control of the debtor, and the debtor should therefore be released from debts. But bankruptcy laws were also far-sighted because they recognized that in order to restore a bankrupt debtor to economic activity; to revive economic fortunes, it was periodically necessary to draw a line under debts, and write them off. Bankruptcy laws arose from the recognition that creditors too had to share in the burden of losses and assist the debtor to re-enter the economy.

Under the government of finance, bankruptcy laws have tightened to make it more difficult for the debtor to be 'released' from debts; and, as in the US, to enlist the state's help in extracting additional repayments from debtors. In the international sphere, as noted above, there is no independent, fair process for the orderly restructuring or write-off of debts, in the event of a nation's effective insolvency. Instead creditors make bad loans; set the terms of the loan; use economic conditionality to guarantee that assets are extracted and debts repaid; and then refuse to release impoverished, insolvent debtor nations from old, often corrupt and odious debts.

The ethics of economic redemption should be revived, and should underpin all financial transactions, both locally and internationally.

Periodic correction to imbalances – the Sabbath

Recent, modest international civil society campaigns (like Jubilee 2000) for a Jubilee year, for the cancellation of debts owed by the poorest countries, and for the justice of a 'fresh start', have resonated with western audiences. This is because they tapped ancient, almost forgotten religious ethics of debt. These include the abhorrent nature of usury and the need to defend the weak against exploitation by the powerful, through the periodic correction of imbalances. This was achieved in ancient societies through the use of 'clean slates' and the periodic cancellation of debts in the Jubilee year.

> Count off seven sabbaths of years – seven times seven years – so that the seven Sabbaths of years amount to a period of forty-nine years. Then have the trumpet sounded everywhere on the tenth day of the seventh

month: on the Day of Atonement sound the trumpet throughout your land. Consecrate the fiftieth year and proclaim liberty throughout the land to all its inhabitants. It shall be a Jubilee for you; each one of you is to return to his family property and each to his own clan. (Leviticus 25: 8–10)

Central to the Jubilee principle is the notion of liberty: liberty from the yoke of creditors and oppressors. It has been the slogan of the oppressed throughout the ages, most recently by those seeking independence from the British empire (which is why the Leviticus text 'sound the trumpet of Jubilee and declare liberty throughout the land' is engraved on the US's 'Liberty Bell' in Philadelphia), and also by the anti-slavery movement of America's Deep South.

Fundamental to both the Judaic and Christian traditions is the notion that God has provided abundantly for his people; that there is sufficient for all, *but* that there should be *limits* or restraints placed on the consumption of God's gifts. The strict rules of the Sabbath tradition prohibit the exploitation of land and labour every seventh day, the Sabbath – a form of regulation that limited consumption and exploitation. The purpose of the regulation was to provide an almost automatic mechanism for periodically correcting imbalances and injustices. A similar injunction of the Torah provides for the land to lie fallow every seventh year. To this day, academics often enjoy a sabbatical, in the seventh year of employment. The Sabbath extends communal disciplines of restraint to the restoration of socioeconomic and ecological equilibrium (Myers, 1998). 'Forgive us our debts as we forgive others' is a fundamental text both of the Jewish Torah, and of the Christian New Testament.

Within modern western economies, these beliefs are widely regarded as eccentric, problematic and atypical; belonging to older, less relevant religious traditions. Indeed defeat of the notion of the Sabbath, and the introduction of the '24/7' working week, was fundamental to the de-regulation of 'liberal' economies, and to the removal of 'rigidities' in the labour market. Biblical or Qur'anic regulations are not considered practical or relevant to arrangements for sovereign or commercial lending and borrowing.

Goods are scarce but consumption limitless

Orthodox economists argue that commodities, goods and services are scarce; and that the efficient allocation of these resources is best achieved through the market. However, while emphasizing the *scarcity* of these goods, mainstream economists do not provide for *limits* to be placed on consumption – whether those be the physical limits on exploitation of the land, in its broadest sense; or forms of regulation to limit the exploitation of people, broadly defined as labour.

High-income, largely de-regulated economies like that of the US and UK are today heavily dependent on high levels of personal and governmental consumption to stimulate and maintain rates of economic growth. They are 'one-legged' in that growth is largely driven by a leg of the economy, personal consumption, which in turn is financed by borrowing, and not by for example the investment of profits or surpluses into research and development; or by government spending. Furthermore, rich countries are heavily dependent on resources from poor countries – defined by many as 'ecological debts' or 'asset stripping' – to maintain this growth (Simms, 2006).

For most economists, business and politics are conducted as if there were no limits to the rates of growth that can be achieved through such exploitation, borrowing and consumption.

> Like Faust, modern man has become blind to the problem of limits – and therefore easy prey to the economic alchemists who promise indefinite growth by turning base metals into gold, transitoriness into permanence, and swamps into farmland. (Herman Daly, 1995)

We need to revive the ethics of 'enoughness'; the ethics underlying the physical reality of *limits* – to the exploitation of both nature and of man.

The rate of interest and co-responsibility

A key principle for any ethical assessment of lending and borrowing *could* be, as in Islamic law, that interest should not be charged on loans, especially money loans. However, the availability of credit has undoubtedly facilitated trade and helped society progress at key points in history. Credit, like bank money, is not the problem, this book argues.

The problem is the rate and the terms on which credit is provided by the finance sector – in the interests of the private finance sector – without regard to society's needs and priorities; without regard to whether profits or losses are made; and without regard to nature's limits, both now and into the future.

Human progress, ecological sustainability and social stability depend on regulated credit and Cheap Money, even interest-free money, regulated by the public, not private, sector. If interest rates must be applied they should be set at levels that are repayable and sustainable; rates that are set and regulated by society as a whole in the interest of Industry and Labour; both humanity and the ecosystem. They must take into account both humanity's and nature's limits – both now and into the future. Above all, rates of interest should underpin and reflect democratically agreed priorities and goals; they should emphasize the co-responsibility of creditor and debtor for the loan; and should subordinate the interests of the finance sector to society and the ecosystem.

Conclusion

If we are to avoid crises; if we are to recover from an international financial crisis, then it will be vital for western values to be reinvigorated by both an understanding of, and abhorrence for, usury.

The very concept of usury will have to be unearthed from the deep recesses in which it has been so firmly buried by the finance sector and its supporters. Our moral leaders will have to emerge from their long night of denial, and from their obsession with the conduct of private lives. Instead they must, in my view, begin to focus on the larger issue of finance and usury, whose impact causes lasting damage for large and small economies, human societies and large swathes of the ecosystem. Indeed I believe it vital for leaders of western Christianity to understand that their obsession with sexuality and the minutiae of private lives serves as a perfect foil for the finance sector, which can proceed to extract and exploit humanity and the earth without threat of reproach or hindrance from the leaders of Christian faiths and their followers.

There can be no doubt that with political and ethical will, society can regain the initiative and use moral principles, law, regulation and accountability to rein in the finance sector, and once again subordinate it to the interests of both humanity and the planet. In other words it is possible, with political will, for society to subordinate the finance sector to its proper role as *servant* of the economy, and not *master*.

Sources and suggested reading

Aristotle, *The Politics*, 1258 a19, p. 87. Penguin Books, 1992.

Bacon, Francis, 'Usury' in *Essays or Counsels, Civill or Morall*, 1601. Copyright © 1998 The University of Oregon. <http://darkwing.uoregon.edu/%7Erbear/bacon.html#41>.

Bank for International Settlements, June 2005 Annual Report.

Barwa, Conrad, *Islamic Banking*. Unpublished. London School for Oriental and African Studies. November 2005.

BBC Radio 4's Broadcast House, 27 November 2005. <www.bbc.co.uk/radio4/news/bh/>.

BBC, 'Niger Leaders deny food shortage', 24 November 2005. <http://news.bbc.co.uk/2/hi/africa/4468108.stm>.

Calvin, John, *Commentaries on Psalm 15 verse 5*. Grand Rapids, MI: Christian Classics Ethereal Library, 1999–11–24, v1.0, URL 1999–11–24. <http://www.ccel.org/c/calvin/comment3/comm_index.htm>.

Daly, Herman, 'Sustaining our Commonwealth of Nature and Knowledge'. Lecture at inaugural presentation of the new Forum on Society Wealth lecture series at the University of Massachussets, Amherst, March 2005. <www.unmass.edu/economics/>.

Daly, Herman. In a 2003 review of H.C. Binswanger's *Money and Magic* (A Critique of the Modern Economy in Light of Goethe's Faust. University of Chicago Press, 1996.) <http://dieoff.org/page71.ht>.

Daly, Herman, 'Globalization and its Inconsistencies'. Chapter 12 of *Real World Economic Outlook*, ed. Ann Pettifor. Palgrave Macmillan, 2003.

Daly, Herman, 'The irrationality of homo economicus'. The Developing Ideas interview, 1995 on <www.iisd.org/didigest/special/daly.htm>.

The Economist, 11 June 2005.

Financial Times, 'Profits in financial services soar', Lex Column, 29 December 2005. 'Hedge fund agitators deserve to be heard', by John Gapper, 17 November 2005. 'CBI/PwC survey', 9 January 2006. 'Warning of £150bn black hole in pensions', 9 January 2006. 'Banks seek Islamic scholars versed in finance', 19 May 2006.

Guardian, 'One man's multimillion-dollar legal battle threatens chaos in art world'. 29 November 2005.

Hahn, Wilfred J., in *Final Combustion: Oil, Islam and the Christian West – Part 1*. April 2006. <www.eternalvalue.com/> and <www.eternalvalue.com/MCM/MoneyMuslimsMayhemII.pdf>.

Himmelstein, David U.; Warren, Elizabeth; Thorne, Deborah and Woolhandler, Steffie, 'MarketWatch: Illness and Injury as Contributors to Bankruptcy'. *Health Affairs*, 2 February 2005. <http://content.healthaffairs.org/cgi/content/full/hlthaff.w5.63/DC1>.

Hudson, Michael, 'The early evolution of interest-bearing debt: some unresolved issues', in *Debt and Economic Renewal in the Ancient Near East*, published by CDL Press, 2002, edited by Michael Hudson and Marc Van De Mieroop.

Hudson, Michael; Miller, G.J. and Feder, Kris, from the Prologue to *A Philosophy for a Fair Society* in Georgist Paradigm Series: editor, Fred Harrison. Published by Shepheard-Walwyn (Publishers) Ltd, in association with Centre for Incentive Taxation Ltd. 1994.

Luther, Martin, *Against Usury*. An die Pfarrherren wider de Wucher zu predigen. Wittenberg, 1540 – 173. Quoted in Karl Marx, *Capital*, p. 604. George Allen and Unwin Ltd. 1971.

Myers, Ched, *Balancing abundance and need*. In 'The Other Side', Sept–October, 1998. <http://bcm-net.org/wordpress/theological-animation/cheds-curriculum-vitae/>.

New Economics Foundation, <www.neweconomics.org>.

Polanyi, Karl, *The Great Transformation*. First Beacon Paperback edition. Chapter 6, 'The Self-Regulating Market'. 1957.

Raffer, Kunibert, *Solving Sovereign Debt Overhang by Internationalising Chapter 9 Procedures*. Studien von Zeitfragen, 2002. <www.jahrbuch2002.studien-von-zeitfragen.net/Weltfinanz/RAFFER_1/raffer_1.HTM>.

Raffer, Kunibert, *What's Good for the United States Must be Good for the World: Advocating an International Chapter 9 Insolvency* published in: Bruno Kreisky Forum for International Dialogue (ed), *From Cancún to Vienna. International Development in a New World*, Vienna 1993. <http://homepage.univie.ac.at/kunibert.raffer/kreisky.pdf>.

Robertson, James, *Monetary Reform – Making it Happen!* (with John Bunzl). 2003. <www.jamesrobertson.com/subject-guide.htm>.

Simms, Andrew, *Ecological Debt – the Health of the Planet and the Wealth of Nations*, Pluto Press, 2006.

Smith, Adam, *An Inquiry into the Nature and Causes of the Wealth of Nations*. Oxford World Classics. OUP, 1998.

Tawney, R.H., *Religion and the Rise of Capitalism*. Peregrine Books, 1984.

Tily, Geoff, 'Keynes's theory of liquidity preference and his debt management and monetary policies'. *Cambridge Journal of Economics*, January 2006.

Tily, Geoff, *Keynes's General Theory, the Rate of Interest and Keynesian Economics*, PhD submitted to University College, London, April 2005, to be published shortly by Palgrave Macmillan.

UK Pensions Commission Report, *Pensions: Challenges and Choices*, 2004, Annex C. Source: Barclays Equity Gilt Study 2004.

Visser, Wayne A.M. and MacIntosh, A., 'A short review of the historical critique of usury', in *Accounting, Business and Financial History*, Routledge. Volume 8 Number 2. July, 1998, pp. 175–89.

Wade, Robert Hunter, 'Poverty and income distribution: what is the evidence?', p. 138 of *Real World Economic Outlook*, ed. Ann Pettifor. Palgrave Macmillan, 2003.

Wall Street Journal, 20 December 2005.

Wood, Mackenzie, *Reviewing Exploration Strategy and Performance – A global review of the exploration performance of 28 leading oil companies over the last 10 years*. October 2005. <www.woodmacresearch.com/cgi-bin/wmprod/portal/energy/highlights>.

Woodward, David, *Debt Sustainability and the Debt Overhang in HIPCs: some comments on the IMF's view*. In Eurodad: World Credit Tables, 1995/96.

Zarlenga, Stephen, *A Brief History of Interest*. Copyright 2000. American Monetary Institute. <www.monetary.org/interest.htm>.

6
Debtonation? When and Why will it Happen?

There can be great hysteria, with people all over the world sitting in front of monitors and computers, and there are all kinds of things being communicated, and at times the action can be too fast for anyone to handle ... The Danish Minister of Finance once said that men in the financial arena often acted like hysterical women, and was criticized for his remarks, and that conforms to my experience that we men can be more hysterical than women, but it is quite right that often there is much ado in the financial markets ...

Iceland's Prime Minister, Halldor Asgrimsson,
commenting on his country's financial crisis:
Iceland Review online, 27 March 2006

Introduction

In this chapter I want to explore and list potential 'debtonators' – events or imbalances likely to trigger a prolonged First World debt-deflationary crisis. Included in the list is the threat posed by events related to climate change, like Hurricane Katrina; house price crashes; a rise in interest rates and a cut in consumer spending; the threat posed by the US deficit and a dollar collapse; and finally the oil price shock.

This list is limited because most debtonators will be unpredictable; they will appear to come from nowhere. We cannot list them here, because we do not know, nor can we know, what or where they are. Walter Bagehot observed at the time of the first global, systemic financial crisis – that of 1873 – that 'every great crisis reveals the excessive speculations of many houses which no one before suspected' (Bagehot, 1873).

In October 1998 the mis-named Long Term Capital Management Fund (LTCM) threatened collapse – and by doing so revealed 'excessive speculations' that no-one before had suspected.

> The losses came from every corner. They were so swift, so encyclopaedic in their breadth, so utterly unexpected that the LTCM partners felt abandoned. They had suddenly lost control, as though the gods of science had been dislodged and some unseen diabolical power had taken hold of their fates. (Lowenstein, 2001)

Alan Greenspan, chair of the US Federal Reserve Bank, stepped in to prevent the collapse that market forces would normally have brought about by arranging a bail-out for LTCM's owners – amid howls of protest at blatant 'cronyism'. (David Mullins, a board member of LTCM, formerly vice-chairman of the Fed, was known to be a friend (Lowenstein, 2001).)

LTCM was bailed out, argued Greenspan, because its demise threatened systemic collapse of the international financial system. If so, the Chairman of the Fed must have had a great deal on his mind. At the time there were an estimated 4,000 largely unregulated hedge funds in existence. By 2006 their numbers had more than doubled, and there is now five times more money invested in hedge funds than in 1998 (Brimelow, 2006).

> There are 9,000 hedge funds out there. There aren't that many smart people in the world. (Michael Driscoll, a trader at Bear Stearns & Co. in New York – Bloomberg, 10 May 2005)

This anarchy in the international financial system parades as prosperity and freedom, as Peter Warburton once observed (Warburton, 1999). But there are spooks in the anarchic global financial forest. The spooks attack like bolts of lightning, unexpectedly and out of the blue. No-one, bar brave economists like Brian Reading, predicted Japan's descent into an economic morass in 1990 (Reading, 1992). No economist in the IMF and World Bank predicted the rapidity or the breadth of the South East Asian crisis of 1997/98. (On the contrary: in its May 1997 *World Economic Outlook*, the IMF wrote: 'apart from the short-term effects of labor unrest in Korea, the prospects for the newly industrialised economies in Asia remain bright ...'.) No-one – least of all the Nobel Prize-winning economists running the Long Term Capital Management Fund – predicted Russia's default in 1998. And no-one, in the spring of 2006, least of all their Prime Minister, predicted that Iceland would experience 'much ado in the financial markets'; a sudden, vehement crisis.

The 'butterfly's wing'?

The debtonator for the panic that hit Iceland was a report produced by analysts at a Danish bank – Landsbankinn – entitled *Is Something Rotten in the State of Iceland?* and published on 22 March 2006.

Investors who had borrowed at low interest rates in Japan, and then used the money to buy Iceland's assets at much higher rates of interest, panicked, pulled back and exited on publication of the report – triggering a massive outflow of funds from Iceland's heavily indebted economy. The panic caused Nicolas Bouzou, the chief economist of Institut Xerfi in France, to suggest that

> Iceland could be the 'butterfly's wing' that sets off serious problems in capital markets around the world ... Because many countries have the same macroeconomic configuration of Iceland ... (including) a real estate bubble, very strong credit expansion and a very high commercial deficit. The same could be said of New Zealand, Australia and even the United States. (Quoted in the *International Herald Tribune*, 15 April 2006)

At the time the Danish report was written, Iceland had low unemployment; inflation was rising and wage growth was above 7%. Interest rates had been rising and at the time were above 10%. Landsbankinn's analysts noted that 'there has been a stunning expansion of debt, leverage and risk-taking ... External debt is now nearly 300% of GDP, while short term external debt is just short of 55% of GDP ... Mortgage debt stood at 165% of disposable income at end-2004.' The Danes concluded that 'Iceland looks worse on almost all measures than Thailand did before its crisis in 1997, and only moderately more healthy than Turkey before its 2001 crisis.' It was this conclusion that set off the debtonator and caused funds to flood out of the small country.

Global economy 'rarely in better shape'

Iceland's crisis did little to disturb those at the helm of the global economy. A couple of weeks later, prominent international economists were upbeat about the risk of a systemic crisis in the global economy. Few predicted a prolonged first world debt crisis. The majority were positive and confident that globalization/liberalization/de-regulation/free trade had equipped the global economy with sufficient 'flexibility' and 'resilience' to absorb shocks and manage crises.

While there was universal agreement that 'imbalances' existed in the global economy – deficits in rich countries; surpluses in countries with large numbers of poor, like China and India; the excess consumption in economies like the US and UK; and the limited demand for goods and services in other countries – there was disagreement over whether this mattered and if these imbalances meant the system was fundamentally fragile. Many believed that, even though unbalanced, the financial system remained strong or 'resilient' enough to resist panics and upheavals.

Unbalanced international systems stay aloft largely because IMF staff, Presidents, Prime Ministers, finance ministers and investors in financial markets have *confidence* that these financial systems *will* stay aloft. The IMF's deputy, Anne Krueger, encouraged more of such confidence in a speech in May 2006 in which she said

> the world economy has rarely been in better shape than it is today … the economic outlook remains bright. The global economy appears to be more resilient in the face of shocks than it was even a short time ago. The policy reforms of the 1990s, above all the reduction of inflation around the world and the improvement in macroeconomic management, have played an important role in this. ('A Remarkable Prospect: Opportunities and Challenges for the Modern Global Economy', IMF, 2 May 2006)

She added a brief qualification to these upbeat remarks; 'the world may be more resilient than in the past but there is no evidence that it has become wholly immune to shocks'; but overall her tone was intended to cheer on the surging bull markets in commodities, stocks and bonds.

There is also considerable confidence in capital markets that central bankers, finance ministers and the big international financial institutions have learned from past experience, and will be able to apply the right remedies to prevent, or moderate any crisis. The decision by finance ministers of some the most indebted nations in the world, the G7, to admit there were serious problems with the economy at their spring meetings in April 2006, cheered many, including the most pessimistic.

The G7 took the bold step of tasking IMF officials to come up with a menu of policy advice that politicians in the US, Europe and Asia might adopt to avert recessions and, ultimately, systemic crisis. It was as if a group of debtaholics had joined Debtaholics Anonymous, and by that very act encouraged others to believe that abstention was nigh, and that G7 offenders were ready to be *prescribed*, if not to take, some harsh medicine. The very mention of 'prescriptions' was enough to reassure some that a cure was at hand. Stephen Roach, analyst with Morgan Stanley, and widely known as the Cassandra of the global economy, told the *Guardian*'s Larry Elliott in May 2006 that 'If anything, the imbalances in the world economy have gotten worse over the last several months. But that's been a good thing, because it has elicited a response from the powers that be, that it's an urgent problem that needs addressing' (*Guardian*, 6 May 2006).

Stephen Roach's renewed optimism brings to mind the stubborn optimism of the Harvard Economic Society which after a period of pessimism, decided, in the summer of 1929 that

> ... business might be good after all ... then came the crash. The Society remained persuaded that no serious depression was in prospect. In November it said firmly that 'a severe depression like that of 1920–21 is outside the range of probability. We are not facing protracted liquidation'. This view the Society reiterated until it was liquidated. (Galbraith, 1954)

Few shared Roach's optimism in the spring of 2006. Many, including this author, were sceptical that western elected politicians facing domestic electorates were going to take the 'medicine' prescribed by the staff of an institution whose influence and power have waned over the last decade; and to take it in appropriate doses that would prevent, not worsen the risk of crises. Correcting the world economy's vast imbalances, as we explain below, requires nuanced action, and far more international co-ordination than world leaders have shown themselves capable of, to date. Without such carefully managed (and regulated) co-ordination the 'medicine' itself could trigger a 'debtonation'.

There are a number of these potential 'debtonators' – events that could result in a prolonged First World debt-deflation crisis. They could suddenly erupt and blow up a vital buttress of the global economy: confidence. Confidence is ephemeral, but key to global economic stability and growth. If confidence in markets, institutions and policy-makers were to erode, then spread quickly and become generalized, no amount of 'resilience' or 'flexibility' would be sufficient to contain the flood waters.

Once generalized, a loss of confidence would be transformed into fear. Fear would drive debtors and investors into 'herds' – and cause them to rush like lemmings for the proverbial cliffs. Because the international financial system is perceived as a self-regulated 'fantastic machinery' that 'automatically' adjusts and links the global economy, there is no way of containing such cascading disruption, when it occurs. 'Market corrections' – i.e. crashes, currency collapses, deflation – would spread across national boundaries at the speed of light – or at least at the speed of 24/7 digitized communication.

This chapter explores potential *debtonation* triggers, i.e. triggers that could undermine the very thing that Ms Krueger was encouraging in her speech: confidence, and which could thereby precipitate a prolonged First World debt crisis.

Potential debtonator 1: climate change shocks

The first candidate for the role of debtonator must be climate change. The build-up in concentration of carbon dioxide in the earth's atmosphere is leading to ever-more violent swings in the climate, and to more frequent calamities: floods; windstorms; earthquakes; droughts; wildfires; insect infestations; wave surges. While big insurance companies are extremely concerned, world leaders like US President George Bush and Vice-president Dick Cheney, and many mainstream economists and commentators have a blind spot for extreme weather events and their impacts.

Like the tourists on Phuket beaches who stood and gazed at an oncoming tsunami because it was outside their experience, society is reacting to the coming wave of climate change without urgency. (Linden, January 2006)

The mega-storms whipped up by Hurricanes Katrina, Rita and Wilma in 2005 could have been the kind of climate change shock that undermined confidence in the ability of the US government to expand its already large fiscal (government) deficit, which in turn impacts on the external deficit. In the event the shock appeared to be absorbed by both the US and global economy without much disruption. Alan Greenspan, then Governor of the US Federal Reserve, in a report in the *Washington Post* of 28 September 2005 explained that the economy was able to respond to the shocks caused by events in New Orleans because of

... deregulation of large parts of the transportation, communications, energy and financial industries since the 1970s ... the lowering of trade barriers, the freedom to fire workers, the development of information technologies that have improved inventory management and the creation of complex financial tools that have enabled businesses and investors to disperse risk.

That flexibility enabled the economy to weather the 1987 stock market crash with no long-term economic stress and helped the economy survive both the credit crunch of the early 1990s and the bursting of the stock market bubble in 2000 with the mildest recessions since World War II. Even the terrorist attacks of September 2001 caused 'severe economic weakness ... for only a few weeks'.

While it is true that the crisis of Hurricane Katrina was successfully absorbed, Mr Greenspan's facts must be contested. For example, the 1987 stock market crash was largely weathered, not by the 'flexibility' of the global economy, but as can be seen in the box on Japan (below) by the determined efforts of the Japanese authorities to ensure that Japan, almost single-handedly, absorbed the shock of that international stock market crash (Cohen, 1997). Japanese central bank officials achieved this, at the behest of the US Federal Reserve, by drastically lowering interest rates, and flooding international capital markets with new lending, or Easy Money. US investors whose fingers had been burned in the crash were thus able to borrow cheaply in Japan to shore up their losses in the US.

Events leading to financial crisis in Japan

The background to financial collapse in Japan in the early 1990s lies in the events that led to the global crash in 1987.

In the early 1980s, the US under Reagan and the UK under Thatcher embarked upon unprecedented financial reform and liberalization. In the US, tight monetary policy supported a strong dollar, which together with tax cuts encouraged higher spending and surging imports. Then in 1984 the Federal Reserve began cutting interest rates. With credit easier to obtain because of de-regulation, levels of borrowing increased and reinvigorated the bull market in stocks, bonds and property. Foreign investors, concerned about the twin US deficits (trade and budget) demanded higher interest rates to provide capital to cover the imbalances. However, for domestic reasons the US authorities kept interest rates low. To support the dollar which was falling, central banks intervened but this injected more liquidity into the global economy causing further speculation and asset price inflation. Then in 1987, Japanese investors began a withdrawal of capital from US investments in order to purchase shares in a major privatization in Japan. This caused huge capital flows

▶

across the world's financial markets, undermining confidence as investors woke up to the massive overvaluation of assets. Heavy selling on the world markets in the autumn of 1987 turned into a deluge on 19 October.

After the 1987 global crash, the US authorities pressured Japan to keep her interest rates low, even though a Japanese asset price bubble was brewing. The US concern was for US agents to be able to borrow cheaply in Japan, to re-finance cheaply after the crash, so honouring their liabilities and avoiding a wider economic crisis.

The Japanese bubble had its root causes in efforts to combat recession in the mid 1980s. Japan had reduced interest rates and this had effectively increased domestic demand but the lion's share of this led to asset price inflation rather than increased consumption. Then towards the end of the 1980s further financial de-regulation combined with lax monetary policy, allowed plentiful credit to inflate all types of financial assets at home and abroad. As the cost of borrowing fell to almost nothing, Japanese companies were diverted from core productive activities to speculation in assets from shares to property to works of art because the rate of return on such assets was higher than the rate of return on production. A couple of examples highlight the extent of the excess liquidity: a Japanese businessman bought a Van Gogh painting at auction for the highest price ever paid for a single work of art; meanwhile, the Mitsui Real Estate Company paid $625 million for the Exxon building in New York, even though it was valued at $310 million, because the company wanted to get into the Guinness Book of Records. Residential and commercial property prices in Japan doubled between 1986 and 1989. With such high house prices, 100-year mortgages were developed with repayments spanning three generations. For the Japanese, wealth was not determined by what you earned but by what you owned.

The bubble finally burst at the end of 1989. This was in part because, in response to much inflated property prices, a new central bank regulation limited the growth of new real estate loans. Some investors in real estate, who were financing interest payments on existing loans by taking out new loans, became distress sellers of property. The combination of more restricted credit for investment in property and sales of property caused prices to decline. Stock prices soon followed the downward trend.

The bursting of Japan's bubble was manifested not by a sudden crash but by a prolonged slide in asset values. Japan has experienced one of the longest and deepest economic downturns seen in a developed country. Bankruptcies surged and unemployment, virtually unheard of in Japan, reached a record high of 3.2% in May 1995. The debt overhang was and is still huge. In 1995, Japan's bad debts were estimated to be some ¥50,000 billion (£355 billion), equivalent to one-tenth of the Japanese economy.

By lowering rates and turning on the lending spigot, the Bank of Japan pumped out money which in turn inflated property and other asset markets in Japan. When that bubble punctured two to three years later, in 1990, Japan endured a prolonged recession, the pain of which was largely borne by ordinary Japanese workers and consumers – innocent of any role in the crisis. Of course Alan Greenspan was not directly responsible for the welfare of Japanese workers and consumers; but it would have been courteous of him to recognize the heroic role they played in shouldering the burden of crisis for almost 15 years, thereby protecting the US, and the global economy, from a severe and prolonged recession after 1987. Instead Greenspan attributes the rescue and recovery to abstract notions of 'flexibility' and 'de-regulation'.

The stock market crash of 2000/01 was also dealt with by a flood of new lending, helped by 13 cuts in the US Federal Reserve's rates (the Federal Funds rate) between 2001 and June 2004. This time it was the US that turned on the lending spigot, effectively subsidizing the financial markets by enabling losses to be re-financed cheaply. And it was the *public* sector – the central banks of Japan, China, Taiwan, India, to name but a few – that released a flood of new lending to the US over that period, by purchasing US Treasury Bills as dollar reserves. At the same time the Republican administration embarked on a spending spree, much to the discomfort of its supporters amongst orthodox economists that had done much to discredit such fiscal expansion. In 2002 and 2003 Federal spending increased at a 7.6% growth rate, more than *double* the 3.4% growth rate from 1993 to 2001. The result is the historically unprecedented annual deficits and total debts of the US government, outlined in Chapter 3.

None of these government-driven policies and actions can be described as issuing automatically from the 'flexibility' or 'de-regulation' of the global economy. On the contrary, all three responses to the 2001 crisis outlined above were triggered by the actions of official – i.e. regulated – governmental bodies backed, ultimately, by politicians, officials and taxpayers.

Can the US and the global economy respond to mounting calamities caused by climate change by even further injections of lending? Will taxpayers continue to bail out financial markets acting recklessly, while seeking to avoid the consequences of risk-taking? I think not.

Potential debtonator 2: house prices crash

Economists argue about whether housing bubbles exist – whether the extraordinary rise in house prices in countries as far apart as Chile and

Britain, the US or South Africa can be described as a 'bubble' or whether they are just a result of prices responding to a shortage of supply and excess demand; of the shortage of upmarket properties, or of properties in areas of development.

Let us not trouble ourselves with these debates. The question is this: if there were to be a sudden shock (environmental/terrorist) leading to a general loss of confidence, would debtors become unnerved, and decide to sell their assets to pay off debts? If interest rates were to rise a tad too high, could this cause house prices suddenly to fall, as they did for example in the UK in the late 1980s? And could house price falls be a 'debtonator' for a prolonged First World debt crisis? In my view yes; because of the enormous debts built up by individuals and households, guaranteed against what many regard as the inflated value of these properties. The most indebted property owners will force prices further downward by selling under pressure to raise the cash to pay off debts and mortgages; the decline in values will bring in buyers who are less indebted, and so the downward spiral will gyrate out of control.

A collapse in house prices will frighten 'debtor-spenders' and persuade them to snap shut their purses, triggering another likely debtonator – a fall in consumption.

Potential debtonator 3: interest rates rise; lending and consumption falls

A First World debt crisis could be debtonated by a hike in interest rates that causes 'debtor-spenders' in the Anglo-American economies to begin to worry about their debts; to ease up on their purchases, and start saving. Now many believe this would be a good thing, and indeed from the point of view of individual borrowers, it would be a very good thing indeed. However, from the point of view of the economy as a whole, especially one-legged economies like the UK and US, heavily dependent on these debtor-spenders, a decline in lending, and therefore in consumption could prove to be a disastrous debtonator.

As Prof. Wynne Godley notes (Godley and Izurieta, 2003) it is income that is a major constraint on borrowing, not, as many economists argue, the value of the debtor's assets. If borrowers are overcommitted 'they become vulnerable to a range of nightmarish possibilities', to quote Godley. Debts have to be serviced; and in order to avoid bankruptcy, debtors have to pay the principal on debts as they become due. Incomes are vulnerable to unemployment, health or age, and as we note above, interest rates may have to rise for reasons to do with the foreign deficit.

If US or UK house prices fell, 'heavily indebted families would likely find their equity exhausted, or negative, making it impossible for them to move or even to trade down, while the obligation to service debt remains.'

This matters because, according to Godley, personal expenditure accounted in recent years 'for more than all the growth in total demand' in the UK – 'something which has never happened before'. In other words, like Atlas, the UK 'debtor-spender' was almost entirely responsible for holding up the UK economy during this period. Over the same time, UK exports fell, and business investment remained stagnant. In other words, Britain no longer relied on exports or investment in research and development for economic growth; it relied almost entirely on the 'debtor-spender' – shopping and spending. Similarly for the US: growth in personal consumption accounted for almost all the economic growth that occurred between 2000 and 2003.

This growth was driven by what Prof. Godley defines as net lending (that is, the rise *in the rise* in debt). There will come a point when these rises in the rate of debt accumulation must slow down. Godley believes that the rise does not even have to go into reverse before it has an impact on economic growth; the rise *in the rise* of debt just has to slow down. Such a slowdown in lending will lead, he argues, to growth-recession:

> The debt percentage only has to level off slowly and then fall very slightly *for the flow of net lending to fall from 15 percent of income in 2005 to 5 percent in 2010.* What effect would this have on activity? The average growth rates for 2005–10 come out at 3.3 percent, 2.6 percent, 1.8 percent, and 1.4 percent. *The last three projections imply sustained growth recessions – very severe ones in the case of the last two.* (Godley and Zezza, 2006)

However, if lending and spending does not just slow down to normal rates; but instead implodes (because 'debtor-spenders' are forced by unemployment (caused by 'shocks' and 'corrections') to drastically cut back; or because a housing crash means they cannot sell their property to pay debts), the result would not just be recession; it would be a prolonged debt-deflationary crisis, from which these economies will, like Japan, take years to recover.

Potential debtonator 4: the US deficit and a collapsing dollar

The US's external deficit (or current account deficit), as noted elsewhere in this book, is a major candidate for the role of debtonator. Here is why.

The United States, which according to the latest census has a population of just 280 million people, has foreign liabilities of more than $3 trillion, and these are expected to rise to about $6 trillion by 2008 (Setser, 2006). All low-income countries, including China, Brazil and India, with populations of more than 6 billion people, have foreign debts of only $2 trillion. With the price of oil imports rising, the US's external deficit is expected to rise, or deteriorate further, in 2006. Brad Setser, an economist at Roubini Global Economics, has done some 'optimistic' sums:

> Suppose the trade deficit peaks at $820bn in 2006 (high oil) and then starts to fall as exports grow at 9% and imports at only 5% in 2007 and 2008. I am still looking at a current account deficit that stays around $1100 billion (above 7% of GDP) for the rest of the Bush Presidency. *Rising rates on the United States existing debt and the normalization of rates on debt contracted earlier combine to push net interest payments from around zero in 2005 to maybe $200bn in 2008.* That drives up the current account deficit even as the trade deficit begins to fall. And between 2005 and 2008 the US net international investment position – the broadest measure of US external debt – basically doubles, rising from say $3.2 trillion to well over $6 trillion – barring big capital gains on our overseas assets ... $6 trillion more in external debts than external assets, and the need to borrow $1 trillion a year as far as the eye can see. That's the legacy the Bush Administration would leave for its successor if – and I still think it is a big if – the policies needed to put the world on a path of orderly adjustment are put in place in 2006 and start to yield results in 2007. If nothing happens and the trade deficit continues to expand, the US external position in 2009 would be substantially worse. (Setser, 2006. Emphasis added)

If foreigners lose confidence in the ability of US debtors – both public and private – to repay their debts, or even to address the problem of debt repayment, they will withdraw their funds and the value of the dollar will fall. The rate at which it falls, i.e. gradually or suddenly, will determine the depth of the likely global economic dislocation. Here is why. A fall in the dollar increases the cost of imports, and means imports will fall. A fall in US demand for imports, or the products/exports of other economies, will lead to a contraction of other economies important to the global economy, e.g. China. Richard Duncan reminds us how much pain was inflicted by a very recent drop in US imports: during the financial crisis of 2001. In that year, imports into the United States fell by US$79 billion, or 6.3%, to US$1.180 billion. The US current account deficit fell by only US$17 billion, or 4.1%, to US$393 billion. That reduction in US demand for foreign products had a profound impact on the rest of the world. World merchandise exports shrank by 4% in value in 2001, the largest annual decrease since 1982.

The economic growth rates of all the United States' major trading partners decelerated abruptly. Stock markets spiralled downward, commodity prices fell, and government finances came under strain. (Duncan, 2003)

As this book goes to press, the global capital markets are demonstrating what could happen in the event of a loss of confidence in the US economy. The new governor of the Federal Reserve, Bernard Bernanke, in evidence to the US Congress on the 27 April 2006, indicated that the Federal Reserve might 'pause' at increasing the Fed's basic interest rate.

The effect of these remarks was a sharp slide in the value of the dollar: in other words foreigners were withdrawing their money at the first hint that interest rates might not keep rising. This was only corrected when two days later, Governor Bernanke, according to a report on the CNBC network, made clear that 'he was interested merely in "pausing" the Fed's series of interest rate rises ... rather than in bringing the rises to a definitive close' (*Financial Times*, 2 May 2006). As the *FT* went on to note, this correction to his remarks helped the dollar stage a recovery.

In other words, Governor Bernanke, in order to satisfy the US's foreign creditors, and prevent the dollar from going into free-fall, cannot 'pause' on interest rate rises too long. The Fed is going to have to keep raising rates as the price for keeping those foreign funds flowing in.

While allowing the dollar to fall could be good for the US, because its exports would be cheaper and easier to sell in global markets, it would be bad for those holding dollar assets – like the central banks of China, Japan, India and many other low-income countries which have built up massive US dollar reserves. These will fall as the dollar falls. Central bankers might then decide to stop buying dollar assets and instead buy euro or yen assets. Some have already indicated they are considering such moves.

However, there is one small problem: like most central bankers, Mr Bernanke has given away the power to fix rates, because, as noted in Chapter 2, interest rates cannot be controlled by central banks and governments, if flows on capital, including stocks and bonds, are not also controlled. While it is widely believed that central banks set 'base rates' and the markets set higher rates for longer-term loans, in fact this has proved to be an illusion. The Federal Reserve has begun to realize that alterations in the base rate, do not result in alterations in longer-term rates, set by the markets, and that therefore the Fed cannot necessarily influence market rates, by increasing the base rate.

As unregulated capital markets are global, there are now global interest rates – set by invisible, unaccountable capital market players. These rates for longer-term bonds do not necessarily respond to the Federal Reserve's changes in the base rate – the Federal Funds rate. Indeed the flooding of international capital markets with petrodollars makes it likely that the interest rates (yields) on long-term bonds are going to stay low (see below).

These are but two horns of the dilemma on which the Governor of the US Federal Reserve, Mr Bernard Bernanke, is caught.

But there is another. To compound matters for the governor of the Federal Reserve and other US officials, higher interest rates might keep money flowing into the US; but higher rates are going to badly hurt the millions of Americans that have built up historically unprecedented levels of debt. If and when interest rates rise, the cost of debt will rise dramatically, causing a fall in lending and a fall in consumption – the debtonators outlined above.

Potential debtonator 5: an oil price shock

This potential debtonator has a history. In the 1970s it was the first 'oil shock' that laid the ground for the prolonged debt crises faced by about 50 low-income countries – debt crises that persist to this day, 30 years later, and that have exacted an incalculable human and ecological toll. As the International Monetary Fund points out in its review of oil prices in April 2006, back then the IMF, official creditors and private banks 'recycled' petrodollars to poor countries in the form of loans – in order to prevent an inflationary spiral in rich countries. In other words, like Japanese consumers after 1987, poor countries helped absorb the oil shock of the 1970s by accepting about $36 billion of loans, money that if left in western banks, would have severely exacerbated inflation in economies already suffering the effects of inflation.

Interest rates turned negative throughout the 1970s when inflation was high. Private banks and official creditors became 'loan-pushers' – anxious to spread the money around – and low-income country finance ministers and presidents became eager borrowers.

The IMF considers that the current high oil price is likely to be less of a shock than it was in the 1970s, relative to world GDP, private capital flows, or the size of financial markets. Nevertheless it predicts that this shock may be 'permanent in nature'.

The difference between conditions then and now is that the US, the 'engine' of the global economy, is far more indebted now than it was then. High oil prices have already had an impact and, according to the IMF, account 'for one-half of the deterioration in the US current account deficit'.

The question now is how the massive funds accumulated by oil producers (estimated at $40 trillion between 1999 and 2005) will be recycled, and what role they will play in forcing interest rates lower in a global economy in which central bankers, finance ministers and citizens have lost control of this key lever of any national economy. And will these flows encourage poor countries and the 'emerging markets' – especially those that are oil importers – to make the same mistakes as were made in the 1970s and early 1980s?

On this the IMF points, unwittingly, to the problem with setting interest rates at a national level (outlined above, and in Chapter 2). In their *World Economic Outlook* (April 2006) IMF economists argue that flows of petrodollars into oil-importing countries like the US will push up prices and therefore be inflationary. Their advice is unequivocal and pays no heed to the plight of debtors: interest rates must be forced *up* to suppress inflation. 'As long as ... central bankers respond by increasing interest rates *significantly* ... the effects on both output and especially, the current account are relatively mild' (IMF, April 2006. Emphasis added).

In the same publication the IMF explores the likely effect of petrodollars on US interest rates. They find it hard, because of lack of data about petrodollar flows, to confirm that these international financial flows will 'exert downward pressure on US interest rates'; but note that their analyses 'treat US interest rates as being determined separately from global interest rates. In an integrated world capital market, oil prices may also affect US rates indirectly, through the impact of recycled petrodollars on interest rates in other countries' (p. 90).

In other words there may not be such a thing as US interest rates; instead the addition of petrodollars to liquid capital markets will determine 'global interest rates'. If these global rates are low, how then can the US Federal Reserve use the lever of higher rates to contain the inflationary pressure caused by the oil price rise? Either way, from the point of view of heavily indebted US individuals, households and government, the IMF points up three threats:

- higher oil prices, which will cut the amount available for consumption;
- higher rates of inflation, caused by energy prices working their way through the economy;
- potentially higher interest rates, raised, on the recommendation of the IMF, to help suppress the inflationary pressure of higher oil prices, and which will both increase the cost of debt, and cut consumption.

Alternatively, the IMF points to the threat that petrodollars could play a role in *depressing* interest rates, especially on the longer-term bonds used for mortgages and re-financing. Such lower rates would imply that inflation cannot be managed by US authorities; and that low rates will prolong and further fuel the credit bubble – storing up more trouble for the future. Inflation will frighten foreign investors, causing them to transfer their financial assets out of the US, and this would cause the dollar to fall, further fuelling inflation through higher import costs.

Poor countries do not have to await such events: they are already suffering the shock of higher oil prices, according to the IMF.

The run up in oil prices since 2002 has caused poverty to rise by as much as 4–6% in some countries, with nearly 20 countries experiencing increases of over 2%. Even the relatively modest hike in oil prices between 2003 and 2004 has implied increases in national oil bills of between 1.5 and 5% of GDP for oil importing countries with high energy intensive economies. A sustained price increase of US$10 per barrel above the $30 per barrel level prior to 2004 would cause an economic shock equivalent to a 1.47 percent loss of GDP for the poorest countries (those with GDP per capita of less than US$300). (*World Economic Outlook*, April 2006).

In other words, in developing countries, one 'debtonator' has already exploded.

Conclusion

It is not possible, and nor is it wise, to predict the timing of a crisis. At the same time a prolonged debt-deflationary crisis is outside the experience of at least two generations of citizens living in countries modelled on the liberalized Anglo-American economies. It is vital that they/we should at least be aware of the risks; and, where possible should prepare and manage individual/household/corporate and governmental finances to give maximum protection in the event of a crisis. Above all, national communities should be allowed to prepare for such eventualities; and to protect their citizens and industries from such likely shocks. The determination of world leaders, both political and financial, to continue giving the impression that all is well in the international forest, helps to maintain insubstantial, ephemeral confidence; but does a disservice to the citizens who have, with their approval and encouragement, taken on enormous debts. The silence, collusion and complacency of central bankers, finance ministers and other world leaders will likely render those that are heavily indebted ignorant and helpless in the face of an international 'financial tsunami'. Given that these victims will be the very 'debtor-spenders' that have sustained the global economy, and by borrowing helped enrich the money-lenders who gained immensely from financial de-regulation – this complacency by world political and financial leaders is unforgivable.

Sources and suggested reading

Bagehot, Walter, in *Lombard Street*, 1873, p. 150. Quoted in J.K. Galbraith, *The Great Crash 1929*. First published by Houghton Mifflin Company, 1954.

Brimelow, Peter, Commentary: 'On watch for the next LTCM: Bridgewater's disturbing predictions'. *MarketWatch*, 11 May 2006. <www.marketwatch.com/News/Story/Story.aspx?dist=newsfinder&siteid=mktw&guid=%7BDA5 20BF5%2D1170%2D4CF0%2D8381%2D8EEF45655B05%7D&link=&keywo rd=hedge%20funds>.

Center for Research on the Epidemiology of Disasters, Belgium. <www.cred. be/>.

Cohen, Bernice, *The Edge of Chaos: Financial Booms, Bubbles, Crashes and Chaos*. John Wiley and Sons, 1997.

Duncan, Richard, *The Dollar Crisis: Causes, Consequences, Cures*. John Wiley and Sons (Asia) Pte Ltd, 2003.

Financial Times, 2 May 2006, 'Stocks fall after "Misunderstanding"', by Jennifer Hughes.

Financial Times, 2 May 2006, 'Strong economic data push US dollar down again', by Steve Johnson.

Galbraith, J.K., *The Great Crash 1929*. First published by Houghton Mifflin Company, 1954.

Godley, Wynne; Papadimitriou, Dimitri B.; Dos Santos, Claudio H. and Zezza, G., *The United States and her creditors: can the symbiosis last?* In 'Strategic Analysis', Levy Economics Institute of Bard College. September 2005.

Godley, Wynne and Izurieta, Alex, 'Coasting on the lending bubble both in the UK and in the US'. Paper presented at the Annual Meeting of the Society of Business Economists, London, 25 June 2003. CERF Cambridge Endowment for Research in Finance University of Cambridge. <www.cerf.cam.ac.uk>.

Godley, Wynne and Zezza, Gennaro, *Debt and Lending: a Cri de Coeur. Policy Note*. The Levy Economics Institute of Bard College. April 2006.

IMF World Economic Outlook, *Globalization and Inflation*, April 2006. Chapter II, 'Oil Prices and Global Imbalances'.

Linden, Eugene, 'Cloudy with a Chance of Chaos', *Fortune Magazine*, 20 January 2006.

Lowenstein, R., *When Genius Failed. The rise and fall of Long Term Capital Management*. Fourth Estate, 2001.

Reading, Brian, *Japan, the Coming Collapse*. Orien Books Ltd, 1992.

Setser, Brad, Blog, Roubini Global Economics Monitor. 6 May 2006. <www.rgemonitor.com/blog/setser/126692>.

Warburton, Peter, *Debt and Delusion – Central Bank Follies that Threaten Economic Disaster*. Allen Lane, the Penguin Press, 1999.

7
Things Don't Have to be This Way

Never doubt that a small group of thoughtful committed citizens can change the world, indeed it is the only thing that ever has.
Margaret Mead, 1901–1978

Introduction

This chapter offers a modest contribution to the debate on how we should move beyond globalization. It outlines in five steps just some of the ethical principles, policies, political organization and personal changes that I believe could form the basis of a new, great transformation: away from debt, avarice, usury and exploitation; and towards a world of balance, stability, justice, equity and peace. It includes a short homily on how we could change and improve our own lives. These steps, I would suggest, are just some of those that must be taken if Finance is once again to be subordinated to the interests of humanity and the earth.

I begin by exploring the ethical standards that will need to affirmed or reaffirmed. I call on faith organizations to lead this new ethical movement and end their obsession with matters private, in particular matters sexual, and instead focus on matters economic, as most of the great prophets have done.

I then assert the need to reclaim democracy; and restore power to democratic institutions, by transferring powers from the private finance sector back to elected, accountable governments and institutions. These powers will include the power to make key decisions for creating money, controlling credit-creation, fixing interest rates and regulating markets and trade.

To achieve this transformation I echo the call made by others for a grand alliance between a group that can loosely be defined as Industry (i.e. all those who research, design, produce or grow goods; all those who assist in the distribution and sale of these goods) and a group that can loosely be defined as Labour (i.e. all those who work by hand or by brain). It is these two groups in the global economy – those engaged in productive activity – that are most affected by the usury, volatility and periodic crises brought about by Finance. The task of the grand alliance will be to bury differences and unite; at local, national and international level. Next these two groups should lead a public debate, and bring pressure to bear on elected governments and central banks to introduce the regulatory changes needed internationally, but also in each country, to ensure that the creation of money and the fixing of the rate of interest are recognized as public, not private goods. That control over these public goods and control over capital flows must be restored to the democratic domain; administered by governments and central banks answerable to society at large, not just the finance sector. In other words, to bring about regulatory changes that will subordinate the finance sector to the interests of humanity and the planet.

The chapter then briefly outlines a range of common sense economic policies that will need to be put in place if money and credit is once again to be regulated and the economy – global, regional and national – managed in a way that is equitable and sustainable.

Step one: personal transformation

Those of us who live in the privileged and exploitative economies of the West, can all play a part in bringing about such a transformation. After all, the finance sector depends on us, the world's debtor-spenders, to come to the ball. We can turn down the invitation. We can decline the credit card, overdraft or loan. We can refuse to dance to Finance's tune. We can live within our means.

We could go further, and make it deeply unfashionable to hold a credit card, and downright embarrassing to have three. We could hold hen-parties where women cut up their credit cards!

We can cut back, be prudent, get out of debt and build up our savings.

We can refuse to play the competitive game of buying 'a bigger house' a 'new registration car' or the very, very latest gizmo. We could refuse to allow celebrities to bait us into buying the latest and most expensive, branded sports shoes, sunglasses or perfume. Indeed we could decline anything branded, and thereby refuse to pay the extra 'rent' that branded goods extract from us, simply by attaching the brand to a product. By so doing we could refuse to reward those who, unlike ourselves, live unproductively, and without working; but instead collect rent and accumulate wealth from brands and branding.

We can resolve to simplify our lives; to cut back our shopping and consumption; to recycle and reuse. We could end the obsession with the 'new' and the novel. Like an MP3 user discovering the authenticity of vinyl, we could begin to 'add value' to the old.

We can slow down the work-and-spend treadmill. We could, for example, decide that time spent with our friends, lovers and families, and time spent in our community, is precious time – more precious than the lonely time spent mesmerized by supermarket shelves, computer games and fashion boutiques. We could refuse to be 'atomized', separated from the things we really want and that we can only get from other people, not from cars, gizmos or computer screens. After all, when it comes down to it, we all crave love, friendship, appreciation, a sense of community, a sense of belonging, a sense of empowerment. Albert Einstein understood our needs well, when he wrote that 'Man can find meaning in life, short and perilous as it is, only through devoting himself to society.'

> The individual has become more conscious than ever of his dependence upon society. But he does not experience this dependence as a positive asset, as an organic tie, as a protective force, but rather as a threat to his natural rights, or even to his economic existence. Moreover, his position in society is such that the egotistical drives of his make-up are constantly being accentuated, while his social drives, which are by nature weaker, progressively deteriorate. All human beings, whatever their position in society, are suffering from this process of deterioration. Unknowingly prisoners of their own egotism, they feel insecure, lonely, and deprived of the naive, simple, and unsophisticated enjoyment of life. Man can find meaning in life, short and perilous as it is, only through devoting himself to society. (Einstein, 1949)

We need to develop the sense that we are not victims, but have dignity and are in control of our lives; that we can take action, to change our own lives; and can join with others and can change society and its impact on nature.

Instinctively we all crave closeness to nature; consciously, or unconsciously, we recognize that we are of the earth. We can begin by paying attention to the environment that sustains us and gives us life. We could periodically remind ourselves, as our ancestors invariably did, that we owe our lives to the earth, its soil, its plants and animals, its water and its atmosphere. Without these we would drop dead in the most fashionable outfit. We can notice how our consumption – our cars, our foreign holiday flights, our extravagant western life-styles – rips open, destroys and extracts valuable 'assets' from the soil, from animal and plant life, from the earth's minerals and from the atmosphere. We could cut consumption, dramatically, and perhaps just begin to restore some of these gifts that we have stolen from nature, *and from the future.*

> I sincerely believe that banking establishments are more dangerous than standing armies, and that the principles of spending money to be paid by posterity, under the name of funding, is but swindling futurity on a large scale.
>
>> Thomas Jefferson (1743–1826).
>> American 3rd US President (1801–09).
>> Author of the Declaration of Independence

We could expand our horizons and consider the future. We could abandon some of the arrogant attitudes that lead us to believe that what we create, what we consume *now*, is of much greater value than anything that could be created or consumed in the future. (This is the basis of the concept of Net Present Value – the device whereby creditors calculate the value of debt.) That by ill-treating the future, by destroying the legacy we should leave for our children and grandchildren, we somehow establish our own superiority as greater. The Greeks understood this as 'hubris'.

We can discover the power and perfection of 'enoughness' – and learn to understand how much that is. (Dominguez, 1999). These are all things that we can do, that would dramatically reduce the power and control that banks, credit card companies and the finance sector as a whole exercise over us.

We need not sit passively by, believing that our man-made structures are 'natural' or permanent; or that financial powers are so entrenched that wrenching them away from the finance sector would require a revolution. While it is true that there will be dogged resistance from those greatly enriched by current arrangements, we need to remind ourselves that in a crisis, the finance sector will be only too happy to transfer its losses and liabilities to the public sector; i.e. to you and me, hard-working taxpayers. Indeed it is already doing so, by transferring responsibility for private pension fund losses to taxpayers.

We need not give up because new technology means that 'the genie is out of the bottle', and cannot be put back again. Not so. We are not after all governed by a monster called technology. We govern technology. We must not assume that the power to create free money and issue endless credit; the ability to use this power to extract wealth from others, and make a claim on the future are powers that are irreversible and fixed in stone. They are not.

The world really does not have to be this way. We can change it.

Keynes put it well when he wrote at the height of the Great Depression:

> If our poverty were due to famine or earthquake or war – if we lacked material things and the resources to produce them, we could not expect to find the means to prosperity except in hard work, abstinence, and invention. In fact our predicament is notoriously of another kind. It comes from some failure in the immaterial devices of the mind, in the working of the motives which should lead to the decisions and acts of will, necessary to put in movement the resources and *technical* means we already have. (Keynes, 1932. Emphasis added)

A group of 'thoughtful committed citizens' can deal with the 'immaterial devices of the mind'; can find the psychological and political will to organize for change; and 'put in movement the technical means, we already have' to help us live within our moral, ecological and financial limits. But first, we have to overcome the sense of powerlessness that is a consequence of the last three decades of finance sector dominance, during which these powers shifted from the public to the private domain.

Overcoming powerlessness

Perhaps one of the most lamentable consequences of the hollowing-out of the democratic sphere is the feeling of despair, helplessness and insecurity it begets in the majority of the world's population. Powerlessness finds expression in apathy; which in turn results in the election of ineffectual, and often corrupt elected representatives. Insecurity compounds the public's distaste for weak government and ineffectual representatives; and causes voters to turn to authoritarian, nationalist and even racist demagogues and political parties.

Some societies, in particular those in which democratic channels for protest are absent, choose to confound their powerlessness through terrorism and fundamentalism; lashing out violently and irrationally. The effect of such mindless violence *increases* insecurity and has, so far, strengthened the forces behind globalization. Osama bin Laden, George Bush and Tony Blair colluded effectively, deepening insecurity within their own societies and reinforcing each other's deluded agendas. But irrational reactions are natural and predictable responses to the pain and degradation inflicted by the wildly utopian policies of orthodox economists who believe that society and nature have no limits or boundaries, and can be exploited in the same way as commodities.; that humanity and the ecosystem can be marketized and subordinated to the interests of a small, greedy financial elite. They are the inevitable political outcomes of a society dangerously polarized between extremes of rich and poor: the asset-holders and the asset-less; the employed and unemployed; the secure and the insecure. Nelson Mandela compared the world we have created to that of apartheid and slavery.

> Massive poverty and obscene inequality are such terrible scourges of our times – times in which the world boasts of breathtaking advances in science, technology, industry and wealth accumulation – that they have to rank alongside slavery and apartheid as social evils. (UNDP, 2005)

He's right. But it doesn't have to be that way.

A modest precedent

The reason I somewhat boldly assert that things need not be this way, and that we the people can change things, is because of a modest precedent. That is, the organization of a group of 'thoughtful committed citizens' that grew into a world-wide movement and helped change the attitudes and practices of some of the most powerful bankers and financiers in the world; the International Monetary Fund and the finance ministers and officials of G8 finance ministries. Indeed this book has emerged from all that I learned about international debt and finance during the extraordinary Jubilee 2000 campaign of 1994–2000.

Privileged to be granted a leadership role in the campaign, and together with colleagues from UK NGOs, we analysed the international financial system and the phenomenon of low-income country debt in great depth. Working with a small group of the campaign's co-founders, together we framed first, a national and then an international campaign, based on clear political and ethical principles (rooted in the Jubilee principle of periodic correction to imbalances). Then, standing on the shoulders of those who campaigned internationally against slavery and apartheid, we designed and put together, initially, a national UK coalition; but ultimately a global coalition. This used electronic communication and organization to mount a campaign, and mobilize millions of other like-minded people. These millions of individuals then took myriad individual and collective actions that ultimately placed intense pressure on world leaders to write off billions of dollars of debt. Jubilee 2000's supporters in more than 60 countries around the world hauled the debt of low-income countries right up the global political agenda – at a time of supposed 'aid fatigue' and despite the sustained opposition of powerful creditors – where it remains to this day. Furthermore, we developed an all-inclusive, highly principled and focussed model for global campaigning that became a template for later international coalitions on poverty and climate change.

Above all, we began to change the world we're in. Sixty billion dollars that should have been transferred out of low-income countries into the coffers of high-income countries as debt repayments have instead remained at home. As this book went to press, the Zambian government announced it was using money freed up by debt relief to introduce free healthcare (Reuters Health, 3 April 2006). It would be wrong to suggest that the campaign achieved all its goals; or that creditors did not use the opportunity to find innovative ways of extracting assets from poor countries. Nevertheless, a campaign that began life in a shed on the roof of Christian Aid's building in London – ended by helping to transform relations between international creditors and sovereign debtors. Countries as diverse as Brazil, Nigeria, Argentina and Russia, buoyed by popular pressure from below, which in turn had been catalysed by Jubilee 2000, did something historically unprecedented in 2006: they used the opportunity of higher commodity prices to pre-pay debts, and get out from under their creditors – in particular the International Monetary Fund. The effect of these decisions was to weaken the power of foreign creditors over these countries; and restore independence and a degree of policy autonomy to both governments and the people.

All of these changes, still on-going, came about because a 'small group of thoughtful committed citizens' got together, and were then joined by millions more, to change the world. Celebrities and politicians played an important role, but they stand on the shoulders of millions of ordinary, dedicated and angry people. Without them there would be no platform for either celebrities or politicians to promote their own roles in the campaign.

As Will Hutton, one of Britain's leading economic commentators, put it in *The Observer*: 'I doubt many readers know the Old Testament books of Leviticus, Exodus,and Deuteronomy any more than I do, but without them there would be no Jubilee 2000, no debt campaign, and no international public pressure. At the end of an increasingly secular century, it has been the biblical proof and moral imagination of religion that have torched the principles of the hitherto unassailable citadels of international finance.' (Wroe, 2000)

Things do not have to be the way they are.

Although it is too late for the millions who have already lost their lives and livelihoods; and although it may be too late to restore biodiversity and reverse adverse impacts on climate change; it is not too late to change the mandate and the power that we, the people have, consciously or unconsciously, explicitly or implicitly, given the finance sector.

We can make the world fit for our purpose, and fit for the ecosystem. We, the people, must and can protect ourselves, our families, our communities and the planet from the 'satanic mill' of market forces and from the overweening power of the finance sector.

Step two: revival of the ethics of usury

> It is usury – the rankest, most extortionate, most merciless Usury – which eats the marrow out of the bones of the raiyat (cultivators) and condemns him to a life of penury and slavery.
>
> Jain, 1929, quoted in Visser and McIntosh, July 1998

One of the first tasks facing those wishing to challenge the finance sector's dominance, will be the reinvigoration of long-established ethical principles. This is a task for us all, but in particular for faith organizations. Condemnation of usury has a long history, stretching back 4,000 years, and as noted earlier its condemnation by Islam has been consistent. Today, thanks to centuries of active encouragement by landowners, bankers and financiers, usury as a sin has been diluted and modified, in particular by the pro-usury counter-movement of the Christian faith.

The manner in which, for example, bankers, hedge funds managers and derivatives traders make money is clothed in cryptology more mysterious than the Da Vinci code. By using methods of camouflage and by adopting esoteric, abstract language players active in the business of money-creation, money-changing, money-gambling and money-lending avoid the moral condemnation and strictures of society. But these men and women are engaged in activities that can rightly be described as usurious, not just of their fellow men and women, but also of the future. The ethics of usury must be rescued from usurers and those who collude with usurers, and its denunciation actively revived.

Theft – of 'the common from the goose'

Condemnation of usury must of course be accompanied by condemnation of downright theft by the rich and powerful – theft not just from individuals and from the community, but also from nature and the future. The lesson of the man punished by the law for stealing 'a goose from off the common', while those who stole the common from the goose went unpunished, must be understood and applied. For as this poem by an anonymous poet suggests, 'Geese will still a common lack/Till [we] go and steal it back.'

THE GOOSE AND THE COMMON

> The law locks up the man or woman
> Who steals the goose from off the common
> But leaves the greater villain loose
> Who steals the common from off the goose.
>
> The law demands that we atone
> When we take things we do not own
> But leaves the lords and ladies fine
> Who take things that are yours and mine.
>
> The poor and wretched don't escape
> If they conspire the law to break;
> This must be so but they endure
> Those who conspire to make the law.
>
> The law locks up the man or woman
> Who steals the goose from off the common
> And geese will still a common lack
> Till they go and steal it back.

ANON

A Global Jubilee

It will also be vital to revive the ethical principles that underline fair bankruptcy laws; or 'clean slates'. In other words, principles that place limits on levels of indebtedness; that draw a line under debts that can only be repaid at the cost of human rights; and that recognize the limits of the ecosystem. Principles that recognize that creditor and lenders are co-responsible, share responsibility with the debtor, for debts; that bad loans make bad debts; that losses as well as gains, must be shared. These principles are already embodied in the Qur'an; and in the Christian principle of redemption, initially an economic term.

The ethics of redemption will provide a sound basis for the cancellation of debts. Because of the build-up of personal, corporate and government debts since the 1970s, the need for redemption of these debts 'vast as space' will be immense. Indeed it is my view that societies will have to introduce a *Global* Jubilee of debt cancellation – an extraordinary amnesty for debtors. The first purpose of such an amnesty or Jubilee will be to release millions of people, business enterprises and governments from the grip of parasitical creditors, currently draining them of every last asset. Creditors and financiers that without a Jubilee of debt cancellation will demand that more individuals commit suicide, more children die, more families are broken, more drugs are sold, more diseases neglected, more forests burned, more export crops grown, more seas fished – to repay debts.

The second purpose will be to restore debtors to viability, and therefore enable them once again to become productive and economically active.

The third purpose will be to restore order and stability to the balance sheets of the finance sector, whose livelihoods too will be destroyed by a severe and prolonged debt crisis.

Without such a Global Jubilee, high-income Anglo-American economies could be mired in prolonged economic degradation caused by debt-deflation for decades ahead; just as low-income countries have been mired in debts since 1982. A prolonged crisis in rich countries will impact more severely on people in low-income countries. A Global Jubilee will release rich and poor countries alike from debt bondage.

Step three: transferring power back to the democratic sphere

> Finance must be the servant, and the intelligent servant, of the community and productive industry; not their stupid master.
>
> National Executive Committee of the British Labour Party
> (June 1944), Full Employment and Financial Policy

Once ethical values have been reinvigorated and asserted, a parallel process will be the appropriation of key financial powers from the private finance sector and the restoration of these to the public sphere: in particular the power to create and control money and credit; and the power to set interest rates. In other words, these powers must be restored to governments that enjoy a mandate from the 'common people' (*demos* in the Greek) to 'rule' (*kratein*). In academic terms this is referred to as 'policy autonomy' – that is, the right of governments to enjoy autonomy, without pressure from international capital markets, to implement policies that represent the interests of those who live within their territorial boundaries.

Such a change would be transformational; it would begin to make democracy meaningful again, and restore power to political institutions. Today governments are routinely attacked and undermined for representing their people and adopting policies that meet the needs of their people and of their territories. These attacks are led by the finance sector, as for example in Brazil before and after the election of President Lula, and supported by the sector's apologists in the media, in politics and in the economics profession.

As noted in Chapter 2, the invention of bank money provided society with a new and extraordinary mechanism for creating money. Bank money ensured there need never be a shortage of money for vital projects: e.g. financing the arts and scientific research, housing the poor; feeding the hungry; or protecting endangered species. The invention of bank money arose from the determination to circumvent the power and greed of the hoarder and the usurer – by providing money to the many, not the few, at very low rates of interest: Cheap Money.

However, the effectiveness of such a mechanism depended on the creation of money and of credit being managed and regulated by the state in the interests of society as a whole: Industry and Labour as well as Finance; those with assets and those without; rich and poor; weak and powerful. By removing controls and regulation over the creation of money and credit, society has inadvertently given away immense financial and political power, and taken upon itself the inevitable consequence: ballooning and, ultimately, unpayable debts.

Usurers were quick to grab these powers from the state, when the foreign deficit of the United States in the 1970s made it vulnerable, and called the US's global economic leadership role into question. Circumstances, and weak political leadership gave the finance sector its chance to transform the money- and credit-creating mechanism, and the financial apparatus that supports it, into one that served the interests of a small, rich elite. This tiny elite now exercises almost complete control over bank money, and over international interest rates; disbursing money and credit at rates of interest that are as reckless and usurious as before the invention of bank money.

The re-appropriation of the financial sphere by society will not be easy. While it may most likely occur after a crisis, even then it will be daunting and will require intellectual and political courage and leadership. However, it will not happen at all until citizens, academics and intellectuals become aware of the existence of these powers, fully understand them, and find the courage to demand that they be restored to the public sphere to be exercised in the interests of society and the ecosystem as a whole.

Step four: the common sense economics of the transformation

Virtually none of the economics practised today would be relevant or helpful to the transformation of the economy, at national, regional or global level. However, this has not always been so. The economics profession has in the past helped humanity make great strides. Economists like Adam Smith, Karl Marx and John Maynard Keynes all agreed on the basics: namely that usury was destructive of civilized life; and that Cheap Money was essential for the maintenance of social order, of environmental sustainability (although they would not have called it such) and of progress. All three recognized that by minimizing usury in an economy, investment, employment and wages could be expanded. High rates of interest lower investment, employment and wages – and create unsustainable levels of debt; this much analysis was shared by all three. All three understood that if money is unavailable or witheld for projects like child health, maternity care, clean water, sanitation; for housing; for educating and employing young people; for scientific research, for protecting the environment, for the arts – and if rates of interest on long-term investment and projects are allowed to rise well above the viability of these projects – then the consequences are highly predictable. Debts will rise and become unpayable; children and mothers will die; dirty water and unfit sanitation will kill millions and spread disease; millions will become homeless; uneducated, unemployed youths will take to drugs and violence; scientific research and biodiversity will decline and the arts will be left to wither on the vine. Societies will disintegrate and war will spread. Economic growth will grind to a halt.

All of this was common sense to Adam Smith, Karl Marx and John Maynard Keynes. It is common sense to you and me. Sadly, it is not common sense to today's finance sector, to the economics profession, to central bankers and to their favoured, sponsored sons and daughters in the political sphere.

Control over capital flows, credit and interest rates

Central to the transformation of national economies and the global economy will be the re-regulation and restriction of the finance sector.

Such regulation implies the reintroduction of capital controls, vital if central banks and governments are to be able to fix and determine the whole spectrum of interest rates, short and long, risky and safe. (Note, capital controls are not the same as exchange controls, although they may be linked. Exchange controls restrict *the trade in currencies*; capital controls are taxes or restrictions on international transactions in assets like stocks or bonds.)

> Capital, which is more mobile than labour, must be taxed less heavily than wages if you want it to stay in the country.
>
> Top economist (who declined to be named) commenting on Christian Democratic economic policy during the German general election campaign, 18 August 2005 (*Financial Times*)

By imposing taxes and restrictions on capital and controlling flows in and out of their borders, governments will regain the power to exercise an independent monetary policy, to fix interest rates appropriate to the home economy. Capital controls will preserve domestic savings for domestic use; help the central bank determine the full range of interest rates – short and long, real, safe and risky – and end exchange rate volatility, which hurts the productive exporting sector.

Such controls will help effect a transfer of the power to create money and to set the full range of interest rates back to a central bank accountable to Industry and Labour, that is the majority of society. From these 'technical' changes, much good will flow. Amongst these goods will be greater stability and balance in international trade.

The spurious reason given for liberalized capital flows by those active in the finance sector, is the need to transfer savings from high-income countries to low-income countries; i.e. for savings to 'trickle down'. I have shown, in Chapter 4, that far from rich countries exporting capital to poor countries, today, thanks to the re-engineering of the international financial architecture in favour of rich countries, countries with large numbers of poor *export capital* to rich countries. Furthermore, we have seen from Chapter 2 that funds for investment or development need not derive from 'savings', that bank money makes it possible to *create* economic activity; that bank money is not the result of economic activity.

Now the proposal to introduce capital controls will either be greeted by a feigned yawn from neo-liberal economists ('it's all been tried before, and failed'; 'the world has moved on, electronic flows of money make controls impossible'); or else the sector will orchestrate public outrage, much as it did when Malaysia successfully introduced capital controls during the 1998 crisis. But the fact is that in a crisis, capital controls will inevitably be imposed. In June 2005, the Bank for International Settlements, perhaps one of the most conservative institutions in the financial system, addressed the problem of global imbalances and aired the possibility that the international financial system could

> revert to a system more like that of Bretton Woods. History teaches that this would only work smoothly if there were more controls on capital flows than is currently the case, which would entail its own costs. (Bank for International Settlements, 27 June, 2005)

Central banks have a range of capital controls in their armoury.

They will be vital to any transformation of the global economy; as they are the instruments that enable central banks to fix rates of interest, short and long, safe and risky. Returning this power to government and central banks will in turn allow them to begin the process of re-regulating the creation of money, of credit, by setting limits.

The creation of money

As explained in Chapter 2, the money that banks put into circulation is actually created by society; it is a 'social construct'. It does not fall from heaven; nor is it dug up from the soil. It is not even linked to something dug up from the soil, as money was once linked to gold. It is based on something quite ephemeral, one of Keynes' 'immaterial devices of the mind' – namely confidence and trust.

Because it is created by society, money is actually the property of society – of all of us – and should not therefore be appropriated by the banks as their sole property. If banks do hold sole rights over this confidence and trust, then they are in fact stealing it from the rest of us.

This is because allowing the banks the privilege of creating money represents a massive subsidy to the tiny minority that own banks, or have shares in banks. A subsidy granted by the bulk of society, which is much poorer, to the rich. Monetarists and other right-wing economists are opposed to subsidies, yet are quite happy to tolerate society's generous subsidies to private banks – amongst the largest of all economic subsidies. As Richard Douthwaite argues, these subsidies distort the way the economy operates (Douthwaite, 1999).

By giving the power to create money *for nothing* to private monopolies like the banking sector, society gives away a massive power: the power to charge rent on this free money. That rent, or interest, is charged to the poor, as well as the rich; to the government, as well as to the private sector. It is like a regressive tax.

Political parties in society are always railing against taxes and taxation. But there are no political parties railing against the regressive tax charged by banks. Why? Could this be a conspiracy? Or is it simply ignorance? I believe it is the latter; very few people understand the workings of the banking system. Furthermore, the finance sector continues to veil its activities in language intended to conceal; and so very few challenge it.

To achieve a genuine transformation of the economy at local, national and international level, it will be vital for society to reclaim this great power, and to insist that a) we (through our elected representatives) set the 'rent' or interest on free, costless money; and b) that our government issues the money (i.e. enters numbers into a ledger) and uses it to fund government projects – 'rent'-free; or in other words at either low, or no interest.

If the state created free money, undertook the task of entering numbers into a ledger for us all, it would do so at a much lower cost than the banks. (For example, banks pay higher salaries and much higher bonuses than are given to government employees!) With the assistance of the central bank, this free money could be used for government projects; Cheap Money could be made available to those engaged in productive activity; with the supply of credit carefully regulated and controlled.

If the government spent the new money into circulation each year (for example by spending money on building housing for the elderly, which would help the construction industry, which would put money into the pockets of builders and their families; which in turn would put money into the local economy) *then the government would save on borrowing from private banks and other financial institutions and taxes could be cut!*

Between 1998 and 1999 the private banks issued about £50 billion of costless money into the UK economy. They issued this money as expensive loans (Douthwaite, 1999). The UK government's budget is £300 billion; if £50 billion of that could have been financed, not by taxes or borrowing from private banks (which is currently what happens), but by the government creating £50 billion of costless money and spending £50 billion into the economy, then taxes could be cut and, for example, old people's homes could be built – a massive benefit to society, if not to the private banks. As things stand, the government is having to a) tax citizens for that money or b) borrow that free money from private banks at high 'rents' or interest. In both cases, as Henry Ford understood so clearly, we the citizens end up paying.

This change is a small 'technical' change that could generate the money that we, society have created, for the needs that we, society consider important. But it is one of those technical changes that will be fiercely resisted by the small, greedy and powerful elite that now controls the creation of money. The history of western civilization is the history of the majority gradually diluting the power of elites, and restoring that power back to the people. We can do it again.

Things do not have to be this way.

Furthermore, these 'technical' changes and economic policies could begin to restore stability to *national* economies. While they sound simple, and hardly revolutionary, they will in effect have extraordinarily beneficial consequences that will quickly ripple through our daily lives; our ecosystem; our financial and consumption habits; and our culture.

Step five: Reforming the international financial system

It will also be vital to redesign and rebuild the international financial architecture. As explained in Chapter 1, since 1971 the international financial system has been skewed in favour of one currency; one nation; one empire. This has not been good for the US, or for the rest of the world. Under the current system, the US does not have to earn the currency needed to repay foreign debts, as for example Nigeria has to do (by investment and export of products such as oil or cassava, earning dollars, and using these to repay foreign debts). Instead the US repays its debt with the currency that it prints. Given that there is no limit to the dollars that can be printed, there is theoretically no limit to what the US can purchase, consume, or borrow.

This helps explain why the US deficit is so high, and keeps climbing inexorably. While US consumption has without doubt stimulated growth in countries that export into US markets, it has also distorted the global economy, by creating imbalances – with countries like Japan, China and Germany holding surpluses and others massive deficits. At the same time economies like that of China are now largely focussed on the US market, and tend to neglect the interests of citizens and consumers within China. In other words, investment in health, in education, in environmental sustainability in China is neglected in favour of investment in exports to the US. This is not a healthy state of affairs, and cannot continue.

The crucial 'technical' fault that causes these economic outcomes, is the dollar's role as the world's reserve currency (that is, the currency kept in reserve by governments for the payment of goods, services and financial assets, and for the repayment of debts).

If we are to thoughtfully redesign the international financial system, and encourage greater stability, we have to address the most basic problem of any international system: how can citizens of one country pay for the goods, services or financial assets of another? What should the rules be? And how should they work? (D'Arista, 2003).

Currently the rules are that in order to trade, countries have to build up reserves of dollars (although countries have recently begun to diversify, into euros for example). They accumulate these by earning dollars from exports, or by providing low-cost loans to the US in return for a financial asset denominated in *dollars*, i.e. a Treasury Bill.

John Maynard Keynes proposed a system – an International Clearing Agency (ICA) – that would treat all nations more fairly, and that would help maintain balance in the international trading system. Jane D'Arista, in a recent essay, describes the rules and operations of the ICA simply:

> an importer in country A would pay for machinery from country B by writing a cheque on his bank account in his own currency. The seller in country B would deposit the cheque in his (commercial) bank and receive credit in his own currency at the current rate of exchange between the two currencies. This would be possible because of the existence of an international clearing process that would route the cheque from the commercial bank to the central bank in country B and from there to the international clearing agency.
>
> At the end of the day, the ICA would net all cheques exchanged between the two countries and pay the difference by debiting or crediting their reserve accounts. Meanwhile, the individual cheques would be returned to the countries of origin and paid in a similar fashion. In this example, the central bank would debit the reserve account of the bank in country A on which the cheque was written and the bank would deduct that amount from the buyer's account.
>
> The process is simple but it does imply certain rules. It would require that all commercial banks receiving foreign payments exchange them for domestic currency deposits with their central banks. The central banks, in turn, would be required to deposit all foreign payments with the ICA. The result would be that all international reserves would be held by the ICA and that the process of debiting and crediting payments against countries' reserve accounts would provide the means for determining changes in exchange rates. As in national systems where the level of required reserves is determined at weekly or bi-weekly intervals, such a structure would greatly reduce the exchange

rate volatility that currently plagues the system. (D'Arista, 2003. Emphasis added)

If the ICA held government assets of its member countries as collateral for international reserves, then it could buy these, and build up its own reserves. This would give the ICA 'fire-fighting' resources, needed at times of financial crises. This would enable it to act as a lender of last resort, and maintain international financial stability – vital 'for balanced growth in the global economy' (D'Arista, 2003).

These changes too are 'technical', but not beyond human ingenuity, intelligence and skill. All they require is widespread understanding and political will – at an international level.

Conclusion

These are the tasks – personal, moral, political and economic – that will be needed to restore Finance to its proper role as servant of society and the global economy, not master. All that is required to fulfil these tasks and implement these changes is the reinvigoration of ethical and moral principles; the personal will to change; political will, and organization; and 'common sense' economic policies.

That does not mean the challenges to those who wish to bring about an economic transformation will not be daunting. They certainly will. But what is the alternative? The alternative is the world we live in now. A world in which the Seven Deadly Sins – Pride, Sloth, Gluttony, Wrath, Envy, Lust and Greed – are alive and well, thriving in a global economy based on 'barren' money, and wreaking havoc with humanity and the ecosystem.

Things *really* don't have to be this way.

Sources and suggested reading

Bank for International Settlements, 75th Annual Report, 27 June 2005, Chapter VIII. 'Conclusion: How might imbalances be fixed?' <www.bis.org/publ/annualreport.htm>.

D'Arista, Jane, 'Creating a new international monetary system', Chapter 24 in *Real World Economic Outlook*, edited by Ann Pettifor. Palgrave Macmillan, 2003.

Dominguez, Joe, *Your Money Or Your Life*. Penguin Paperbacks, 1999.

Douthwaite, R., *The Ecology of Money*. Schumacher Briefings, published by Green Books for the Schumacher Society, 1999.

Einstein, A., 'Why Socialism?', *Monthly Review*, New York, May 1949.

Visser, Wayne A.M. and McIntosh, Alastair / Centre for Human Ecology, 'History of Usury Prohibition' – a short review of the Historical Critique of Usury. First published in *Accounting, Business and Financial History* 8:2, Routledge, London, July 1998, pp. 175–89.

Jubilee 2000, December 2000, 'The world will never be the same again'. <www.jubileeresearch.org/analysis/reports/J2REPORT.pdf>.

Keynes, J.M., *Essays in Persuasion*. Harcourt, Brace and Company, 1932.

Neely, Christopher J., 'An Introduction to Capital Controls', in Review: Federal Reserve Bank of St Louis, December, 1999.

Reuters Health, 3 April 2006, 'Zambia introduces free health care after debt relief', by Shapi Shacinda.

UNDP, 7 September 2005, *Human Development Report 2005*. <http://hdr.undp.org/reports/global/2005/>.

Wroe, M., 'An irresistible force: Jubilee 2000. A look at how and why it caught fire', *Sojourners Magazine*, May–June 2000.

Index

Compiled by Auriol Griffith-Jones

Note: Page numbers in bold refer to Boxes

Africa
    development models for 117–19
    see also Mozambique; Niger;
        Nigeria; Zambia
anti-semitism 96
Argentina 29
    financial crisis (2001) 11, 115
Aristotle 19, 23, 129
art, as collateral for debt 126
Asgrimsson, Halldor, Prime Minister
        of Iceland 145
Asia
    and US Treasury loans 45, 48–9
    see also China; India; Indonesia;
        Malaysia; South Korea; South-
        East Asia; Thailand
asset inflation 7, 9–10, **79**, **80**, 152
    credit and 78–80
assets
    and deflation 92–3
    see also property
Attlee, Clement, UK Prime Minister 27
Australia, debt levels 102
Austria, Jewish bankers in 34

Babylon 127–8
Bacon, Francis 130
bad debts 4, 136
Bagehot, Walter 4, 110, 145
Baker, James, US Treasury Secretary
        114
Baker Plan, on Third World debt 114
Bank Charter Act (1844) 30–1
Bank of England
    and interest rates 63–4, 69, 74
    nationalization of 27
Bank for International Settlements
        (BIS) 5, 8, 10, 176
    2005 report 29, 122
bank money (intangible) 59–60, 173
    democratization of 66–9
    and economic activity 60–1, 62–3, 67
    as free good 64–6

interest rates as price of 63–4, 67–9
and trade 70
virtues of 67, 81
see also money
banking services, provided by retailers
        17, 77
bankruptcy
    credit cards and 123–4
    state 113, 126–7
    see also insolvency
Bankruptcy Abuse Prevention and
        Consumer Protection Act (US
        2005) 123
bankruptcy laws 123–4, 171
banks
    bad debts 4
    cash reserves 61–2
    charges 65–6, 176–7
    and creation of money 176–7
    debt write-offs 114
    international (IFIs) 136
    Islamic 133–5
    and money as free good 64–6
    oligopolies 78
    and power to set interest rates
        69–70, 137, 157–8
    profits 4, 124
    and rates of interest 63–4
    ratio of cash to deposits 62–3
    reactions to debt crises 81
    shariah advisory boards 134–5
    subsidies to 176
    US Treasury loans held as reserves
        45, **46–8**, 178
Barings Bank 10
barter, and emergence of money 57
Barwa, Conrad 133
Bernanke, Bernard, Governor of US
        Federal Reserve 43, 157–8
Blair, Tony, UK Prime Minister 116
Block, Fred 33
Boer War (1899-1901) 31
Bolivia, debt cancellation 115

Bouzou, Nicolas 147
Brady Plan 114–15
Brazil 29, 173
  financial crisis (1999) 115
Bretton Woods system 13, 27–8, 37–9
  displaced 28, 39–40
  US withdrawal from 41, 108–9
British Empire, and gold standard
    30–1
Brown, Gordon, UK Chancellor 126
Browne, Lord 17
BT, pension scheme 95
Buffett, Warren 10–11, **99**
Buira, Ariel 5
Bush, George W., US President 98,
    150
  and US external debts 156

Calvin, John 14, 130–1
capital
  Islamic view of 133
  taxation of 175
capital flows
  controls lifted 113
  and gold standard 33
  and interest rates 71–2
  from poor countries (to US) 46,
    46–8, 49–50, 175
  regulation of 27, 38, 82, 174–6
capital gains 131–2
  and profits 18–19, 136–7
car title loans (US) **20**
central banks, influence of 70, 176
Cheney, Dick, US vice-President 150
Chile, house price inflation **79**
China
  oil demand 17
  and US Treasury loans 46, 178
Christian Aid 169
Christianity
  and forgiveness 138–9
  and sin of usury 14, 129–30, 138
  see also Islam
Churchill, Winston, and gold
    standard 35
climate change, as potential crisis
    trigger 150–3
Clinton, Bill, US President 116
Cologne Debt Initiative (HIPC 2)
    116–17

colonialism
  and development 110–11
  and liberty 140
commodity prices 89
  collapses (1980s) 111–12
community
  and economic system 15
  importance of 165
competition, and oligopolies 52
compound interest 91, **92**, 137
confidence
  and debt crises 148–50
  in international financial system
    147–9
  and money creation 176
  in US 45, 156–7
consumption
  dependent on debt 90–1, 100
  and economic growth 2, 6, 44–5,
    141
  fall, as crisis trigger 154–5
  and hubris 166
  personal action on 164–5
  and scarce resources 140–1
corporations
  effect of high interest rates on 76
  insolvency 10
  mega-mergers of 51–2
'corrections' (shocks) 21–3, 149–50
  climate change 150–3
  fall in interest rates and
    consumption 154–5
  house prices 153–4
  oil prices 158–60
  US deficit and fall in dollar 155–8
corruption 123
  and corporate debt 10
Costello, Peter, Australian Treasurer
    102
credit
  and asset price inflation 7–8, 9–10,
    78–80
  control over 82, 141–2
  cost of 6, 56–7, 82
  created by borrowers 19, 60–1
  de-regulation of 6, 76, 77–8, 82
  falling standards **78**, 100
  and gold standard 31–3
  see also debt; interest rates
Credit Action 97

credit cards 8, 62–3, 98, 164
   and bankruptcy 123–4
   UK debt level 97

Dalton, Hugh 13, 27
   and Great Depression 36
Daly, Herman 23, 32, 123, 129, 137–8,
   141
D'Arista, Jane 179–80
de-regulation
   of credit 6, 76, 77–8, 82
   effect on financial systems 8
   and increase in wealth gap 9–10
debt
   compounded by interest 91
   ethics of 122–4
   forgiveness of 138–9, 172
   government-owned 8–9, 11, 42
   and interest rates 154–5
   national levels 96–105
   personal 1–2, 8, 84–5
   personal action on 164–70
   and poverty 127–8
   in pre-urban societies 127–8
   responsibility for 121, 123, 138–9,
      171–2
   as way of life 97–8
debt consolidation 91
debt crises 11, 86
   bank reactions to 81
   blame for victims 3, 96
   compromises to unwind 12–13
   expert warnings on 5–6
   and international confidence
      148–50
   Japan 80–1, 86, 151–3, **151–2**
   need for preparation for 160–1
   threat of 16, 52–3, 82, 105
   triggers for 145–7
   unpredicted 146–7
   see also corrections ('shocks');
      financial crises
debt relief initiatives 115–17, 169–70
deflation 7, 33, **87**
   and interest rates 93–5
   and social unrest 95
   and value of cash 91–3
   see also inflation
democracy
   and bank money 66–9

   and financial regulation 15–16
   and interest rates 72–3
   and restoration of financial power
      172–4
derivatives, trade in 10–11
development
   and colonialism 110–11
   models for poor countries 117–19
Dikshit, Anurag 85
distributive justice 123, 137
Drexel Burnham Lambert 10
Duncan, Richard 156–7
Dyson, James 68

Eck, John 129–30
economic growth
   and consumption 2, 6, 44–5, 141
   dangers of continuing boom 2–3,
      5–6
   dependent on consumption 90–1
   and fall in lending 155
   global 1, 12
   and gold standard 32–3
   under Bretton Woods system 27–8
economic justice 14, 15
economics
   orthodoxy of 122–3
   for transformation 174–8
Edison, Thomas 66
Einstein, Albert 137, 165
Elliott, Larry 149
Enron 10
environment
   and natural resources 137, 166
   sustainability 15, 165–6
   and threat of climate change 16
   see also resources
ethical standards
   absence of 120–2
   need for 13–15, 22–3, 121, 125
   see also usury
ethics
   of debt in pre-urban societies 127–8
   of usury 170–2
European Union, Maastricht Treaty 97
exchange rates
   fixed 37–9, 41
   lifted 42

financial crises 11, 29, 34–7
   2000/01 stock market crash 153

and 'corrections' (shocks) 21–3,
149–50
see also debt crises
financial institutions
application of law to 125
increase in 17, 77
financial sector
and 'corrections' 21–2
and global economic growth 3–4,
120–1
and Global Jubilee of debt
cancellation 172
lack of ethical constraints on 121
need for controls over 174–6
as parasite 16–17, 19–21, 81
power of 14–15, 28, 124
pressure on Keynesian policies 74–5
and responsibility for interest rates
141, 175
and rise in interest rates 74–7
role in highly indebted nations
20–1
role in international crises 29
trade in derivatives 10–11
see also international financial
system
First World War 34–5
Ford, Henry 61, 66, 177
France, debt levels 96, 101–2
Franco-Prussian war 34
Fugger family, bankers 130
Fukuyama, Francis 29

G7 summits
and confidence-building 148–9
Naples (1994) 115
G8 summits 13
Birmingham (1998) 116
Cologne (1999) 116–17
and Jubilee 2000 campaign 168
Galbraith, J.K. 2, 4, 86, 149
gambling 84, 85–6
Geithner, Tim 5
Gelinas, Jacques, *Freedom from Debt* 118
General Motors 10, 13
Germany 178
debt levels 96
and gold standard 35
Peasants' Revolt (1524) 138
and rise of Nazism 96

Global Jubilee, concept of 117,
171–2
GlobalCrossing 10
globalization 26–53
compared with Bretton Woods 28
and dismantling of Bretton Woods
39–40
first crisis (1873) 34
and gold standard 31–3
and interest rates 73
and legacy of debt 52–3
origins of 26–9
second crisis (1914) 34–5
third crisis (1929) 36–7
transformation of 163–4
and US Treasury loans 42, 45,
46–8
and wealth gap 49–50
see also liberalization
Godley, Wynne 5, 101, 154–5
gold mining 31
gold standard 28, 31–3
Bretton Woods and 37, 42
machinery of 30
return to (by 1925) 35–6
Goose and the Common, The 171
governments 11, 40, 82
bankruptcy of 126–7
compensation schemes 95
and control of capital 71–2, 175
cost of borrowing 76, 177–8
and end of Bretton Woods system
28
and financial accountability 16, 39
and gold standard 31–3
and interest-free money 66, 67–8,
177
need for intervention 12–13
and restoration of financial powers
172–4, 177
US Treasury loans held as reserves
42, 45, **46–8**, 178
see also democracy; politics; low
income countries
Great Depression (1920s and 1930s)
12, 13, 22, 36
Bank of England and 74
optimism before 149
Roosevelt and 26–7

Greenspan, Alan, governor of US
    Federal Reserve 2, 73, 79, 101,
    146
  on Hurricane Katrina 150–1
  and Japan 153
Gross, Daniel, article **46–8**
Group of 24 5

Hahn, Wilfred 132
Haiti, debt levels 116
Havard Economic Society 149
healthcare systems, debts 8
Heavily Indebted Poor Country
    Initiative (HIPC 1) 115–16
  evaluation of 117
hedge funds 146
Hitler, Adolf 34, 96
Hong Kong Shanghai Banking
    Corporation (HSBC), profits 4
house prices *see* property
Howe, Sir Geoffrey 77, 109
Hurricane Katrina 145, 150–1
Hutton, Will 169

Iceland
  debt levels 104–5
  financial crisis (2006) 145, 147
income
  average 79–80, 101
  and debt repayment 154–5
  restrictions on wages 7
  unearned 136
India
  Kerala debt crisis 128
  and US Treasury loans 46, 48
individualism 15, 165
Indonesia 11, 29
  tsunami (2005) 150
Industry
  alliance with labour 23, 39, 57, 121,
    142, 163–4
  decline of 16, 17
  need for low interest rates for
    investment 68, 70, 174
inflation 87–9, **87**, 112
  of asset prices 7, 9–10
  and oil price rises 159
  and prices 88, 94–5
  see also deflation
insecurity, increased 167–8

insolvency 10, 113
  see also bankruptcy
interest
  forbidden by Islam 132–4
  on money 56–7
  origin of 19, 58, 70–1
  in pre-urban societies 127
  see also usury
interest rates
  bank powers to set 69–71, 137,
    157–8
  and capital flows 71–2, 81, 175
  Christian view of 130
  and debt crises 80–1
  and deflation 93–5
  and democracy 72–3
  effect of oil prices on 159–60
  ethical levels 141–2
  as price of bank money 63–4, 67–9
  and return on investment 131–2
  rise in 74–7, 112, 154–5
  and role of politicians 73–4, 175
International Clearing Agency (ICA),
    Keynes's proposal 179–80
international financial system 136
  need for reforms 178–80
  and origins of globalization 26–9
  political confidence in 147–9
  see also financial sector
International Monetary Fund (IMF) 5,
    37–8, 146
  and confidence in international
    system 148
  debt rescheduling schemes 114
  and Jubilee 2000 campaign 168
  and loans to developing countries
    109, 111
  on oil prices 158
  poor countries' debts to 114, 115
  and South Korea 103
  and sovereign debt restructuring
    mechanism 127
  World Economic Outlook 146, 159,
    160
investment
  need for low interest rates for 68,
    70, 174
  rate of return on 132
Islam
  and interest-bearing money 132–5

and sin of usury 14, 121, 130
and trade 136

Jacobs, Jane 23
Japan
  debt crisis (1990) 11, 80–1, 86,
    151–3, **151–2**
  debt to US 49, 100, 178
Jefferson, Thomas 166
Jubilee 2000 campaign 4–5, 11,
  116–17, 123, 139–40
  success of 168–70
Jubilee year
  concept of 139–40
  see also Global Jubilee
Judaism, and Sabbath tradition
  139–40
justice, economic 14, 15

Kaunda, Kenneth, President of
  Zambia 111
Keynes, J. Maynard 7, 14, 23, 167
  and Bretton Woods 37–8
  and gold standard 35
  and interest rates 71–2, 74
  International Clearing Agency
    (ICA) proposal 179–80
  on money 58, 65, 68–9, 174
  theory of liquidity preference 71,
    74
King, Mervyn, Governor of Bank of
  England 126
Kohl, Helmut, German Chancellor
  116
Krueger, Anne 5–6, 148
Krugman, Paul 5

labour 16–17, 18, 164
  and interest rates 70
  alliance with Industry 23, 39, 57,
    121, 142, 163–4
Labour Party (UK) 172
Laker, Freddie 75
land
  and debt 127–8
  as resource 16, 18
  see also property
Latin America
  debt moratoria 115
  debt problem 114

under Bretton Woods system 39
  see also Argentina; Chile; Mexico;
    Venezuela
law
  ethical boundaries 125
  and principles of lending 129
  see also bankruptcy laws
Law, John 67
Lawson, Nigel 77, 115
Levitt, Kari (Polanyi) 23
liberalization
  1880-1914 period 34
  and end of Bretton Woods system
    39–40
  and regulation 140
liberty, and principle of Jubilee year
  140
Lincoln, Abraham 70
loans
  car title (US) **20**
  and creation of deposits 60–1
  and profit 130–1
  student 8, 98
  to developing countries 109, 111
London
  banking centre 4, 30, 31, 33
  National Gallery 126
Long Term Capital Management Fund
  (LTCM) 10, 146
lotteries 86
low income countries
  access to bond markets 114
  capital flows (to US) 46, **46–8**,
    49–50, 175
  commodity trap 112
  corruption in 123
  debt levels 114–15
  debt relief initiatives 115–17,
    169–70
  development models for 117–19
  effect of oil prices 160
  foreign debt levels 156
  insolvencies 113
  and Jubilee 2000 campaign 169
  lending to 109–11, 113
  and structural adjustment policies
    111–12
  see also Heavily Indebted Poor
    Country Initiative
Luther, Martin 130, 138

MacDonald, Ramsay 26, 37
McIntosh, Lord 60, 61
Major, John 115
Make Poverty History campaign 5
Malaysia, capital controls 175–6
Mandela, Nelson 168
markets
    need for regulation 125
    see also stock markets
Marx, Karl 174
metals, as money 128–9
Mexico 29, 111
    debt crisis (1982) 108, 110, 113–14
Milanovic, Branko 12
Mill, John Stuart 23
Milner, Alfred, Lord 31
money 57–9
    additional cost of 19–21
    bank money (intangible) 59–64
    as barren 137–8
    cash 61–2
    creation of 176–8
    and debt creation 56–7, 82
    as end (not means) 135
    as fictitious commodity 129
    as free good 64–6
    functions of 57–8
    growth of 17, 18–19
    metals as 128–9
    privatization of 74–7
    ratio of cash to deposits 62–3
    regulation of 122
    and wealth 85
    see also bank money; interest rates
mortgage arrears 4
mortgage debt 8
Mosley, Oswald 96
Mozambique, debt relief 115–16
Muentefering, Franz 124
Mulford, David C. 114
multilateralism 28

Namibia, house price inflation **79**
nationalism, and protectionism 28–9,
    34
nations *see* governments
neo-liberal economics 28
New Economics Foundation 60
NGOs
    and Jubilee 2000 campaign 168
    and pressure for debt relief 115

Niger, drought (2005) 128
Nigeria
    compounded debt 92
    debt to US 178
Nixon, Richard, US President 41, 50,
    108
Noland, Doug 5
Norman, Montagu, governor of Bank
    of England 35, 36

OECD, and loans to developing
    countries 110
oil, exploration 17
oil prices 88
    1973 shock 109, 110, 112–13, 158
    as trigger for debt crisis 158–60
oil revenues 108, 109
oligopolies
    banking 78
    corporate 51–2
Oxford Review of Economic Policy (1999)
    76

Paris Club 115, 126
Parmalat 10
Payne, Will 4
pension schemes
    compensation for fund shortfalls 95
    deficits 13
personal consumption 1–2, 44, 154–5,
    164–5
personal debt 1–2, 8, 84–5
    action on 164–70
Polanyi, Karl 23, 34, 125, 129
politics
    and interest rates 73–4
    and modern economic system 120
    and power of finance 124
poverty
    and debt 127–8
    mass 168
powerlessness, overcoming 167–8
prices
    and deflation 93–5
    inflation **88**
    retail discounts and sales 89
    see also asset inflation; property
private investors, loss of confidence
    in US 45
privatizations 21
    of money 74–7

production, compared with finance
16
profits
banks 4, 124
and capital gains 18–19
from loans 130–1
from trade 136
property
asset inflation 78–9
and credit de-regulation 77
house price falls, as trigger 153–4
price falls 93, **93**
price inflation 10, 153–4
see also assets
protectionism 28–9, 34
Protestant Revolution 138

racism 96
Raffer, Kunibert 126, 136
Rahman Babu, Abdul 118
Rajan, Raghuram, IMF 5
Reagan, Ronald, US President 42, 113
recycling 165
redemption, principle of 172
Refco hedge fund 10
refugees 12
Reid, Tim 100
resources
land 16, 18
need for allocation of 140–1
see also environment
retailers, banking services 17, 77
Rhodes, Cecil John 31
risk, in Islamic finance 133
Roach, Stephen 5, 149
Robertson, James 129
Roman Catholic Church, and usury
138
Rooney, Wayne 84
Roosevelt, Franklin D., US President
26–7
Roubini, Nouriel 5, 156
Russia 11, 29
financial crisis (1998) 115, 146
and gold standard 35
Pushkin Museum 126

Sabbath, tradition of 139–40
savings, in western development
model 118

savings rates 8
Schröder, Gerhardt, German
Chancellor 116
Schumacher, E.F. (Ernst Friedrich) 23
Schumpeter, Joseph 60
Setser, Brad 5, 156
Smith, Adam 32, 126, 174
on usury 130–1
social unrest, in deflationary periods
95
Soddy, Sir Frederick 81
South Africa, Witwatersrand goldfields
31
South Korea 11, 29
debt levels 103–4
South-East Asia, financial crisis
(1997/98) 114, 146
sovereign debt restructuring
mechanism, proposed 126–7
Stamp, Josiah Charles 65
Stewart, Roger, US senator 20
stock markets 4, 153
access to 114
global 1
see also financial sector
store cards 8
interest rates 76–7, **77**
Strong, Benjamin, governor of US
Federal Reserve 35
structural adjustment policies 111–12
student loans 8, 98
Sumerians 127
Summers, Larry, US Treasury Secretary
42
supermarkets 17, 18–19
Switzerland 126

taxation, of capital 175
technology, proper use of 166–7
Thailand 11, 29
financial crisis (1997) 115
Thatcher, Margaret, UK Prime
Minister 42, 75, 113
Third World
debt crises 11
debt debates 4–5
debt financing 48, 114
role of finance sector in 20–1
see also Africa; Latin America;
Mexico; low income countries

trade
  and bank money 70
  and capital transfers 50
  permitted by Islam 136
Tsunami (2005) 150
Turkey, financial crisis (2000) 115

Uganda, debt cancellation 115, 116
United Kingdom
  and Bretton Woods system 27
  Competition Commission 76, **77**
  debt levels 96–8
  as development model 118
  and gold standard 30–1
  mortgage arrears 4
  national debt 11, 97
  Pensions Commission report (2004)
    76
  sale of gold reserves to pay debts 40
  trade deficit 43, 97
United Nations Conference on Trade
    and Development (UNCTAD)
    89, 113
United Nations High Commission for
    Refugees (UNHCR) 12
United States 29, 40, 46
  bankruptcy laws 123
  credit standards **78**
  debt financing 5
  debt levels 98–101
  and debt system 39
  default on debt (1971) 40–2, 108–9,
    173
  dollar devaluation 43, 48–9
  dominance of 178
  gambling revenues 85–6
  and gold standard 35
  household debt 1–2, 8, 10, 100–1
  loans to 42, 45, **46–8**, 153, 157, 178
  national deficit 11, 43, 44–5, 48,
    98–100, 155–8, 178
  and oil prices 159–60
  personal consumption 1–2, 44
  trade policy 51, **90**

US Federal Reserve 35, 74–5
  and interest rates 157–8, 159
  rate cuts (2001-04) 153, 156
usury 135–7
  and bank money 69–70
  definition 135
  and natural resources 137
  need to reject 142
  and profit 136–7
  religious views of 14, 121, 129–30,
    138, 170
  and revival of ethics of 170–2
  as theft 171
  and wealth transfer (to rich) 137

Venezuela 111
Vietnam War, and US debt 40, 108
violence, and increased insecurity
    167–8

wages *see* income
WalMart, banking services 77
wealth gap
  increase in 9–10, 120, 168
  poor and rich countries 49–50
  within countries 50–2
wealth transfer, to rich 137
welfare projects 177
  and bank money 70, 174
women, financial mobilization of 118
World Bank 109
  debt relief initiative 115–17
  Global Development Finance
    reports 49–50
  poor countries' debts to 114, 115
World Lottery Association 86
World Trade Organization 7
WorldCom 10

Yeltsin, Boris, Russian President 116

Zambia
  debt relief 169
  debts 110–11

8543

8543

DATE DUE

Demco, Inc. 38-293